FORGOTTEN FATHERLAND

THE SEARCH FOR ELISABETH NIETZSCHE

BEN MACINTYRE

MACMILLAN
LONDON

First published 1992 by
MACMILLAN LONDON LIMITED
a division of Pan Macmillan Publishers Limited
Cavaye Place London SW10 9PG
and Basingstoke

Associated companies in Auckland, Budapest, Dublin, Gaborone, Harare, Hong Kong, Kampala, Kuala Lumpur, Lagos, Madras, Manzini, Melbourne, Mexico City, Nairobi, New York, Singapore, Sydney, Tokyo and Windhoek

ISBN 0-333-55914-2

A CIP catalogue record for this book is available from the British Library

Photoset by Parker Typesetting Service, Leicester
Printed by Billing & Sons Ltd, Worcester

The author and publishers would like to express their gratitude to the following who have very kindly given their permission for the use of copyright materials:

Penguin Books for permission to quote from: *Ecce Homo* by Friedrich Nietzsche, translated by R. J. Hollingdale (Penguin Classics, 1979)
Twilight of the Idols/The Anti-Christ by Friedrich Nietzsche, translated by R. J. Hollingdale (Penguin Classics, 1968)
Beyond Good and Evil by Friedrich Nietzsche, translated by R. J. Hollingdale (Penguin Classics, 1975)
Thus Spoke Zarathustra by Friedrich Nietzsche, translated by R. J. Hollingdale (Penguin Classics, 1969)
A Nietzsche Reader translated by R. J. Hollingdale (Penguin Classics, 1977)

Peters Fraser & Dunlop Group Ltd for permission to quote from *Nietzsche: A Critical Life* by Ronald Hayman (Weidenfeld & Nicolson)

Faber & Faber for permission to quote from *The Four Quartets* by T. S. Eliot.

Crown Publishing Group for permission to quote from *Zarathustra's Sister* by H. F. Peters.

Every effort has been made to trace all copyright holders but if any have been inadvertently overlooked, the author and publishers will be pleased to make the necessary arrangement at the first opportunity.

FOR MY FATHER AND MOTHER

ACKNOWLEDGEMENTS

I am grateful to many people in several countries for their help. In Germany, my thanks to Dr Roswitha Wollkopf and the staff of the Goethe–Schiller Archive for the long hours spent trying to tease some sense out of Elisabeth's peculiar handwriting and to Ulrich Brochhagen for his tireless research and translations. In Paraguay, to staff of the Gran' Hotel del Paraguay, to Jakob Davies, to the crew of the *Blanca Doña*, Colum Lynch (whose modesty forbids me from bringing him into the story) and most of all to Pastor Detlev Fenhaus, Dr Christoph Schubert and the people of Nueva Germania. In Britain thanks to Rachel Delaney and Julie Read for their help with translations; Richard Gott; to Dr Baljinder Mankoo of University College School of Medicine and Dr Steve Jones of University College Galton Laboratory for their help over genetics and to the numerous scholars I have met in the last two years who kindly cut a path through Nietzsche for me to attempt to follow. Particular thanks to Dr Keith Ansell-Pearson, Lecturer in Political Studies at Queen Mary College, University of London, for his comments and advice and to Mr and Mrs Albie Rosenthal for permitting me to quote from their private manuscript collection.

This book would have been impossible without the support and skill of Candida Pryce-Jones and the BBC's Timewatch Unit. Roland Philipps of Macmillan, friend and publisher, has been as ever supremely generous with his time and encouragement. And finally thanks and love to Kate Muir, for putting up with me and the Nietzsches for so many months.

CONTENTS

LIST OF ILLUSTRATIONS

I know my fate. One day there will be associated with my name the recollection of something frightful, of a crisis like no other before on earth, of the profoundest collision of conscience, of a decision evoked *against* everything that until then had been believed in, demanded, sanctified. I am not a man. I am dynamite.

FRIEDRICH NIETZSCHE,
Ecce Homo, 'Why I am Destiny', I

Foreword

THIS book is the story of two journeys, one through a remote, largely forgotten part of central South America, the other through the thickets of the vast, sometimes impenetrable literature which surrounds Friedrich Nietzsche: both were in search of his sister, Elisabeth.

More has been written, more bafflingly, about Nietzsche than about perhaps any other modern thinker. Scholarly biographies have traced the philosopher's life in depth and detail; but his sister, whose life was in some ways rather more remarkable than his, usually lurks malignantly in the footnotes, the undergrowth of history. It seems as if her lamentable influence on Nietzsche and the grim prescience of her ideology have often been too much for his supporters to contemplate, too easy a weapon for his opponents to beat him with.

The story of Elisabeth Nietzsche is important partly because of the effect she had on her brother and his philosophy, both during his life and most emphatically after his death. She made him famous and she made him infamous; with her connivance, his name became associated with Nazism; but, without her, he might never have been heard of at all outside a small circle of scholars. But her life is also illuminating in itself. Her ideas foreshadowed one of the darkest periods in human history, but for more than forty years she enjoyed fame and wealth as one of Europe's foremost literary figures; no woman, except perhaps Cosima Wagner, was more celebrated in the cultural world of prewar Germany. She died just at the moment when people who shared many of her views were about to plunge Europe into devastating war and unleash the Holocaust of European Jewry.

Most fascinating of all to me was the unwritten story of New Germany, the racist colony Elisabeth helped to found in the middle of South America over a century ago. That community was a reflection and realisation of those beliefs – anti-semitism, vegetarianism, nationalism, Lutheranism – which Elisabeth shared with her husband, Bernhard Förster, one of the most notorious anti-semitic agitators of his day. Elisabeth later tried to graft these ideas on to Nietzsche, the anti-anti-semite, anti-nationalist and self-proclaimed 'Anti-Christ'. A measure of her success is the fact that Nietzsche's name has still not fully shaken off the taint of fascism.

It is not the primary intention of this book to discuss, once more, whether the Nazis had any justification when they cited Nietzsche in support of their evil aims. The consensus today is that they did not. I believe Nietzsche would have been appalled at the use which the fascists (ably abetted by his own sister) made of his philosophy. His own words are, I think, sufficient to show that he would have damned Nazism comprehensively. Nietzsche had made no secret of his distaste for his sister's Paraguayan colony, and he refused to have anything to do with it from the start; in his last years of sanity he distanced himself from his sister, her husband and the South American project, and his biographers have tended to follow suit, largely ignoring Elisabeth and wishing her colony and her ideas into oblivion.

Nietzsche never doubted that he was 'a destiny'. His ideas continue to shape our own, the problems that obsessed him are as relevant now, perhaps more relevant, as when he first addressed them. Our own world is more anomic even than his was, our need for Nietzschean individuality still more pressing. It is as easy to disagree with Nietzsche as it is hard to dislike him, in spite or because of his cussedness. He is feisty and irritating and fiercely challenging, permanently either moving the goal posts or trying to brain you with them. Some of his thoughts are mistaken, but he has views on everything; all are worth hearing, none is boring and some are surely right.

What follows is in part a personal reading of Nietzsche, not an interpretation of him, still less an explanation. (Nietzsche was constantly worried about not being understood, but would probably have sneered at those who claimed they do.) If this book sheds light on his books or still better encourages the reading of them, then so much the better. But this is not a philosophy book. Anyone who expects to find here another diagnosis of Nietzsche will be disappointed and those who already believe they understand Nietzsche will be disgruntled, as such people normally are; but, as the man said, 'one has to get rid of the bad taste of wanting to be in agreement with many'.

This is rather the story of a journey in search of a singular, if singularly nasty, woman. But Elisabeth Nietzsche was not just bigoted, ambitious and bloody-minded (although she was all of these things and more), she was also a woman of extraordinary courage, character and (she would have been gratifyingly annoyed by the word) *chutzpah*. Through sheer willpower she founded one New Germany in the middle of Paraguay and then helped to found another, half a century later, in the shape of the Third Reich. She was awful, in both senses of the word.

What T. S. Eliot wrote about footfalls applies as well to footnotes:

> Footfalls echo in the memory
> Down the passage which we did not take
> Towards the door we never opened
> Into the rose garden. My words echo
> Thus, in your mind.

The footnotes which had told, tantalisingly, of Elisabeth's experiment in South American *Lebensraum*, fifty years before the Nazis, echoed in my mind. I decided to follow in the footnotes of Elisabeth Nietzsche to Paraguay, a savage and beautiful country that deserves its anonymity as little as Elisabeth herself. There can be few peoples, except perhaps the Germans under Hitler, who have been more brutalised by history than the Paraguayans; but there are fewer still, again excepting the Germans, who have overcome their past with more courage and determination.

THE revolution overthrowing the communist regime in East Germany in 1989 opened up that region's history to close self-scrutiny for the first time in nearly half a century. In December 1946, the large house in Weimar where Elisabeth had lived and which she had turned into a shrine to her brother's work, was closed and sealed on the orders of the Red Army; the German staff of the Nietzsche Archive was disbanded and the head archivist, Elisabeth's gallowglass, was arrested and later disappeared, presumed killed. Soon after, the Nietzsche Archive was incorporated into the Goethe–Schiller Archive, the Nietzsche Foundation (established in 1908) was dissolved and Elisabeth's house, Villa Silberblick, was used from time to time as a guest house. The study of Nietzsche, the adopted philosopher of fascism, was discouraged by the self-proclaimed anti-fascist state.

In 1991 Villa Silberblick was finally reopened on the orders of the unified German government (it is now a museum), and unrestricted public access was permitted to the Nietzsche papers, still in the Goethe–Schiller Archive in Weimar. The primary source for the biographical sections of this book (Chapters IV–VIII) is that collection; citations and some secondary sources are specified in the Notes; other material was gathered from interviews in Paraguay, Switzerland and Germany. Where I have seen the relevant unpublished documents, translations are my own; in all other instances, translators are cited in the Notes. In quoting from Nietzsche's works, I have relied on the excellent translations of R. J. Hollingdale.

Elisabeth was a passionate, if selective, hoarder of documents, and the Elisabeth Nietzsche Collection in Weimar contains a wealth of unpublished material: Elisabeth's diaries and memoranda; her own letters (more than 30,000 in all), letters from her brother, husband, mother and the colonists of New Germany; newspaper clippings and photographs spanning the years 1844–1935; souvenirs and business records. From these, as well as a number of other collections and the published writings of the Nietzsche family, I have tried to create a narrative of Elisabeth Nietzsche's long, eventful life.

CHAPTER I

Asunción Docks, Paraguay, 15 March 1886

LATE in the afternoon the little Montevideo steamer docked at the decrepit quay below the Plaza de Palma, and fourteen families of sweating, travel-weary German immigrants climbed unsteadily down the gangplank into Paraguay. People said later it was the hottest day that year.

Their leader was immediately identifiable. A tall, gaunt man with emphatic eyebrows and a thick spade beard which started high on his cheekbones and jutted straight out from his face. His mouth was almost entirely concealed behind a bushy carpet of hair. He wore, as always, a tight frock coat with an Iron Cross pinned on the lapel, and his booming voice and fierce manner gave him the air of an avenging prophet; which is exactly what he thought he was. His name was Doktor Bernhard Förster of Charlottenburg, and he was in the Utopia-building business.

His wife Elisabeth was equally conspicuous. A small, restless woman with her hair tied back in a tight bun, and topped with a lace bonnet. She was dressed in black, as formal and severe as her husband, and seemed oblivious of the heat. At thirty-nine years old she was still beautiful, her face round and unlined with a slightly snubbed nose, though her looks had always been marred by a squint. One piercing black eye looked directly ahead, while the other seemed to focus on something several feet to the right. In German they call it a 'Silberblick' or silver view. Even her best friends used to say that the effect at close quarters, through her pince-nez, was thoroughly unnerving. She had been born Elisabeth Nietzsche, the second child of a Lutheran pastor from

Saxony, and the sister of an eccentric, and as yet quite unknown, German philosopher, Friedrich Nietzsche.

Elisabeth, although she considered herself to be cosmopolitan, had seldom set foot outside Germany, and never outside Europe. Until her marriage to Bernhard Förster, less than a year earlier, she had lived a sheltered bourgeois life with her mother in a small house in Naumberg. Yet of the hundred or so Germans who disembarked at Asunción docks in the heat of that March afternoon, it was Elisabeth who was probably the least put out by her new surroundings. Her penetrating voice, with the provincial Saxon accent she had tried but never been able to conceal, grew shrill as a gang of mulatto peons clumsily manoeuvred her large piano down the gangplank.

Asunción in 1886 cannot have been a welcoming sight. Much of the city was still in ruins after the War of the Triple Alliance, an unwinnable blood-bath waged by Paraguay against three far more powerful neighbours. The years of carnage had left three-quarters of the male population dead, and the countryside devastated by famine and disease. The skyline above the port was still dominated by the half-built edifice of the Presidential palace. This was to have been the imperial seat of Francisco Solano Lopez, the country's war-hungry President, and a symbol of Paraguay's military power. He had died an ignominious death in the last battle of the war and building had stopped abruptly; now there was neither the money nor the manpower to finish it. It loomed, a rotting testament to the dictator's vanity.

If some of the German settlers stared in understandable horror at the crumbling, malodorous remains of the Paraguayan capital, Elisabeth and Bernhard Förster certainly did not. They were, by nature, a couple immune to second thoughts. Paraguay was to be the setting for the most glorious moment of their lives, the culmination of a dream no less grandiose and hopeless than the one which had inspired the dictator Lopez to model himself on Napoleon. Bernhard Förster was by inclination, indeed by profession, an anti-semite who, like another of his type fifty years later, sought to build an empire out of race hatred; Elisabeth Nietzsche was a willing accomplice – to both of them, as it turned out. A few European settlers had come to Paraguay before, impelled by poverty, greed or adventure. Most, it is true, had perished or disappeared. The Försters' motivation was both more simple, and more terrible, than any who had preceded them.

Every one of the German men and women who now loaded their few possessions on to ox carts, the great-wheeled *carreteras*, and moved with painful slowness along the quay had been selected on the basis of their genetic purity, their Aryan racial characteristics. Most were from Saxony, victims of an economic crisis in Germany that had left much of the peasantry landless and nearly destitute; but many also shared the Försters' ideal of a community cleansed of Jewish influence, of the taint of Jewish capitalism. It was the Jews, they all agreed, who had forced them out of the Fatherland. Förster spoke of Germany as a 'step-fatherland', a place where honest German virtues were being blighted, where culture was at the mercy of Zion. In South America, he said, they could found a New Germany, where Germans would be able to cultivate the genuine German *geist*, where fruit and vegetables grew in abundance (the Försters were militantly vegetarian), and where their Lutheran religion could prosper in pristine isolation. New Germany, in the midst of the Paraguayan wilderness, would be the nucleus for a glorious new Fatherland that would one day cover the entire continent.

In 1883 Förster had been sacked from his Berlin teaching post for racist agitation, and had travelled through central South America in search of a suitable site for his colonial project. He had chosen Paraguay, depopulated, fertile and above all uncontaminated by Jewry. For two years after his return he had peddled his message through the cities and villages of Germany, while Elisabeth Nietzsche distributed his racist pamphlets and collected funds for the venture. In Berlin they had been ridiculed, but in rural Saxony, over foaming *biersteins*, they had been heard and understood. The Fischer family had been among the first converts, then the Schuberts, who claimed to be of the composer's family, and the Schüttes, who made musical instruments in Chemnitz. Some agreed to vouchsafe their savings, as a downpayment on the land Förster said he could find at cheap rates, but most had no savings to offer. Förster said it did not matter; they could pay after their first bountiful harvest in the promised land. Fritz Naumann, a young, intelligent artisan came from Breslau with his family; Oscar Erck, a big-fisted farmer from the south, sold his land to become Förster's henchman. The number of Förster's followers grew slowly but steadily; they were a mixed crew, but all claimed pure Aryan ancestry.

There had been a few last-minute recruits. Max Stern, for example, a dark-haired carpenter who said he was from Frankfurt, had appeared while they were loading their possessions and families on to the steamer *Uruguay* in Hamburg harbour. Förster and his wife had welcomed him aboard. 'Others will follow,' they promised, as the boat prepared to set sail. Elisabeth was sure that her intellectual brother, whose health, she said, would certainly benefit from the excellent Paraguayan climate, would one day agree to join them, even though he had repeatedly denounced the anti-semitic venture. Once the colony was established, Förster assured his disciples, thousands would flock to the new Fatherland from the old one where they were 'wasting away in sickness and poverty'.

The voyage from Germany had been one of the purest horror: a month at sea on a rotting hulk, alive with cockroaches, awash with vomit, living off weevily biscuits and rancid cheese. They had spent a few days plunged into the bemusing hustle of Montevideo while Doktor Förster arranged their passage, and then five days up the Paraná River in a swaying, clanking steamer. At night, animal howls echoed from the dense riverbank undergrowth as the boat churned past; the dark-skinned boathands spoke a language of twittering birds, they mocked the Germans' discomfort, frightened the children and spat horribly. At night the mosquitos had pounced in dense fizzing clouds, and microscopic bugs, which the boathands called '*polverinos*', burrowed under their skin and laid tiny yellow eggs which festered at once if scratched. Two days before they reached Asunción, the Fischers' youngest daughter had suddenly died. At Montevideo she had been pale but talkative; then one night she had vomited blood and started a fever; the next morning she was dead, curled up in the hold next to her sister. They had buried her on one of the few clear patches of riverbank, under a huge tree with red flowers.

That first evening in Paraguay Elisabeth and Bernhard Förster checked into the city's only remaining hotel, while the rest of the immigrants bedded down for the night in makeshift huts next to the customs house, the *Aduana*, an incongruously grand building and another of the dictator Lopez's architectural innovations. It had been built so that its lines followed the contours of the steep river bank, and it looked ready to topple into the water at any moment. Across the river the Gran' Chaco stretched away to the west, a vast tangle of sharp undergrowth, tall trees and deep swamp. It was through this sort of terrain that the settlers would have to travel before they reached the area, about one hundred and fifty miles to the north, that Förster had already christened 'New Germany'. The final part of the journey would take at least another week, by boat up the broad Rio Paraguay and then across country, by horse and oxcart.

Förster had already lectured his colonists on the correct attitude: 'Despite the many difficulties, the emigrants will know they have partaken in a great project. This mission has a name: the purification and rebirth of the human race, and the preservation of human culture.' Perhaps those words ran through their minds, as the handful of Aryan pioneers sat in the foetid atmosphere of Asunción harbour and waited for another boat to take them upriver.

CHAPTER II

Terra Incognita

'I'M GOING to the Paraguayan jungle to find a one-hundred-year-old Aryan colony set up by the sister of the great German philosopher Friedrich Nietzsche and I need some sun cream, mosquito repellent and a hat.'

The man in the survival shop in London's Euston Station batted a laconic eyelid, just one, for the sake of form. These shops are used mainly by two sorts of people: those who think they might be in danger of getting killed and want to prevent it; and those who think they might want to kill someone else and want to do it efficiently. Survival, to judge from the racks of guns, knives, gougers, stabbers and garrotters on display, tends to involve homicide.

Nietzsche himself might have approved of this violent approach to survival. 'My way of thinking calls for a warlike soul,' he wrote in *The Gay Science*, 'a desire to hurt, a joy in denial, a hard hide.' The man in the survival shop had Nietzsche down to a tee. 'It's a jungle out there,' he said, probably not for the first time that day. 'What factor would you like?' I bought a large tub of something which he promised would stop anything from coming near my hide: water, insects and burrowing worms as well as ultra-violet light. It smelled faintly of silage.

The Euston survivalist thought it might well rain a fair bit, so I bought a rather dashing panama hat, a jacket which promised to keep the rain out while allowing my pores to breathe (the few that would still be breathing after applying my suncream) and half a dozen waterproof notebooks. I later practised with one of them in the bath.

In between the literature on potholing, unarmed combat and body-building was a slim pamphlet entitled *Jungle Survival*, a military guide to sub-tropical conditions and how to stay alive in them. It stated: 'Whatever the type of country in which you are unfortunate enough to crash-land . . . your chances of survival and eventual rescue depend on a few definite factors. By far the most important of these is the first, "determination to live".' And it carried on:

> The greatest dangers lie in the demoralizing and cumulative effect of sometimes rather insignificant factors which may be summarized under the following headings:
>
> a) panic
> b) sun and heat, and sickness therefrom
> c) sickness and fever
> d) demoralizing effect and danger from all forms of animal life
> e) poisoning.

The book was peculiarly depressing, although it did explain which sea anemones are edible and how to make essential clothing out of your parachute. I bought a copy anyway. If I ran out of food and there weren't any sea anemones about, I could always eat it.

'What colour are they in Panama then? Black?' asked the survivalist.

'It's Paraguay, and they're sort of brownish mostly.'

He looked doubtful.

'But the ones I'm going to find are white, I think.'

He looked relieved. 'That's all right then.'

ACCORDING to *The Present State of All Nations*, written in 1739, 'It must be acknowledged that *Paragua Proper* is a perfect *terra incognita.* I meet with no author or traveller that pretends to give any description of it, or know the extent of it; and our map-makers are so ingenious as not to incumber their maps with the name of one town in all the country.' The situation has only marginally improved.

Elisabeth and Bernhard Förster had called their colony New Germany, Nueva Germania in Spanish. A journalist had visited the area some years earlier, but Nueva Germania didn't appear on my atlas, nor in the only guidebook I could find which covered Paraguay, nor in any novel by any South American author, living or dead. There was New Italy, New Australia and New Bordeaux, but New Germany seemed to have vanished. The staff at the Paraguayan Embassy politely but firmly insisted that no such place existed, at least not in Paraguay. They suggested trying the Brazilian Embassy instead. 'Actually the only one of us who has been to Paraguay in the last thirty years is the Ambassador,' said the receptionist, 'and he's in Wales at the moment.' The only map I could find which actually pinpointed Nueva Germania was Elisabeth Nietzsche's own. In 1891 she had published a book called *Bernhard Förster's Colony New Germany in Paraguay*. It was an exercise in self-justification, the first of many, printed in Germany and intended to recruit more colonists. It contained a map, an updated version of one drawn up by Bernhard Förster himself based on a military chart made by the Hungarian expatriate, Colonel Heinrich von Morgenstern de Wisner.

THE name Colonel Heinrich von Morgenstern de Wisner looms large in Paraguayan history; he was also partly responsible for the creation of New Germany. Once a noted wag at the Imperial court of Vienna, a Hungarian aristocrat, suspected pederast, military adviser, amateur historian and cartographer, Morgenstern ended up as Immigration Minister for the Republic of Paraguay at the time that Bernhard Förster was deciding where to start his colony. It was partly Morgenstern's propaganda talents that persuaded him, and Morgenstern's maps that guided him.

Morgenstern was highly suited to the job of Immigration Minister since it involved, among other things, a talent for extreme mendacity; his main role in the years after the War of the Triple Alliance was to lure Europeans to depopulated Paraguay with apparently generous land deals and an extensive tissue of misinformation about the country's natural advantages. The Colonel's 'Report on the State of Paraguay' had been printed in European newspapers, including *The Times*, inviting European colonists to apply for land. One who did was Bernhard Förster. The German colonist and the

Hungarian émigré must have met on several occasions, and as a foreigner who had survived for forty-six years the vicissitudes of life in Paraguay, the aged Colonel may have provided Förster with a remarkable, if rather bizarre role model. What Förster cannot have known, however, was that Morgenstern's real name was in fact Morgenstein and that he was probably Jewish.

As a young man Morgenstern had used his aristocratic connections to gain a place at the Viennese court, which he was then obliged to leave in a hurry after an unseemly scandal. But Europe had proved too small for this professional, courtly *flaneur*, and he turned up in Paraguay in 1845 as part of a Brazilian military delegation to the Paraguayan dictator Carlos Antonio Lopez. Though the climate was foul, the opportunities were boundless for a man with a little refinement and a lot of ambition. Morgenstern quickly became the toast of Asunción's undemanding high society. As a foreigner there was a simple recipe for success in the upper reaches of Paraguayan society of the mid-nineteenth century: you grossly flattered the dictator of the time, or ran the risk of being executed by him. This became particularly essential when Carlos Antonio was succeeded by his son, a portly young sadist with poor teeth by the name of Francisco Solano Lopez, who butchered his way to the presidency in 1865. Morgenstern went one better than the avid sycophants who buzzed around the new dictator: he captured the attractive ear of the only person who had influence over the President-for-life – his mistress, a talented Irish courtesan called Eliza Lynch, whom everyone knew as La Madama.

Morgenstern, with his snobbish manners and urbanity, was exactly what Eliza Lynch needed to put the noses of the Asunción ladies firmly out of joint; they persisted in calling her *La Concubina Irlandesa* behind their fans and snubbing her at parties. Morgenstern treated her with extravagant Viennese courtliness; in return she persuaded Lopez to make him Lord High Chancellor. When Eliza threw one of her masked balls, Morgenstern chose the wine and pruned the guest list and advised her on which silks were *à la mode* in London. President Lopez, his megalomania reaching imperial proportions, announced that he was another

Napoleon and that he intended to rule the whole of South America. Morgenstern was promptly made his chief military adviser. He soon became one of the largest, and certainly the fattest landowners in Paraguay. The high point of Colonel Morgenstern's career came at the grand opening of the National Theatre in Asunción, an exact replica in miniature of La Scala in Milan. The President and his mistress both attended. Behind them in the presidential box sat the beaming figure of Colonel Morgenstern de Wisner, wearing the uniform of a Hungarian Hussar, a doublet embroidered with silk frogs and an Astrakhan collar; and what is even more extraordinary, no one dared to laugh at him.

Together the dictator, his beautiful Irish mistress and the Hungarian adventurer plotted the conquest of South America. The result was the War of the Triple Alliance, waged simultaneously against Brazil, Argentina and Uruguay. Morgenstern had been one of the few foreigners to survive; he had been found cowering in a wood with eleven of his Paraguayan 'slaves' by a troop of Brazilian cavalry, who for reasons unknown decided not to stick a lance through him. He was soon back in government and spent his last years drawing maps of the country and, as Immigration Minister, encouraging other Europeans to colonise it.

BERNHARD FÖRSTER had used Morgenstern's map as a basis for his own, tracing the routes he had followed through Paraguay between 1883 and 1885, while a smaller inset map showed the Grand Duchy of Mecklenburg, to give it a sense of scale and importance. Elisabeth had taken a pen to Förster's map and inked in the relevant bits. 'Col. Nueva Germania' appeared as a triangular strip of land, between two glottal rivers, the Aguarya-umí and the Aguarya-guazu, about one hundred and fifty miles north of the capital Asunción. The route she sketched followed the wriggling Rio Paraguay to a point just above where the Rio Jejui flows into it; from there she had drawn a line east by north-east, clearly the largest and straightest road in Paraguay. Unnervingly, the road stopped dead after Nueva

Germania, which, according to the scale on the map, seemed to cover an area about the size of London.

I knew enough already about Elisabeth's cavalier approach to accuracy to view the map with some distrust; her description of the journey from Asunción, intended to entice settlers to the colony, made it sound impossibly easy: 'Several small boats travel up the Rio Paraguay but there is only one ship that goes regularly, the *Posadas*, which leaves Asunción on Wednesdays.' The river journey, she claimed, would take a couple of days, counting stops, then 'you change to the ship *Hermann* which flies under a German flag' as far as San Pedro on the Jejui, and continue the last part of the journey by horse and oxcart along a forest track. This final stretch, wrote Elisabeth, was 'hard going' and would take several days. Even taking into account Elisabeth's tendency to play down the obstacles, and the fact that her description was a century out of date, I estimated it would still take a week or more to get to the colony from Asunción by following her route; if, that is, anything like a colony still existed.

Elisabeth Nietzsche's bizarre experiment in the name of racial purity had envisaged thousands of settlers, a New Germany covering, initially, a territory the size of a dukedom and later spreading throughout South America. The hordes of willing converts never materialised, and Elisabeth's new Germany was, by all accounts, a failure. But what had become of the fourteen German families she had taken out there in 1887, and what of their descendants? Had they survived? And, if so, what sort of people were they now? More importantly, what would they make of me?

What is left of my hair is fair, my eyes are blue and I speak an Indo-European language. That is about as Aryan as I get. But it struck me that after a century of isolation, the people of New Germany might not be too choosy any more about who did or didn't pass the Caucasian test. The more I thought about it, the more likely it seemed that I would be captured by this lost tribe of Aryans and kept chained up for the rest of my days to be used for breeding, a captive pump for the genetic pool. At dusk, jungle Brünhildes, perfect Teutons in every way with bright-blue eyes, would emerge from the forest to the clearing where I lay strapped naked to a trestle table; one by one they would line up... It was too horrible to think about. I packed some sleeping pills.

The Försters had gone into minute detail about what the prospective colonist should bring in the way of equipment. On Elisabeth's advice I packed a poncho, boots, linen trousers, a straw hat, medicine, needles, cooking equipment and a blanket. Bernhard Förster recommended 'the odd luxury ... as presents to establish friendly relations with the neighbouring family, souvenirs of the Fatherland'. Quite what would remind a nineteenth-century peasant in the middle of a South American jungle of the Fatherland, I wasn't sure; I packed some postcards of Berlin nightlife and a three-cassette pack of Wagner's music for the Walkman.

After some reflection I decided against carbolic to keep off the vampire bats and in favour of the multi-purpose silage-flavoured goo from the survival shop. Förster was graphic about the various carnivorous insects I would get to know, and one in particular:

> The next worst bug [after mosquitos and bloodsuckers] is called a 'sandfly' by the Germans. A fairly small insect, it bores into the epidermis of the foot on people and animals and gradually lays eggs. The boring is barely perceptible, and it is only when the insect grows during the egg-laying period that it becomes noticeable. Then every sensible person will have it removed by an operation which can be learned, with a little practice and the aid of a pointed knife ... anyone who allows these small parasites to multiply, which usually attack newcomers, can pay for his lack of hygiene with extreme pain.

I scanned the medical dictionaries for the sandfly, and found the *Phlebotomus* (Greek: *Phleps = vein; tomos* = a cutting), sole carrier of *Leishmania*, and where I was going, *Leishmania brazilhiensis*: 'the initial cutaneous sore [is] followed after a relatively long interval by ulceration of the mouth and palate extending through to the nose'. It is also called the oriental sore, Baghdad boil, Aleppo boil, Sart sore, Delhi boil or *bolsa de Biskra*, depending on where you are when it bites you. On the other hand, Förster could have been talking about bilharzia, which, according to a medical friend, enters the body through the skin after spending a while in a snail and then reappears as a worm out of your eye. (A German doctor born in 1825 called Theodor Bilharz discovered bilharzia in Egypt around 1850. Poor Theodor; the praise heaped on him for his 'excellent diagrams of a pair of copulating flat-worms', which helped to identify the disease, meant little to him; he always thought his work on the electrical organ of the thunderfish was much more interesting. He died in Ethiopia at the age of thirty-seven, bitter, disillusioned and looking for thunderfish.)

I went back to the survival shop and bought a knife which looked like a knuckleduster with a small scythe stuck on it, just in case self-surgery should become necessary; it was confiscated by the airline authorities before I left Heathrow.

Reading matter was clearly going to be important, since there is a strict limit to how long anyone can exist on an unrelieved diet of *Jungle Survival.* I decided to take a combination of Friedrich Nietzsche, R. B. Cunninghame Graham and the Försters.

Both Bernhard and Elisabeth had written books about Paraguay, he with the intention of founding a new Fatherland in South America, she with the purpose of maintaining it. For two years before he settled on a site for his colony, he travelled a country left almost deserted after the War of the Triple Alliance; he noted everything that might have been of interest (and rather a lot that probably wasn't) for prospective German colonists: flora, fauna, the river routes and how to get the best out of your mandioca plantation. He had a talent for snappy titles, and the resulting tome was called *German Colonisation in the Upper La Plata District with Particular Reference to Paraguay: The Results of Detailed Practical Experience, Work and Travel 1883–1885*. It was an advertising tract, intended to persuade good German workers of the advantages of his colonial vision. The long, strangling German sentences are interlaced with anti-semitic asides, encomia on vegetarianism, Lutheranism and Wagner, rotund with grandiloquent rhetoric about the future of the German race. But it is thoroughly engrossing, and slyly revealing about the author: fastidious and pedantic, driven equally by pride and prejudice. The frontispiece is an etching of Bernhard Förster himself, with his square beard and fanatic's eyes, and scrawled beneath it is the Goethean motto, written in Förster's elaborate hand: 'Over all obstacles, stand your ground.'

At that time Förster had unwittingly toured on horseback the precise area where the colony would later be founded. Had he known that, he would surely have painted a less daunting picture of his promised land:

> My first worry was to find the most direct route to San Pedro. Until now I had only heard that it was impossible. The whole way was supposed to be one great swamp, almost impassable for a single person and full of dangers. My own experience confirmed these reports. . . . the horses had to cross deep swamps of mud. Only occasionally was there high land, firm underfoot. Moreover the area was completely uninhabited, and there are great numbers of deer, foxes, tigers, monkeys, ostriches etc. . . . To emigrate here would surely be a Herculean task, though the ground appears fertile. Along the way, a few tiled houses, now collapsed, bore witness to the fact that there must have been a cattle-raising livelihood here before the war. . . . Part of the population are negroes, former slaves. The chief one of these was an old blackamoor who understood neither Spanish nor anything else. He couldn't be bothered to help me, so I was forced to sleep in the open. . . . the dangers here are said to be tigers, Indians and snakes. I saw numerous tiger tracks and several snakes, but was never attacked. The only Indians I saw were in a very miserable, domesticated state. . . . the Indians are scarcely dangerous, and would make good servants. But the Lengua are more dangerous, and occasionally cross the Gran' Chaco on raiding parties. The real difficulties faced by a traveller unacquainted with the country are losing your way, bad weather on lonely paths, and the feeling of solitude brought about by the complete beauty and horror of the place, and, last but not least, hunger. . . . If you are simultaneously suffering from hunger, the beating rays of the sun on your head, the wetness of the marshes and streams, and the effect of the tough, high

> grasses on your feet, the illness may affect you for days. A weak constitution may easily collapse with the fever, to which I remained immune.

Förster was motivated by what Nietzsche would have called *Ressentiment*, a combination of envy, jealousy and revenge. A morality defined by contrast to other moralities, which it labelled evil, Nietzsche called a slave morality. Christianity was, for him, the ultimate slave morality, but nationalism and racism were others. Bernhard and Elisabeth Förster were slave moralists *par excellence*.

In his *Genealogy of Morals* Nietzsche wrote, 'While every noble morality develops from a triumphant affirmation of itself, slave morality from the outset says No to what is "outside", what is "different", what is not "itself": and *this* No is its creative act. . . . The man of *Ressentiment* is neither upright nor naive, nor honest nor straightforward with himself. His soul *squints*, his spirit loves hiding places, secret paths and hiding places. . . .'

Nietzsche is like no other writer, in German or any other language. He is rude, violent, a rebel and an iconoclast. To read him is to enter a world shorn of all moral certainties; he urged his readers to live dangerously, to embrace the conflict which he saw as the motive force in human affairs. Humanity was motivated by a will to power, he said; whatever increased power it accounted good; even the slave morality was a form of this will. It was the brave, the strong, the self-possessed who would inherit the real world, the only world there is, while the meek, the pious and the kind would inherit, and deserved to inherit, nothing. He scorned and feared the mediocre, the mass, and beliefs that acquired the status of morality through sheer weight of numbers. Nietzsche's philosophy took a hammer to ideologues, dogmatists whose 'truth is supposed to be a truth for everyman', Christians, politicians, preachers and populists of any sort. He believed above all in the individual, the strong, purposeful, independent-minded free-spirit who rode roughshod over morality, the 'herd instinct in the individual', and who, if he could overcome his own *Ressentiment*, might attain the status of a Superman, or more exactly Overman.

It is refreshing but dangerous stuff. His imagery is often violent and his style prone to some of the worst myth-making tendencies that found their apogee in Nazi rhetoric, the ultimate in *Ressentiment.* But cant and hypocrisy were his sworn enemies, and if he tended to use a claymore where he might have used a scalpel, that was only because of the originality of what he had to say and the urgency with which he needed to say it.

Despite his opposition to codified systems of belief, Nietzsche's name has been associated with practically every 'movement', intellectual or otherwise, in this century: feminism and structuralism, Marxism and anarchism and behaviourism, as well as fascism. If you put into one room everyone who considered themselves a Nietzschean, there would be a bloodbath. Nietzsche saw it coming: 'Whoever believed he had understood something of me', he wrote in his autobiography *Ecce Homo*, 'had dressed up something out of me after his own image – not uncommonly an antithesis of me, for instance an "idealist"; whoever had understood nothing of me denied that I came into consideration at all.' And he admitted that it pertained to his nature as a philosopher 'to *want* to remain a riddle in some respects'.

He saw his contemporaries, the Europeans of his day, being emasculated by their own piety, 'a shrunken, almost ludicrous species, a herd animal, something full of goodwill, sickly and mediocre . . . .' He urged freedom above all, and self-realisation, and spurned 'the contemptible sort of well-being dreamed of by shopkeepers, Christians, cows, women, Englishmen and other democrats'. As so often with him, the tendency to lash out, the very violence of his language, offends and angers – which was exactly what he wanted, to jolt his readers out of their torpor and force them to scale, as individuals, the heights he thought they were capable of. For in spite of his lascerating language he loved humanity and believed that by 'writing with blood' he could do apathetic man 'a great service by bringing out the hidden sickness of his heart and making it visible'. His was an anguished cry for individuality. Thus spoke Nietzsche: 'Overcome, you higher men, the petty virtues, the petty prudences, the sand-grain discretion, the ant-swarm inanity, miserable ease, the "happiness of the greatest number!"' He is contradictory and contrary, and at times thoroughly dubious; he knew he was dynamite – a horrible explosive in the wrong hands. But he was no dogmatist: 'We would not let ourselves be burned to death for our opinions: we are not sure enough of them for that. But perhaps for the right to have our opinions and to change them.' What Oscar Wilde wrote about Dorian Gray applies equally to Nietzsche: 'he never fell into the error of arresting his intellectual development by any formal acceptance of creed or system, or of mistaking for a house in which to live, an inn that is but suitable for the sojourn of a night in which there are no stars and the moon is in travail. . . . no theory of life seemed to him to be of any importance compared with life itself.'

As an antidote to the constipated moralising of his sister or her husband, Nietzsche's very contrariness is a purge; as Montgomery once said of Chairman Mao, 'He would be a good man to go into the jungle with.' And if, like Tony Last in Evelyn Waugh's *A Handful of Dust* reading Dickens in the jungle, I was imprisoned and made to read nothing but Nietzsche for the rest of my life, I would at least go mad fairly quickly.

IN 1864, the same year that Friedrich Nietzsche was made Philology Professor at Basle University, an aristocratic Scottish youth of seventeen, who had learned Spanish at his grandmother's knee on the Isle of Wight, set off for Argentina to find adventure and make his fortune. For much of the next sixty years, Robert Bontine Cunninghame Graham wandered through South America living dangerously: in Brazil, Uruguay, Argentina and, above all, Paraguay, he worked as horse-breaker and cattle rancher, traveller and writer. Sporting the pointed beard and long hair of a *hidalgo*, he could throw the *boleadoras* as well as any of the hole-eyed gauchos who were his companions and who called him 'Don Roberto.' He was constantly in trouble, in debt and, I think, in hysterics. His life was a series of hilarities and close calls. In Uruguay he was kidnapped and pressed into service by some revolutionary gauchos; while riding through Paris, he knocked down a pretty Chilean girl of eighteen, Gabrielle de la Balmondière, and promptly married her; on their honeymoon in Texas, they were attacked by Apaches. He voyaged to Morocco in disguise, to find the lost city of Taroudant, but was captured by a Kurd.

And he scribbled it all down, in thirty books of sketches and short stories, histories and travelogues. His writing is odd but poetic, a tumbling scree of half-built phrases and hiccuping grammar, vividly redolent of his own chaotic life. He was equally happy on a horse or at his desk, but most contented of all riding through the forests of Paraguay.

Rejecting the confinement of Victorian life, a gypsy-philosopher, Cunninghame Graham came closer to being Nietzschean man, in a way, than Nietzsche himself ever was; he may even have read Nietzsche, for his autobiography begins with an epigraph from Zarathustra: 'Remain true to the earth, my brethren.' (The other epigraph is from King Alonso XII: 'You know well that when I am needed in any place, I am there, and if there is danger, I am there the sooner.') He was one of that great British tradition of travellers and writers – Byron, Doughty, Burton, Wilfred Thesiger and Patrick Leigh-Fermor. Even in old age the *hidalgo*–laird fulfilled Nietzsche's prescription for the youthful soul: 'A drive and impulse rules and masters it like a command; a will and desire awakens to go off, anywhere, at any cost; a vehement dangerous curiosity for an undiscovered world flames and flickers in all its senses. "Better to die than to go on living here" . . . a rebellious, arbitrary, volcanically erupting desire for travel, strange places, estrangement, coldness, soberness, frost . . . that superfluity which grants to the free spirit the dangerous privilege of living experimentally and of being allowed to offer itself to adventure: the master privilege of the free spirit.'

He loved life and loathed bigotry, and there was barely a trace of *Ressentiment* in him. Nietzsche believed that such men gravitate to political power, as to a birthright. In about 1880 Don Roberto returned to Britain and was elected Liberal MP for North Lanarkshire in 1886. He became a close friend of Joseph Conrad (who re-read Cunninghame Graham before writing *Nostromo*); he shared a speaking platform with Engels and created the Scottish Labour Party with Keir Hardie. On 'Bloody Sunday', 13 November 1887, Cunninghame Graham insisted on going to a banned demonstration in Trafalgar Square. A policeman hit him on the head with a truncheon, cracking his skull, and he was sentenced to six weeks in Pentonville Jail. 'His getting into prison', wrote his friend George Bernard Shaw, 'was as nothing compared to his getting into the House of Commons. How he did it, I know not, but the thing certainly happened, somehow.' Only one word of Cunninghame Graham's appears in *Hansard*: 'Damn.' It was a curse on the hypocrisy he saw on both sides of the House. When asked to withdraw the remark he replied, 'I never withdraw,' and was suspended. Shaw then promptly stole the phrase – for the Bulgarian hero of *Arms and the Man.* Like Nietzsche, Cunninghame Graham distrusted demagoguery. 'I care not in the least for theories,' he said, 'for this or that dogma of politicians and theologist, but take my stand on what I heard myself. . . .'

So he returned again to the beauties and dangers of South America. As a foreigner he never claimed to be part of Paraguay, but his books about the country are eccentric and vivid, if syntactically abstruse:

> When I think on them, pampa and Cordillera, virgin forest, the 'passes' of the rivers, approached by sandy paths bordered by flowering and sweet smelling trees, and most of all the deserted Jesuit Missions, half buried by the vigorous vegetation, peopled but by a few white-clad Indians, rise up so clearly that, without the smallest faculty for dealing with what I have undertaken, I am forced to write.

Again like Nietzsche, he mourned that he had not been born to sail with Columbus; he died at the age of eighty-four in Buenos Aires. The following might stand as his own epitaph, to an anti-didact:

> I have no theory of empires, destiny of the Anglo-Saxon race, spread of the Christian faith, of trade extension, or of hinterlands; no nostrum by means of which I hope to turn Arabs into Christians, reconcile Allah to Jahve, remove the ancient

> lack of comprehension between East and West, mix oil and vinegar, or fix the rainbow always in the sky. . . . I fear I write of things without a scrap of interest to right-thinking men. On the contrary, of lonely rides, desolate empty places, or ruined buildings seen in peculiar lights, of simple folk . . . in fact of things which, to a traveller, his travels o'er, still conjure up the best part of all travel – its melancholy.

I packed four of Cunninghame Graham's books – two on Paraguay's history and two of short stories. He and Bernhard Förster had travelled in Paraguay at about the same time. They almost certainly never met, for, if they had, there would surely have been a fight. Förster ended his book with an appeal for Aryan disciples to his prospective colony, the sort of thing that would have made Nietzsche and Cunninghame Graham want to spit:

> The main things you must bring with you are courage and resignation, strength and endurance – the moral fibre from the old Fatherland to pass on to the next generation.

I didn't have any of the above. What I did have was a suitcase full of old books, several pints of foul-smelling and possibly toxic mosquito repellent, a vague idea of where I was going, and a feeling that if that sort of moral fibre *had* been passed on to succeeding generations, I might not want to get there at all.

I agreed with Nietzsche completely on one thing: 'To make plans and project designs brings with it many good sensations; and whoever had the strength to be nothing but a forger of plans his whole life long would be a very happy man; but he would occasionally have to take a rest from this activity by carrying out a plan – and then comes the vexation and the sobering up.'

CHAPTER III

Up the Creek

I SAT in one corner of Madame Eliza Lynch's summer ballroom, now the Gran' Hotel del Paraguay, and listened as David Williams, a half-German-Swiss, half-Welsh Paraguayan, told me about growing up under President Stroessner.

David had spent his youth in a colony called Primavera, founded in 1941 in the north of the country by a religious sect called the Society of Brothers, an offshoot of the Hutterites, which believes in communal living, strict rules of devotion and pacifism. David had grown up speaking English and German, as well as Spanish and the indigenous Indian language, Guaraní. His accent swung between his father's Welsh-valley lilt and the guttural tones of his mother's tongue. 'Look, boyo,' he said, 'you can't imagine what it's like living under that kind of ideology. Your life was controlled by the decisions of other people, and you never knew why they made them, you just did what you were told.' Primavera had been disbanded while David was still young, but the effects of the religious regime lingered. 'It'll take me the rest of my life to recover, I expect,' he said cheerfully. He had lived in Europe for a while, but had returned to Paraguay. He couldn't really explain why.

The barman brought another beer, called Bremen. All the beer in Paraguay is German, brewed according to the Rheinheitsgeböt, the old German recipe: Bavaria, Munich or Bremen are the alternatives. Above the bar was a framed photograph of President Rodriguez, the man who, exactly two years ago to the day, had overthrown one of the longest-running dictatorships in modern history. Somewhere in Asunción, a celebration was taking place but no one was sure where. Life was better under the new President, said David, and he had promised to institute democracy. To judge from this photograph, the new President certainly smiled more easily than the old one.

Alfredo Stroessner carried out his coup d'état in 1954 and he exhibited a combination of 'will to power' and *Ressentiment* to such effect that he managed to cling to power for thirty-five years. So used had he become to dictatorship, to the daily and brutal exercise of absolute authority, that he could hardly believe it when it was over, and became largely senile. Like the Paraguayan President Bernardino Caballero, who had welcomed Elisabeth Nietzsche and her Aryan colonists to Paraguay more than a century before, Stroessner was not particularly choosy about whom he let into the country. Like flies to dung, right-wing extremists settled on Paraguay. Italian neo-fascists lectured to Stroessner's Colorado Party, and right-wing Croatian militants trained the President's personal bodyguard. After being ousted in 1979, the deposed right-wing dictator of Nicaragua, Anastasio Somoza, was flown to Paraguay by Stroessner's own pilot. He lived comfortably in the former South African Embassy and on a vast ranch in the Chaco, until he was gunned down in Asunción for failing, it was said, to keep up payments to the President.

Himself the son of a Bavarian brewer, Stroessner had a soft spot for his fellow countrymen, including Nazis. When Josef Mengele, the Auschwitz 'Angel of Death', applied for Paraguayan citizenship in 1959, he did not even bother to use an assumed name. It was seventeen years before his citizenship was revoked, by which time he had long since disappeared. The fleeing Nazis settled in quickly, said David. 'The place is still full of them – oh God yes,' he said, leaning forward confidentially, 'hundreds of them.' After his family had left Primavera, he had been sent to the German school at Asunción. There he had completed a history project on the Nazi period and told his schoolmates many things they didn't believe. That had earned him the nickname 'Jew'. 'I had a pretty bad time, I can tell you,' he said. At least a hundred thousand Germans, or descendants of Germans, are dotted throughout Paraguay, one person in forty, most of them completely assimilated into the life of the country.

As my companion talked, an asthmatic air-conditioner

wheezed over the cracked French windows, unequal to the task of cooling the vast room. The hotel's German owner thought it had been built in the 1860s: Madame Lynch's ballroom, imperial bourgeois run to seed, hallmark of the Paraguayan Pompadour. The dusty chandeliers were intact, but the murals, great trellises of fruit and flowers in pastel blues and greens, were crumbling into powder. A family of bats had set up home somewhere in the rotting roof. You could still hear them faintly arguing when the pianist started playing 'The Girl from Ipanema'. The night before, one of the bats had fallen out of a chandelier. It lay like a crumpled mitten until a waiter in a starched white uniform with no buttons had scooped it up with tongs and put it in a bucket. 'It's the heat,' he explained.

Here Madame Lynch had held her *bals masqués*, extravaganzas designed to intimidate the potentially treacherous and impress the poor. Madame herself, crunchy in Parisian silk and with her hair in two golden loops, usually came as Queen Elizabeth I of England, while her High Chancellor Colonel Heinrich von Morgenstern de Wisner dolled himself up as Lorenzo de Medici. Francisco Solano Lopez, Commander of the Armed Forces and President-for-life, dressed as Napoleon, which came as a surprise to no one, because he always did. Madame was a dictatorial hostess. Not only did she decide who was to come and what they were to eat and drink and hear, but she even chose their costume. It was an excellent opportunity to humiliate her enemies, saving a special venom for the female members of the Lopez family, who still mocked her openly. The President's sybaritic sisters were obliged to come as Guaraní Indian maidens, which meant they couldn't wear their jewellery, and their mother, a spiteful mastodon with a luxurious moustache, threw a tantrum when told she must dress as Diana the Huntress. But she came anyway. Failure to get an invitation to one of Madame's balls was social death, but turning one down could be an invitation to death itself.

Paraguay's *haut-monde* raged at her impudence. The French Consul, Monsieur Laurent Cochelet, announced that he 'would as soon break bread with a nigger as accept a morsel from that devious Irish slut'. He was still more appalled when Eliza invited a couple of colleagues from her courtesan days,

Mesdames Bolet and Duport, to open a 'finishing school' in Asunción to raise the cultural tone of the capital. She herself taught the Paraguayan upper classes to polka, and under the gaze of her courtiers she swept around the ballroom screeching prettily in French. And when Lopez's megalomaniac war was drawing to its disastrous conclusion, with the presidential treasury stripped bare, Eliza turned her parties into fund-raisers: the good ladies of Asunción were made to bring their jewellery and donate it to the war effort. Eliza patriotically shipped it all off back to a friend in Paris as an insurance policy.

The echoes from the piano plinked through the humid air and shimmied off the ceiling. The acoustics must have pleased Madame Lynch when she gave recitals on the Pleydel she had brought from France. The audience always clapped heartily, and when the dictator himself was present the applause was deafening. The pianist finished playing and bowed to the near-empty ballroom; through the French windows I watched a pair of small grey parakeets chasing each other over the warping terracotta tiles, and David ordered another beer, Bavaria this time.

I had been in Asunción for two sweltering days and had discovered one encouraging piece of information: Nueva Germania existed. The concierge, a mestizo, had produced a tattered map, with President Stroessner still in the corner looking sleepy. Approximately where Elisabeth's map had indicated, it said 'Nueva Germania' in very small letters. The concierge had no idea who, if anyone, lived there now. 'It's a poor area,' he said, 'lots of trees. You might find a bus,' he had suggested doubtfully, 'but the road should be closed by now because of the rain. When it rains they put chains across the tracks in case they collapse.'

He traced a thumb over the map, reading the names off slowly: San Ignacio, San Estanislao, Santa Rosa, remnants of the Jesuit missions, the country's most famous colonists. Stroessner had built thousands of miles of road through Paraguay; it was his favourite boast. Mostly dirt tracks, perhaps the only enduring monuments to his regime, these squiggled all over the official map of Paraguay; they had cost thousands of dollars to build; the only problem was that very few Paraguayans have cars.

'Oh yes, you can get almost anywhere in Paraguay now,' said the concierge, 'so long as it doesn't rain.'

'When is the dry season?' I asked.

He shrugged. 'There isn't one really.'

I explained that I was following the route taken by the sister of a German philosopher a hundred years ago, so I would be going by boat up the Rio Paraguay and the rest of the way on horseback or by oxcart. 'You're mad, *loco*,' he said. He wasn't being rude, just stating the obvious.

THAT morning I had gone to the Floto Mercante d'Estado, the state shipping agents, to book a passage upriver.

Asunción in daylight looked hung-over, rich with odours that had been obscured by hot January rain the previous night. The newer buildings seemed half built, the older ones half decayed. Great buses rumbled blindly down the narrow streets, their bells crashing. By ten o'clock the heat was already bouncing off the cracked pavements, and the streets were raucous with market people, a bewildering goulash of races mostly selling each other Taiwanese electronic gadgetry. There didn't seem to be much else on offer.

There is no racial type in Paraguay, no 'pure' races except a few thousand Indians in the remote north and west, quickly being wiped out and their forest felled. With at least twenty Indian women apiece, gifts usually from the local Indian *caciques*, the conquistadors had mixed their Spanish blood so fast that Paraguay was not a hundred years old before a mestizo race was a fact. One enlightened governor even encouraged the races to mix, but it wasn't really necessary. Like ink in a bucket, the Spanish blood rippled outwards from the capital, sometimes through marriage to noble Indian women, but more often through rape and concubinage. Other immigrants added their genes to the cocktail – European adventurers, negroes and the mamelucos, fierce Portuguese-speaking land-pirates from São Paulo, part-Indian, part-negro, who descended on the Jesuit missions and carried off the Indian neophytes as slaves.

Nietzsche had applauded mixed races, using the Greeks as

his example; he thought they produced the hardiest, most productive artists and minds. The racial distinctions in Europe he wanted to subsume into the model of the 'good European'; though he spoke of a master race, he did not have a specific race in mind and certainly not the German. He envisaged a group of individuals displaying masterful qualities, not a race as we would recognise it, for it is clear that his ideal men can arise in any race at any time: no one race is supreme. For all his championing of the 'prowling blond beast', the creature of conquest, he would have found in the hardy mestizo culture something admirable and enduring.

Illegitimacy carries little stigma in Paraguay. 'It is somewhat ungenerous to speak of the morals of one's friends,' wrote an English émigré of Lopez's time. 'I will only say that incontinence before marriage is not looked upon there as a serious fault.' Far from that, it was looked on as a national pastime. Cunninghame Graham concurred: 'The Paraguayan women were extraordinarily prolific, and nature had arranged that they should bear Eve's burden with the least amount of pain. Chastity may have been a counsel of perfection, recommended by the priests, but certainly was little practised, even by those who recommended it.' Lopez himself set an example, producing an enormous illegitimate brood, including several by Madame Lynch. The War of the Triple Alliance accelerated miscegenation, leaving, by one estimate, just 28,000 Paraguayan men alive and four times as many women. Society became, briefly, polygamous, as it had been in some tribes before the Spaniards arrived.

Other colonists, Elisabeth and Bernhard Förster included, came to fill the void left by the war: Jesuits, Mennonites, French farmers, Australian communists, European anarchists, Irish and German refugees, Japanese peasants and 'Lincolnshire farmers'. The last-named were the most pathetic of all: it had been impossible to convince anyone from Lincolnshire to come to Paraguay, so the 'farmers' were mostly derelicts picked up off the streets of London in order to fill an official quota. Once in Paraguay they soon disappeared without trace.

Within a few generations, almost all the immigrants had

been absorbed and assimilated, through death or intermarriage, their languages replaced by the versatile Guaraní tongue, their memories of home slowly blotted out by the will to survive. To remain independent required aggressive self-reliance, energetic cultural self-defence. Aggression and energy died quickly in Paraguay's genetic soup; the distinctions quickly vanished.

It was true of most breeding experiments in Paraguay. The Spaniards had brought with them fierce Andalucian bulls, and bullfighting became very popular in the seventeenth century. But the immigrant bulls had been mixed with local cattle, and the ferocity was bred out of them. The bulls simply couldn't be persuaded to fight vigorously enough, and the sport almost died out.

But at least one racial group stood out as I passed along the streetside stalls of Asunción market; the Mennonites, like stragglers from a hoe-down in white shirts and dungarees. They sold a soft cheese, made from an imported recipe, or leaned on battered pickup trucks and burbled in a strange dialect. Like the Amish in Pennsylvania, they had cut themselves off from the modern world and its sin in the Chaco and Paraguay's other deserted places; a hundred and sixty thousand Mennonites lived in Filadelfia alone, the Mennonite city five hundred miles along the desolate Gran' Chaco highway towards Bolivia. They kept to themselves, locked away in their enclosed islands of belief.

Were Elisabeth and Bernhard's Aryans so robust in their convictions, I wondered? Or had racial amnesia come to New Germany too?

A tiny Chinese man in a straw hat was selling Korean sunglasses on the corner. He spoke Guaraní, and a little Spanish. 'Where are you from?' I asked.

'Out of town a little.'

And before that?

He just pointed downriver.

A friend had told me of meeting an Indian family in the far north of Paraguay, at Bahia Negra. The Indian mother had three children, two were dark-skinned with brown eyes and high cheekbones, but the third, the youngest, had blond hair and blue eyes, a genetic reminder of a forgotten night between some ancestor and a European, a railway engineer perhaps, or a gold prospector. The family couldn't explain why their youngest child looked so peculiar, but they were very proud of it and called him *el rubio*, the blonde one.

Elisabeth and Bernhard Förster had chosen to build a racially pure colony in a country where the words meant nothing, where, if you didn't actually like your neighbour, you had no problem loving his wife or daughters, whatever colour they were. The atmosphere was sultry, after all, and the Guaraní maidens generous with their favours; white men quickly forgot to be different, lapped by a gentle tide of brown genes. In Paraguay you either mixed and copied the ways of the Paraguayans or you watched yourself dandering ineluctably towards extinction. Presumably Elisabeth Nietzsche's tribe of Aryans had gone the same way. If any of the original settlers had survived, what could be left? Perhaps just a few pairs of blue German eyes, and a couple of surnames, mangled unrecognisably by Guaraní pronunciation.

But the Aryan myth is a strong one. According to an influential nineteenth-century essay on the 'Inequality of Human Races' by Arthur Gobineau (whose work Elisabeth read and much admired), the Arya were an ancient, gifted people who migrated from their homeland to settle Europe: according to the myth, 'everything great, fruitful and noble in the work of man on this earth springs from the great Aryan family', and that included the ancient cultures of Egypt, Rome, China and Peru. Social Darwinism helped to turn the notion that races were unequal into the biological fiction that some were more fitted to survive than others. The German embryologist Haeckel and his Monist League told the world, and in particular Germany, that 'the whole history of nations is explicable by means of natural selection'. Hitler and his twisted theories turned this pseudo-science into politics, attempting to destroy whole races in the name of racial purity and survival of the fittest.

Förster had left Germany before the establishment of the Monist League, but he was clearly influenced by the views of Ernst Haeckel, which had already gained a large following in Germany during the 1880s; Monism, part-philosophy, part-science, was by definition the belief in one central idea (i.e. Darwinism) but was actually an explosive cocktail of many: racism, nationalism, anti-clericalism, eugenics and misapplied evolutionary theory. For men like Förster (and Hitler) such notions were immediately attractive: Haeckel stressed the evolutionary dominance of an Aryan master race, and warned that racial mixture was leading to 'biological decay'. He followed Gobineau in positing an evolutionary ladder with the white races at the top, yellow in the middle and the black (or Jewish) ones at the bottom; those at the top were there by a natural evolutionary process; those at the bottom were destined to die out. Hitler called his book *Mein Kampf*, 'My Struggle', echoing Haeckel's translation of Darwin's phrase 'the struggle for survival'. The myth of Aryan dominance, initially an attempt to trace the lost language of the Aryas, began as a set of undemonstrable racial assumptions, and ended in a colossal, perfectly unscientific lie: '*I* decide who is Jewish and who is Aryan,' announced Goebbels. That is what the Nazis meant by natural selection.

IT TOOK me an hour to fight my way through the market crowds to the shipping office. Outside a man was selling New York Jets baseball caps. He pronounced it in Spanish, 'Newyork*hets*'. New York, New Germany. Adapt and survive. In his stifling and windowless office, the jefe of the Floto Mercante d'Estado was engrossed in a battle with his own nose hair and didn't want to be disturbed. With intense concentration, and the aid of a mirror and a large pair of tweezers, he was carefully rummaging around inside a vast Roman nose, which seemed to be melting. By his elbow, a cloud of flies avidly attended to the remains of a lamb chop, and a wooden ceiling fan barely moved the hot air. The only decoration was another map of Paraguay, but a photograph of President Rodriguez had been tacked over that of President Stroessner. I asked him for the time of the next boat to Antequera, the port on the river due west of New Germany. He didn't look up – which was sensible in the circumstances since the tweezers would almost certainly have entered his brain. 'It's gone,' he said, without taking his eyes off the mirror.

After a pause of several seconds, and a little more excavation, he tugged violently and extracted something from his left nostril, and laid down the tweezers with triumph. He patted the side of his nose. 'It's gone,' he repeated and picked up the mirror again. 'Why do you want to go to Antequera anyway?' he asked, checking out his nose in profile. 'There's nothing there. The Iguassú falls are much more beautiful, and there's a hotel.'

'I'm trying to find a place called Nueva Germania. Have you heard of it?'

The jefe repeated the name, rolling it around his mouth. 'No.'

'Please just tell me when the next boat goes upriver.'

With obvious reluctance he laid down his mirror and pulled a piece of paper from the desk drawer and studied it. 'March,' he said with finality, and returned to his nose.

So much for the *Posadas*, which left every Wednesday. It was two months before the next boat.

I sat on the crumbling waterfront at Asunción and looked over to the Chaco side. Parched, I bought a bottle of something cold, green and fizzy from a stand; I drank it too fast so that it bubbled back out of my nose. The old woman sitting next to me on the wobbly bench screamed gently and stalked away. When I had finished choking, I saw there was something black at the bottom of the bottle.

The City of Our Lady of the Assumption. Assumption was right; I had assumed it would be easy to get to New Germany, that it would be worth getting there. The city itself had been founded on an invalid assumption: that it would be the centre for exploration of fabulous silver mines in the interior, that it would be somewhere important. On a hill looking out over the vast Chaco plain, it marks the meeting of the Rio Paraguay and the Rio Pilcomayo, where they travel together down the Rio Paraná to Buenos Aires and the great river of silver, Rio de la Plata. There wasn't any silver, of course. Once Asunción was to have been the centre for the great conquest of South America, the first great city of the La Plata. But the Chaco Indians and the Indian river pirates had been too hostile, the climate too cruel, and the capital had moved to Buenos Aires, where the air was better.

You could see the rain from a hundred miles away, rolling in off the Chaco, a great grey blanket, blotting out the forest on the far bank. I took shelter under the walls of the Presidential Palace, obscenely whitewashed amid the surrounding mildew. Just a few feet below it on the banks of the river was the shanty town, roofs beaten out of rusting Volkswagen car bonnets with smoke drifting through the cracks. A Colorado Party anthem blared through a distorting wireless. I leaned on the balustrade and watched two children throwing mud at some scrofulous chickens pecking in the rubbish. The vast building was Lopez's last great *folie de grandeur*. Designed by an English architect, Alonso Taylor, it looks like an English country church with delusions of grandeur. Those delusions made Elisabeth's racist dream possible; perhaps if the Paraguayan people had not been so brutalised by their own leaders, they would never have let Elisabeth into the country. The palace was conceived as the imperial seat of Lopez's South American empire. The work was slow and dogged with difficulties. An Irishman, John Moynihan, did the original sculpture work, but Lopez considered the results to be in poor taste, so he put it in the basement. Taylor himself got only halfway through the building programme before, like most of the dictator's foreign advisers, he fell under the suspicion of his xenophobic employer and was thrown, along with Moynihan's sculptures, into a cell under the palace where he was excruciatingly tortured.

Lopez was an imaginative man, particularly in the ways of inflicting pain. Taylor described the dictator's favourite torment, the *Cepo Uruguyano*, from personal experience:

> I sat on the ground with my knees up, my legs were first tied tightly together, and then my hands behind me with the palms upwards. A musket was then fastened under my knees; six more of them tied in a bundle were then put upon my shoulders and were looped together with a hide rope at one end; then they made a running loop on the other side, from the lower musket to the other, and two soldiers hauling on the end of it forced my face down on to my knees and secured it

> so. The effect was as follows: first the feet went to sleep, and then a tingling commenced in the toes, gradually extending to the knees, and the same in the hands and arms until the agony became unbearable. My tongue swelled up and I thought my jaws would have been displaced. I lost all feeling in one side of my face, for a fortnight afterwards. The suffering was dreadful. I should certainly have confessed, if I had had anything to confess. . . .

Taylor somehow survived the *Cepo Uruguyano* and the construction of the palace, which is more than most of its builders did.

Like everything that Lopez and Madame Lynch built, the palace conformed to the latest European taste. The ceilings were high and the windows large, to admit the breeze off the river to cool the sweaty President and particularly his mistress, more used to the misty rain of Ireland. It was built by an army of child slaves, boys between six and ten years old, just too young for Lopez's army. The foundation was to be of freestone, Lopez decreed, dragged from Empedrado, thirty miles away, and the upper storeys would be of brick with a stucco frontage. The child labourers died in scores building the palace, the National Theatre, the National Library and Eliza's several ballrooms. Charles Ames Washburn, a gold-prospector, novelist, lawyer and newspaper editor sent by President Lincoln to be American Ambassador in Asunción, described Lopez's infant construction workers: 'It was a sad sight to see the little fellows made prematurely old by the labour to which they were condemned. They were constantly watched, that they should never idle away a moment, and in passing through the grounds, where they wrought, they appeared like worn out slaves, in whom all hope is so utterly extinguished that they never looked up or ceased a moment from their labour.'

But for the dictator's own children no extravagance was too great. When Eliza Lynch provided Lopez with an heir, Juan Francisco, he ordered a 101-gun salute to be fired off the palace battlements: eleven buildings were destroyed in Asunción and half a gun battery perished because one of the cannons backfired. Lopez, however, was delighted. As the rain eased, I wandered through Alonso Taylor's intricate gardens. Half a dozen soldiers, teenage boys with outsize rifles, lounged in the shrubbery smoking cigars. The President no longer lived there, but in a larger residence which was easier to defend. Further along the riverbank was a bronze statue of Francisco Solano Lopez on horseback, put there by Stroessner to commemorate the man he had declared a Paraguayan hero. There was a votive shrine at the base but it was empty. Nietzsche noted that 'he who wants to live on after his death must take care not only of his posterity but even more of his past: which is why tyrants of every kind (including tyrannical artists and politicians) like to do violence to history, so that it may appear as preparation for and step ladder to them'.

Under Lopez's statue a couple of prostitutes whistled and primped. In the old days they called them the *peinetas de oro*, for the gold combs they wore in their hair. Towards the end, when Eliza Lynch was really down on her expensive handmade uppers, she herded together the prostitutes of Asunción and made them give up their combs.

Madame Lynch left Asunción, still elegant but now under military guard, fifteen years before Elisabeth Nietzsche arrived, but they had much in common. Both were courageous, resourceful and utterly determined to get what they wanted. But they were also ambitious and ruthless, and were born, moreover, into an age when women were expected, as a point of good taste, to be powerless. Both had greatness in them, as well as greed and cruelty. Both realised early in life that the only hope for fulfilling their ambitions was through men; they both enjoyed men, as profoundly as they disliked women, and with their intelligence, beauty and determination, they played with them like puppets.

Eliza Lynch was nine years older than Elisabeth, born in a little town in County Cork. Although she claimed to be descended from Richard I's favourite catamite as well as the royal executioner who beheaded Charles I, it was not an encouraging start for an ambitious girl. She set off for England at the age of fifteen, and married a French army vet, Manaud Xavier Quatrefages, in Folkestone. The life of an army wife in Algeria did not appeal to her; it was both hot and boring, but at least it wasn't County Cork. She stuck it for a year or so, before running away, it was said, with a Russian cavalry officer called Mikhail, who installed her in the Boulevard Saint Germain. Mikhail soon disappeared but other men took his place, lots of them, usually rich and always influential; for Madame Lynch had found her *métier* as a professional courtesan; it was hard work, but she was good at it, advertising herself as an 'instructress in languages'.

Her popularity was understandable. 'Her eyes were of a blue that seemed borrowed from the very hues of heaven,' said one admirer, 'and had an expression of ineffable sweetness in whose depths the light of Cupid was enthroned.' But at nineteen Eliza began to look for something more permanent than the wealthy strangers who trooped in and out of her bedroom on the Boulevard Saint Germain. Her opportunity arrived in the bulbous shape of Francisco Solano Lopez, who came to Paris in 1853. He had been despatched from Asunción by his father, President Carlos Antonio, who vainly hoped a stint in Europe might knock a little culture into the youth and raise Paraguay's reputation abroad.

Cunninghame Graham gave a brief character sketch of the younger Lopez: 'Sadism, an inverted patriotism, colossal ignorance of the outside world, a megalomania pushed almost to insanity, a total disregard of human life or human dignity, an abject cowardice that in any other country in the world but Paraguay would have rendered him ridiculous, joined to no little power of will and of capacity, were the ingredients of his character.' At twenty-seven, he already had that 'gross animal look that was repulsive when his face was in repose. His forehead was narrow and his head small, with the rear organs largely developed. His teeth were very much decayed, and so many of the front ones were gone as to render his articulation somewhat difficult and indistinct.'

Lopez, then, was not an ideal language student, but Eliza was enchanted by her new pupil. After twenty-four hours, which cannot have been too pleasant, she informed the landlord she was leaving France to become Lopez's mistress. They may even have fallen in love. 'Even the meanest intelligence and the coldest heart still feels something of the lustre of this word,' thought Nietzsche, 'the shrewdest woman and the commonest man think when they hear it of the relatively least selfish moments of their life, even if Eros has only paid them a passing visit.'

The young Lopez's tour of Europe was, he thought, a triumph, even though Queen Victoria had announced she was 'quite too busy to see the little savage', and there had been a sticky moment during his audience with the French Emperor Napoleon III in Paris. The Emperor himself was formal but welcoming; after presenting Lopez with the *Légion d'honneur*, he murmured, '*J'espère que vous vous amusez à Paris.*' But the Empress Eugénie seems to have reacted less politely; it was said that when the hideous Lopez bent over to kiss her hand, she vomited all over the Emperor's ormolu desk and had to retire. But Lopez was delighted with his imperial reception: then and there, he decided to model his clothes, his life and the uniforms of his army on those of the French Emperor. He and his new mistress went shopping. He bought seventy pairs of leather boots with high heels and silver trim, and she bought silks and glassware and a Pleydel piano; after a brief visit to the Crimea to watch the European armies massacring each other, they set off for Paraguay with the avowed determination to create a new domain, over which they would reign as Emperor and Empress. Their imperial designs were not so different from those held by Elisabeth and Bernhard Förster, twenty years later.

Back in Eliza Lynch's ballroom, Dai Williams was practising his Welsh on me as the electricity flickered and the pianist started to play 'La Palomita', a jaunty *Habañera* which had been the favourite tune of Francisco Solano Lopez, who liked to have it played during executions.

THE next morning I wandered down to the dock, where a variety of ramshackle craft – canoes, punts and a couple of larger boats – jostled for position at the tiny jetty. Mestizo porters, bare-chested and mahogany brown, staggered up the slipway under their loads. Others sat in the shade drinking *yerba maté* or flirting with the women selling river fish and fried mandioca root, a vegetable so full of starch it is used to stiffen petticoats. Some naked children played happily in the sewage at the water's edge, and tiny fish plucked at the oily surface.

A huge barrel-chested man in frayed cotton cut-offs and a peaked sailor's cap was directing two peons as they painfully manoeuvred a freezer wrapped in plastic across a narrow gangplank on to one of the larger boats.

'That is the man,' said a grizzled Indian under a straw hat. 'Captain Ramirez, he goes to Antequera.'

Ramirez doffed his cap and pronounced himself not only happy to take me to Antequera, about a hundred and thirty miles upriver, but positively honoured. 'Welcome to my ship,' he said, and bowed. He had a huge red face, covered in odd lumps from which sprouted thick tufts of black hair, and he spoke Spanish almost as badly as me. Over one eyebrow was a particularly large protuberance, which jumped up and down when he laughed. If you half closed your eyes he looked like a sunburned Hans Holbein. His feet, which were almost broader than they were long, with crenellated toenails, inspired immediate confidence.

Which is more than could be said for his boat. A converted barge about forty feet long, it was massively overloaded and plainly rotting. The wheelhouse perched on top looked like one of those too-small party hats the boss puts on at office parties, wonky and out of place. The engine was making a tubercular grunting sound, like a large animal in pain, and a small diesel slick spread out from the stern. The legs of a tall Paraguayan hung out from the innards of the engine, the rest of him having been completely swallowed. He was hitting something with a hammer, irregularly and very hard. He extracted himself briefly to flash a wide, oil-smutted grin, and went back to his hammering. A mountain of food had been stashed in the hold, onions, mandioca, sugar, potatoes, flour and crates of empty beer bottles. A three-piece suite, upholstered in algae-green, was arranged at the bow, along with a small oil-tanker on wheels. With the addition of the freezer, the boat sank still lower, leaving perhaps three inches between the lapping brown river and the gunwhale.

The trip would take two or three days. Ramirez said, barring unforeseen circumstances, and the cost would be whatever I deemed appropriate, payable now. His personal chef, Ector, would be ready to provide me with whatever I wanted in the way of victuals, or I could bring my own. He pointed to a small Paraguayan boy slicing strips off a carcass hung over the stern.

'Is there a bed?' I asked.

'Yes,' said *el Capitán*, slapping a sack of onions and winking at the boathands. The lump on his eyebrow shrugged.

Once again I explained that I was looking for a group of German peasants who had been settled in the northern forest a century ago by a white woman called Elisabeth. He paused, then broke into a grin. 'Then you will certainly want to travel with us,' he said, pointing to the wheel house, 'it is a good sign.' A painted board had been nailed on to the roof of the wheelhouse bearing the boat's name: *Blanca Doña*, the White Lady.

That afternoon a small crowd assembled on the slipway to see us off. Francisco, the engineer, seemed satisfied with his repairs, even though dense clouds of black smoke billowed out of the ship's funnel, at one point completely obscuring the Presidential Palace as it retreated behind us. Within minutes everything was covered in a thin film of diesel smuts. We rounded Nanawa point at a walking pace, the white of the palace stark against the skyline. The half-built skyscrapers behind were another of Stroessner's legacies; most had been projects owned or controlled by the Stroessner family. After the coup, work had stopped, and the process of transferring ownership into the hands of the Rodriguez family, according to the more cynical Paraguayans, was still under way.

Here the river was at its widest, a fast-moving sliver of grey. As we moved into mid-channel, the clumps of detached water-hyacinths, *camelote*, grew thicker and more numerous, interspersed with *neñufares*, floating islands of waterlilies. Snakes and monkeys sometimes travel downriver on these natural rafts detached by the rain. Lopez's more daring soldiers used to hide in them with incendiaries in order to catch the Brazilian ironclads unawares. Sir Woodbine Parish reports that a tiger once floated all the way to Santa Fé by this method, where it disembarked, prowled the streets of the town and finally devoured a Christian. Sir Woodbine, former

British minister in Buenos Aires, later helped to restore the Bourbon dynasty in Naples after the fall of Murat, and personally handwrote the peace treaty of 1815 between Britain and France. He was also a member of the Royal Society, so his tiger tale must be true.

'It will not take more than three days,' Ramirez assured me, although we seemed to move impossibly slowly against the current. The Rio Paraguay is as dangerous as it looks; even in the broader reaches, fast undertows can pull you down in minutes. 'The colour is generally that of grey mud,' wrote the great explorer Richard Burton, 'full of vegetable matter, it never strains clear and colourless; some say it is good to drink, others, myself included, that it causes trouble.' The Indians claim that the waters of the Paraguay clear the throat and purify the voice. I would soon find out; in the intense heat, I calculated that my stock of drinking water, stolen from the fridge at the Gran' Hotel, would last a day at most.

To our left, the Gran' Chaco wilderness, a dry Pleistocene sea, stretched away to the Bolivian border, largely uninhabited, fertile, dangerous and damp. Cunninghame Graham described it, and from what I could tell it had changed little:

> As a steamer slips along the bank, nothing for miles and miles is seen but swamp, intersected by backwaters, in which lie alligators, electric eels and stinging rays. Far as the eye can reach are swamps, swamps and more swamps, a sea of waving pampas grass. After the swamps come thickets of tacuaras (canes), forests of thorny trees, chañares, ñandubay, jacarandas, urundey, talas, and quebrachos, each one hard enough to split an axe, some, like the black canela, almost like iron. . . . the climate [is] heavy and humid, the air dank with vinchucas [*Conorhinus gigas*, a smelly, triangular bug], mosquitos and the little black infernal midget called the jejen; no roads, no paths, no landmarks, but here and there at intervals of many leagues, a clearing in the forest where some straggling settlement exists. . . .

I listened to Wagner's *Tristan* and thought about Wagner's Peccary. Quite recently a zoologist by the name of Wagner (no relation) discovered a species of pig unique to the Chaco. If Wagner's Peccary could stalk Paraguay undiscovered for millennia there seemed every likelihood that all sorts of other beasties, discovered and undiscovered, were wandering around waiting for the arrival of a tender European, already basted in sun-cream.

I re-read the relevant parts of Bernhard Förster's book. On the subject of the piranha, an orange fish with a Habsburg chin and sharp teeth, he becomes almost excitable: 'A large round fish, it uses its jaws set with long, pointed teeth to rob the bather with the greatest deftness of pieces of flesh or a limb. But I wish to say that anyone who thrashes strongly in the water is fairly safe from this thief.' Then there is the rana fish, which has 'a long tail with a pointed spike about the length of an index finger. If wounded with this poisonous shard, the victim suffers the most indescribable pain and the wound is hard to heal.' He is dismissive, however, of the crocodile, or *yacaré*. 'They flee on the sight of human beings, and the Lengua [Indians] of the Gran' Chaco eat their flesh.'

The forest, which grew thicker as we left Asunción, is said to house a positive menagerie of mythical beasts: swine-like creatures, which grow navels on their backs and hunt in packs, and the unknown animal with a ruby stuck in it which, according to my *History of Paraguay*, shines 'with marvellous splendour through the darkest of nights. No one ever saw this elusive creature, since exposure to its eerie light caused one to lose all sense of direction.' And the *quirquincho*, 'a hoggish-appearing animal protected by a hard shell ... so fond of deer meat that it would lie on its back, make a trough of his belly to catch rain water, then seize and kill any deer so unwise as to drink from this improvised tank'. Travellers all agree on avoiding the *mboya jagwa*, or dog-snake, a thirty-foot-long water serpent, which has the head of a dog and yelps like a puppy. Father Antonio Ruiz de Montoya, one of the earliest Jesuit missionaries, who in his own words spent thirty years in Paraguay 'in order to find Indians and bring them to the true sheepfold of the holy Church', described its anti-social habits. An Indian woman, who was 'carelessly washing some clothes on the banks of the Paraná, saw one of these beasts and it unexpectedly attacked her for the purpose of violating her. The woman was speechless with fright on seeing the huge snake so licentious, and the latter, carrying her to the opposite bank of the river, carried out its lascivious purpose.' The snake guarded her for three days as she lay dying on the riverbank, until Father Montoya appeared, and, like the good journalist that he was, got an exclusive on her story before administering the last rites.

This riparian rapist was bad enough, but it was the *ow-ow* which made the blood run cold. Alexander Macdonald, an Australian settler who had come to Paraguay at the turn of the century as part of a failed communist colonial scheme, describes it as 'a white, long-haired animal about the size of a sheep, which hunts in packs and attacks human beings'. I have always lived in fear of a hilarious death. Being mauled to death by a mutant South American merino comes into this category. Nor was I safe on the boat. Father Montoya calls it 'an amphibious animal . . . like a sheep, but with the difference that its teeth and nails are like a tiger's, which animal it equals in ferocity. The Indians never look on it without terror, and when it sallies from the marshes where it lives (which it does ordinarily in troops), they have no other chance of escape but to climb up a tree, and even then sometimes they are not in safety, for this terrible creature sometimes uproots the tree, or sometimes stays on guard until the Indian falls into its jaws.' I asked Captain Ramirez about the *ow-ow*. 'I've never seen one,' he said, 'but the Indians say they exist, up by the Brazilian border and in the Chaco.' He jerked a thumb towards the tangle of lianas on the left bank. Later Francisco, one of the peons, approached me where I lay in the bow under the shade of the oil tanker. 'There are *ow-ow* here in the forest, I know because a man in our village was killed by them.'

'Why is it called an *ow-ow*?'

He gave me the sort of look reserved for distracted people in airports who mistakenly try to walk the wrong way up escalators.

'Because that is what you say when it eats you.'

Francisco was the most sociable of the four-man crew. He had a pencil moustache, pot belly and shoulders like a gorilla. He wanted to talk in English, but knew only one word, 'fuck', which he repeated constantly with different Guaraní intonations. His opposite number was called Alberto, a great bullock of a man who took pleasure in torturing Ector, the cabin boy and cook.

Ector was the most intriguing of the boathands. Fourteen years old, he had the eyes and slightly simian face of an old man. Ector, I felt, had seen ugly things. His muscular arms and legs seemed stunted, almost dwarfish, as if he had been stopped in the process of growing up and suddenly aged for the purpose of being put to hard work. I offered him a piece of melted chocolate as he passed me in the wheelhouse. He grabbed it as if expecting to have it taken away again and stuffed it in his pocket. Only later did he shoot me a sly grin of thanks. He was the butt of the crew's humour, which made him scowl and retreat with the ship's dog to a cubby hole he had constructed under a tarpaulin.

There were some half a dozen other passengers. Two young Indians who listened to Guaraní music on a Walkman as if in a trance, each taking one half of the headphones; an amazingly old woman, with a parchment face and dewlaps like plucked chicken skin, and her blonde granddaughter, a couple of Paraguayan *campesinos* and Captain Ramirez's mother. Señora Ramirez was in charge of ship's discipline. Every so often she would hit one of the crew extremely hard on the head with a piece of wood. They didn't seem to notice.

By late afternoon the heat had begun to slacken. The *chacras* and fields that had dotted the river's east bank became fewer, and the river narrowed; tributaries darted off to left and right. The fishermen, an old man and a young boy in pairs, had started to pull in their nets, held up by bobbing plastic bottles, and make for the shore. Tiny yellow birds darted across the water in pursuit of dragonflies. We slowed, and the drumming of the engine seemed to slacken a little. On the Chaco side a plume of yellow smoke rose where the forest was being burned.

I sat in the wheelhouse with Captain Ramirez. He wore my hat, and we shared some *yerba maté*. It was my first taste of

Paraguayan tea, or *Ilex paraguayensis*, the herb indigenous to the country which is drunk all the year round, all day, by everybody. It is also the main topic of conversation, the social glue that holds the country together. Masterman, one of Lopez's personal physicians, wrote a short treatise on the subject:

> Sipping the infusion of the *yerba maté* was the great excuse for idling time away. Early in the morning and after the siesta were the legitimate hours for indulging in it; but those who had plenty of *yerba* and, as usual, little to do passed half their waking hours *maté* in hand. *Yerba* is the dried and powdered leaf of the *Ilex paraguayensis*, a tree in size and shape resembling the orange (that is, as the latter grows there, thirty feet high) and with small white clustered flowers. It belongs to the holly family but contains a bitter principle similar to, if not identical to, theine, the alkaloid found in tea and coffee. It is taken in a somewhat singular way. The *maté*, a gourd stained black, which would hold three or four ounces of water, is nearly filled with the coarsely powdered *yerba*. The *bombilla*, a silver tube with a bulbous end pierced full of fine holes, is then inserted, the gourd filled with boiling water, and the infusion sucked through the tube immediately, exactly as one would take a sherry cobbler except, of course, that it is scalding hot.

The protocols of *maté*-drinking are simple, but strict.

> If the ceremony be conducted in the accepted and time-honoured fashion, the same *maté* and the same *bombilla* will be made to serve for two drinkers, or half a dozen. Like the pipe of peace of the departed Redskin warriors, it is passed from hand to hand, and each sips his fill, while the bowl is replenished as often as may be necessary. In the more populous centres of these modern days it may occur that two or three *maté* enthusiasts, drinking together, may each be provided with a separate bowl and *bombilla*. But this, from the hardened *maté* toper's point of view, is the rankest degeneracy. It is most emphatically against all the ethics of *maté* sociability. . . .

We passed the *maté* cup back and forth, Ramirez refilling it from a flask. The faintly narcotic effects of the drink seemed to calm him. The eyebrow wiggled less frequently and the gales of laughter blew less fiercely. Ector came and sat at his feet, dangling his legs over the side of the wheelhouse and staring wordlessly at the bank. Ramirez rested the *maté* cup on his head.

The taste of the *maté* was not unpleasant, smelling slightly of marijuana and freshly cut hay. It was first drunk by the Indians, who collected it from the wild plantations, *yerbales*, which grew in the forest. Ramirez pointed out the different varieties as we chugged past the west bank. The Spaniards had taken to it quickly, and the gauchos drank it to alleviate the constipative effects of a diet of meat. Even Bernhard Förster, never much of a one for foreign customs, had only praise for it: 'the effects of *yerba maté* are not only beneficial to the stomach, but all complaints can be cured by it and it has a pleasant effect on the nerves. As is supposed, this custom was found among the Indians by the first immigrants, and taken over from them.' The Paraguayans claim it has medicinal powers, relieving rickets, beri-beri, malaria, piles, diphtheria and impotence. The only effect I noticed was an almost instantaneously laxative one. Its magical properties are enshrined in the complex religion of the Guaraní Indians. Ramirez and the crew embarked on a lengthy religious discussion about *yerba* and the gods. Catholics all, they talked of Guaraní gods as if they were only marginally less believable than the Christian God, second-rung deities which could be invoked if the Catholic God failed to deliver. Nietzsche held that polytheism was a sign of individuality and thus applauded it:

> The one god was not the denial of or blasphemy against another god! It was here that the right of individuals was first honoured. The invention of gods, heroes and supermen of all kinds, together with that of fictitious fellow men and sub-men, of dwarfs, fairies, centaurs, satyrs, demons and devils was the invaluable preparatory exercise for the justification of the selfishness and autocracy of the individual: the freedom one accorded the god in relation to other gods one at last gave oneself in relation to laws and customs and neighbours.

Ramirez talked of the Guaraní pantheon as of old friends; their names cropped up regularly in his blasphemies. The Guaraní creation goes something like this: first there was Tupa, who created the forests and the streams and the animals, and his enemy Aña, who lived with the goddess Yaci in the crescent moon and who visited misfortune and devastation and death when he felt like it; a sort of devil, only funnier. Tupa made man last, from red earth brought to him by I-Yara, master of waters. He made two brothers, Pitá, who was red in colour, and Moroti, who was white, and he gave them two sisters as companions. Pitá and Moroti, the red man and the white man, were made to be brothers, yet they fought with the lances they had made to spear meat for the pot, and Tupa summoned Osununu, god of thunder, with a storm to ravage the forest for three days and nights. When the sun reappeared, his emissary I-Yara came again, disguised as a dwarf, and ordered the brothers to embrace. They merged, and became the lily of the forest: red blossomed in summer, turning to white with the winter. Like the mixed race of the mestizos, the men of different colour became one.

I wondered what Elisabeth and Förster would have made of this man's casual approach to his gods. 'The population is Christian by name,' said Förster archly, 'but I doubt there are many people in Paraguay who are actually Christian.'

Ramirez sucked on his *bombilla* happily. Caa Yara, he thought, is the goddess of the *yerba*, young and blonde, who wanders the forest, protecting those who gather the plant. It is said that Tupa was wandering the country he had made when he came across an Indian hut where lived an old man who was so poor that he had only a beautiful daughter and a hen for company. The Indian sacrificed his hen to make a meal for the sake of his divine guest, who repaid him, rather ill, by granting immortality to his daughter and turning her into the *yerba* tree.

Francisco said that was nonsense. It was Yaci the moon goddess who, like Caa Yara, takes human shape as a beautiful fair-haired maiden and walks the forest at night with only her white handmaiden, Arai, for company. One night they were cornered by a jaguar which threatened to devour them.

But an arrow sped through the night air, striking the beast in the side. Enraged and dying, it lunged at the attacker, an old Indian hidden behind a tree, who plunged another arrow through its heart. That night Yaci and her maiden visited their protector and made him a gift of the *yerba*, in thanks.

ECTOR produced a meal of *soo-yosopy*, or tough meat and noodles. It took rather longer to digest than it did to prepare.

Captain Ramirez sat in front of the wheelhouse and clipped his spoon-like toenails by the light of an oil lamp. The others lounged around him drinking *maté* and smoking, oblivious to the sharp fragments which occasionally whizzed off his feet like shards of glass. Guaraní conversation clicked and buzzed around me. Father Dobrizhoffer, a German and the first Jesuit to leave a full account of this time in Paraguay (printed in Latin in 1784), claimed 'that the sounds produced by the Indians of the Chaco resembled nothing human, so do they sneeze and stutter and cough'. But it is an extraordinarily robust language that has somehow survived the marauding Spanish tongue largely unchanged: of the South American countries Paraguay alone can claim to be truly bilingual, and in the wilder areas Guaraní is the first, indeed the only, language. It is truly disconcerting to hear. In every sentence there seems to be an English word that couldn't possibly be there. My notebook contains this bemusing phonetic exchange.

CAPTAIN RAMIREZ: 'Ootunondumi rabo Caaguazu.'
FRANCISCO: 'Bokinmaginum sinking.'
RAMIREZ: 'Help.'

I learned my first Guaraní blasphemies: Añan me buy (mother of the devil), Aña ra quo (devil's arsehole) and A Kam bu ce ndet titire (I want to suck your tit). My rendition of the last phrase seemed to cause particular mirth. Ramirez laughed so hard his eyebrow threatened to detach itself. Even Ector grinned, though Señora Ramirez brandished her piece of wood menacingly.

I asked them whether they knew about the colony established by Germans about seventy kilometres east of the river at Antequera. Los Mennonitas? Certainly there was a large community not far from Antequera, Colonia Volendam, where they grew pineapples, but a German colony? They looked doubtful. There had been Germans this far north, sure enough. Francisco said his surname was Eisenhut and that he was descended from a German. He didn't know where, or when, but his great-grandfather had crossed the sea in a big boat, much bigger than the *Blanca Doña*. But he had been born in the south, he said, near the Argentine border. Señora Ramirez joined in. Yes, she said, she knew about Nueva Germania: it was through the *montes* on the way to Santa Rosa. There were many *rubios*, blonde people, pretty girls with long, fair hair, and people who spoke a language no one understood. It would not be hard to find. I plied her with questions, but that was all she knew; she had been told by someone, but she had never been there. I should ask in Antequera, they would know. Embarrassed, she hit her giggling son on the head with her truncheon to signify that she had had enough questions.

YACI, goddess of the moon and protector of Aña, the death-bringer, had risen above the Chaco shore. I leaned on a box of empty beer bottles in the stern and watched our churning brown wake. It was suddenly gloomy, and cold.

We were hugging the east bank now, an unbroken cliff of tangled creepers, leaning over the water and rising thirty feet overhead. The mangroves curtsied in our wake, and the lily leaves bobbed. The crew and passengers had spread out in the hold on bags of onions, or with their heads resting on their arms. Above the engine's throb, someone was snoring. I lay by the wheelhouse, feeling my body cool at last, but couldn't sleep.

So Nueva Germania did exist. And if Señora Ramirez was right, I would eventually find the human remnants of that bizarre racist experiment. If they were still there, in the middle of this inhospitable wilderness, did they have any notion why? Was there even a faint recollection of the racial theories and poverty that had propelled their ancestors from their homes? And, if there was, did they know what the Nazis had done with those ideas half a century after they had departed Germany? Did the name Nietzsche mean anything to them?

More likely the people of Nueva Germania had eaten the fruit of the great *aguabirá* tree Ramirez talked of. One bite of its yellow fruit, says the Guaraní myth, and the traveller will forget his own people and be content to stay forever in the forests of Paraguay, a natural racial amnesia.

Guabira was an Indian girl who wanted to be a sorceress. A favourite of the gods Tupa and Yaci, she had been given supernatural powers. She had to fast, remain chaste and finally drink the *jugo de muerte*, death juice, made from herbs and *yerba maté* and a liquid distilled from the bodies of Indian warriors decomposing in their funeral platforms in the trees. She passed all the tests easily, and became a medicine woman, a *cuña-tai*. If she inhaled enough tobacco smoke, Guabira could understand the present and see into the future, and she could tame the most dangerous snakes in the forest. One day she ran away with a Spaniard whose life she had saved with her magic, on his wedding night. They disappeared into the forest and enjoyed their passion for many years. But the Spaniard grew restless. He longed for his homeland and the pretty white maidens of his youth. He left the brown-skinned Guabira, and returned to Spain to marry a white woman.

Guabira was broken-hearted and an outcast now for having broken her vows of chastity. But Tupa took pity and gave her immortality too, in the shape of the *aguabirá* tree. Once a person has tasted the fruit, he will forget all about the land of his birth. I somehow expect Elisabeth Nietzsche banned *guabirá* from her vegetarian menus.

IT WAS now pitch dark, though I could just see the outline of the far riverbank by the flickering light of the brush-burning on the Chaco side. We had moved into mid-channel again, Ramirez seeming to know instinctively our position in the current, needing no light to see the way. To our right you could feel rather than see the forest. A bat darted overhead, chattering angrily, and I remembered the words of the explorer Christopher Gibson, on his first night in the Chaco: 'Sleep was out of the question. Vampire bats, obscene, evil creatures, kept fluttering round, clinging to the mosquito net, trying to force an entrance. As they attack man in the big toe, or above the eyebrow, I was careful to keep these portions of my anatomy as far from the net as possible.' Perhaps that explained the shape of Captain Ramirez's eyebrow. I pulled my hat lower, and wrapped the poncho around me.

From the shore strange night noises wafted across the water. Pombero, the boozy Guaraní gremlin-god of starless nights, was somewhere out there. Working by the light of the firefly, Pombero was a nuisance, never seen but heard all around on the night breeze. He was short and squat, with a dwarfish shape and an impish face. He had soft hair on the palms of his hands and feet, and he could run upright or on all-fours at the speed of an idea, to let your horses loose or unlatch the gate on your cattle pen. Like his allies the river snakes, he could glide across the water, to untie your boat and leave you at the mercy of the swift water. He liked to panic lonely people on long journeys with blood-chilling screams on hot nights. Pombero's voice echoed across forest and river, for he could make himself invisible as the night gnat, but throw his voice behind your back to startle the uneasy, like the caraya monkey, or howler. Keep Pombero happy, by putting a plug of dark tobacco in a hollow tree, and he would guard your sleep and protect you on dangerous night excursions; but annoy him, and he would happily visit you with disaster.

The air over the water seemed so clear that my hearing suddenly became perfectly acute. I thought I could hear the heart of the forest beating.

Nietzsche called the ear 'the organ of fear', and believed that the sense of hearing 'could have evolved as greatly as it has only in the night and twilight of obscure caves and woods, in accordance with the mode of life in the age of timidity, that is to say the longest human age there has been:

in bright daylight the ear is less necessary. That is how music acquired the character of an art of night and twilight.'

I was jolted from my half-sleep, propped against the back of the wheelhouse, by an angry revving of the engine and a lurch as the boat picked up speed and turned sharply. Someone, Ramirez I think, was shouting orders in Guaraní from the wheelhouse. His voice was urgent and frightened. The passengers and crew were all awake, shouting and staring intensely over the boat's side and beyond into the murky night. From somewhere, Alberto the bull-peon had produced a spot light. Attached to the ship's battery it cast a pale spot on the water about twenty feet beyond the bows, as we sped back downriver with the current behind us.

Ector had disappeared and, like most of Paraguay's river people, he couldn't swim.

He had last been seen washing dishes from the stern, half an hour before, perhaps more. His cubby hole had been found empty, except for the ship's dog now furiously barking at the noise. The boat slowed suddenly, and we strained to see through the night, the spotlight hopelessly panning across the empty water's ripples. But Ramirez was already shaking his head and muttering in Guaraní under his breath. Francisco whispered: 'El Niño fell off the boat once before, but then it was daylight and we managed to find him. Now it is too dark. There has been rain upriver and the water is fast.' He stared back over the bow.

For hours we trailed the river bank, looking for a flash of clothing or an ancient little boy's face illuminated by the feeble spotlight. Ramirez turned off the engine, and we strained to listen. Only the whistles and hoots of the night forest, the mocking voices of Pombero, drifted back from the tangled bank.

CHAPTER IV

The White Lady and New Germany

AT MIDDAY the *Blanca Doña* docked at Porto Rosario, a jumble of huts and a broken jetty, face down in the river. Smoke from the forest-burning tainted the air and snagged my dry throat. It was deathly hot. A mutter of thunder threatened from the Chaco side. I felt my face stretched and swollen from lack of sleep; an angry little flurry of insect bites was spreading along my left cheek. Ramirez waded ashore and climbed the steep bank to the village to report the man overboard. Years of judicial death under Stroessner taught that formalities must be observed.

Small grey birds hopped among the jagged stones at the river bank, and the two Indian men, with hair cut square on the forehead, lay on each others' arms like lovers, listening to the scratching of their Walkman. Only Francisco and the ship's dog, a stunted little brown object with a shrill bark, seemed much affected by Ector's disappearance. The dog kept returning to the hot cave under the tarpaulin and whining, until Francisco kicked it hard and it yelped away into the hold. Francisco was not sure where El Niño came from – Antequera, he thought, where the boy might still have a mother. Captain Ramirez had found him a year ago, hungrily wandering the Asunción docks. He wasn't paid, but he lived on the boat and ate for free. He was a strange boy, said Francisco, one of the *gente perdita*, the lost people.

An ancient Indian bumped alongside in his canoe and stared up at the *Blanca Doña* without a word. Francisco tossed him down a packet of *yerba*, and he paddled slowly down-river, stopping now and then to look back.

Ramirez returned with the news, broadcast on the midday

radio, that Ector's body had been found by fishermen, about twenty kilometres downriver from where we had lost him. He had drowned, Ramirez said, and his hands and face had been gnawed away by piranhas.

For the first time I wondered whether to abandon the journey. Where last night it had been a worthwhile adventure, it now seemed obscenely trivial to hack through this cruel country in pursuit of a tribe of white people that probably didn't exist and arguably should never have existed. Ector had fallen to his death a few feet below where I sat, probably slipping on the rotting wet planks of this infernal White Lady. He must have died watching the boat grinding uncaringly into the darkness. And, lost in my own preoccupations, I had been deafened by the forest and had heard nothing.

The peons began unloading some of the cargo, wobbling along the narrow gangplank under great bags of mandioca and sugar, and a small crowd of children, dressed in ragged clothes of identical material, gathered on the bank to watch. One played tunelessly on a reed-whistle. The sound was infuriating. Francisco soon abandoned the hard work and threw himself down on the floor of the wheelhouse next to me. 'Fuck,' he said, 'fuck, fuck, fuck.'

Beyond Porto Rosario, the Rio Paraguay grew wide again. To the west the country was supposedly flatter, but it was impossible to see what lay beyond the forest-lined shore. Far to the north-east, beyond Nueva Germania, between Pedro Juan Caballero and Cerro Corá, is a town which carries the indelible mark of Eliza Lynch.

President Lopez's vain war lasted half a decade. Surrounded and outgunned, the Paraguayans for some reason fought on with suicidal determination. The remains of the white Spanish aristocracy, always under suspicion from Lopez, were pressed into the army – the 40th Battalion – and were immediately wiped out at the Battle of Estero Bellaco. It was a war fought partly over the colour of different skins. The white Brazilian aristocracy traditionally looked down on the Paraguayan mestizos as savages. There was more than a hint of racial supremacy in their genocidal enthusiasm for the war; both sides referred to the other as monkeys. Even

Cunninghame Graham was inclined to look for a racial explanation for Lopez's fanatical will to power: 'in the blood of most mulatos, mestizos, or to whatever mixed blood Lopez belonged, there is a lust for power, but power with all the pomp of military rank, medals and crosses, gold sashes, silver helmets decked with plumes, in fact a perpetual carnival, with a brass band always a-braying to direct their people's eyes to them, when they ride down a street.' Like Nietzsche, Cunninghame Graham was a raging snob. The President's mother was a mestizo, his father the offspring of an Indian–negro slave mother and Creole father, a shoemaker. 'That Lopez, with his Indian blood, was influenced by the insane hatred of the white races that has inspired so many half-breed tyrants was not altogether strange,' thought Cunninghame Graham. Nietzsche would have called it the slave morality of rebellion, doomed to failure, the *Ressentiment* of the oppressed.

The allies, Brazilian, Argentinian and Uruguayan, killed the Paraguayans so fast they couldn't get rid of the bodies. Funeral pyres were built, alternate layers of wood and dead soldiers. But the Paraguayans were so thin they would not burn, so the invading troops left them for the *perros cimarrones*, the wild dogs of the plain. To Madame Lynch's fury, the expensive carpets from her ballrooms and palace were cut up and turned into ponchos for an army composed of old men, young boys and women. Measles, smallpox and cholera killed those out of range of the allied guns.

By 1870 the dictator's army was running so short of munitions that books from the National Library were cut to pieces and used for rocket and squib cases; makeshift cannon were constructed from the hollowed trunks of the great *quebracho* tree. These could be fired three, at most four, times, before they shattered, tearing the cannoneers to shreds with a blast of burning splinters. Women, too old to fight, or too pregnant, were made to reinsert fuses into any unexploded enemy shells. Often they exploded too.

In the midst of the battles, Eliza Lynch gave some 'capital dinner parties', where, according to one English guest, 'she could drink more champagne without being affected by it than any woman I have ever met'. The entertaining went on even as the Brazilian artillery shelled the fortifications at Las Lomas Valentinas, where the President had retreated after the fall of Asunción. Most of the foreigners who had been engaged to help Lopez had already been executed in the President's *tribunales de sangre*; the remaining ones were invited to dinner. Colonel Morgenstern de Wisner selected wines to complement the gourmet food of a petrified French chef. The dictator himself sat at the head of the table, swallowing copious draughts of brandy and ordering more, to still the pain from his rotting teeth and gums. When he had drunk to excess, 'he would indulge in the most revolting obscenity and would sometimes give orders for the most barbarous acts'.

After dinner, his mistress played the piano, while shells sang overhead. Eliza boasted that Liszt had heard her play in Paris and had tried to persuade her to follow a musical career, and she became furious when her recitals were interrupted by the sound of the army's *turututus*, loud Paraguayan horns which they played to keep up their spirits. They were stopped immediately. But the allies were closing in, so the President and his mistress headed north, she in an old Spanish carriage with high wheels and leather springs, he in an American four-wheeled buggy. They took the remains of the army and 600 carts, loaded with the national archives, all the gold from the treasury and enough wine and provisions to last the dictator and his family several months. And they took Eliza's Pleydel piano. Lopez's mother and sisters, Raphaela and Innocencia, the vast 'Bavarian eggs' whom Eliza loved to humiliate, fell under suspicion of treachery and were locked in wooden cages on wheels and rolled along with the rest of the heavy baggage, just behind the piano; every so often Lopez would take them out for an airing and have them flogged, as the column wound northwards, harried by advance units of Brazilian cavalry. At a point between Las Lomas and Cerro Corá in the far north, the President's final resting place, the Pleydel was unceremoniously dumped near the river, the horse drawing its carriage having died and been eaten.

The town is still called Piano, or Isla Madama.

*

THE progress of the *Blanca Doña* was slower now. Every few miles a tiny hut, or merely a path, broke the monotony of the forested banks. Usually there was a canoe waiting, on to which the crew would load provisions. No money seemed to change hands.

We left the main branch of the river and detoured down a winding tributary, stopping at a larger *estancia*, the Rancho Negro, to take on two more passengers. One was a taciturn, leathery gaucho with deep, distant eyes and a heavily scarred face. The other was a live puma nailed into a wooden cage which the crew gingerly carried to the bow and then avoided. She was a pathetic sight, about five feet long with a tawny coat, spattered with her own excrement. The cage was too narrow for her to turn, and she spat and hissed furiously if anyone approached her. Except her captor. When he menaced her with a raised hand she would cower in terror, shrinking back against the slats. The hunter, whose name was Roberto, made an illegal living as a puma-hunter. This one had been lassoed with *boleadoras* from horseback; more often he would merely trap them. 'They are difficult to find,' he explained, 'but easy to catch.' When trained and domesticated they could fetch $80 in Asunción market, sold on the quiet as the plaything of some gorged Asunción housewife. The government knew all about the trade in rare animals and animal skins, but turned an eye blinded by bribery.

I couldn't decide which of the two new arrivals was more threatening. The puma's cage looked distinctly unsafe, but Roberto looked more so. His skin looked peculiarly white next to the other Paraguayans. Of the two he would have been more at home in a zoo. A great knife was stuck in the back of his belt. He took it out as we left the shore, and stuck it absent-mindedly in the wheelhouse door.

THE first European to set foot in Paraguay also came up the Rio Paraguay in search of a possibly non-existent tribe of white-skinned men.

Don Alejio Garcia was a conquistador, a credit to Portuguese manhood and a brave crusader for the holiest of Churches. None of which alters the fact that Don Alejio was actually a violent and greedy pirate, which he might have admitted if you had asked him. A Florentine bank-clerk called Amerigo Vespucci was Garcia's inspiration. Vespucci was manager of the Seville branch of the Medici bank, a boring job which he abandoned after hearing tales of the wonders of a new world, to take up exploration, cosmology and geography. He crossed the Atlantic and sailed down the coast of Brazil, discovering what was later to be called the Rio de la Plata. Vespucci became convinced that somewhere on this vast coast was a strait leading through the continent to the spice islands on the other side, but he abandoned the search at some point on the Patagonian coast. There was another reason for wanting to colonise South America, apart from the money to be made. By biblical prophecy, the conversion of the 'hidden Jews' would be the prelude to the ending of the intermediary age, when Christianity would become truly catholic. What could these half-clad savages be other than the Jews of the Diaspora of the period of Salmanazar? Stealing their precious metals, raping their women and converting them was all part of God's plan, an excellent way of combining business, pleasure and piety.

Alejio Garcia sailed with Juan Diaz de Solis, pilot major of Spain, to discover the passage through the new continent, which would bring with it untold wealth. The explorers arrived at the Rio de la Plata estuary in the summer of 1515 and began to explore where Vespucci had left off. On the island of Martin Garcia, a group of Charrua Indians hospitably beckoned the pilot major to come ashore. Juan de Solis landed on the beach and, sadly for him, was immediately eaten.

The leaderless party decided to set sail for home, but one vessel ran aground near the island of Santa Catharina. Only eighteen men made it to shore, one of whom was Alejio Garcia. Garcia rapidly gained a working knowledge of the Guaraní tongue, and with it tales of a vast and wealthy kingdom, ruled over by *el Rey Blanco*, the White King, lying far to the west, which the Guaraní had periodically invaded over the preceding centuries. Garcia's Guaraní informants were talking about the Inca Empire. His avarice piqued by the fabled wealth of this White empire, Garcia left Santa

Catharina around 1524, with a handful of Spanish and Portuguese companions, and some Indian slaves. They headed west, discovering *en route* the great Iguassú falls and crossing the Paraná river. At about the point where Asunción was later founded, Garcia persuaded 2000 Chiruguano warriors to join him in his planned raid on the riches of *el Rey Blanco.* They sailed up the Rio Paraguay into what is now Bolivia, before striking west through the Chaco swamps. On reaching the outskirts of the Inca Empire they settled down to some plundering, and in a short time amassed a vast quantity of booty. But the troops of Huayna Capac, the reigning Inca, fought back, forcing Garcia to retreat to protect his spoils of war.

The conquistador headed south again to the safer banks of the Paraguay and sent word to his former companions in Santa Catharina to join him and help in the plunder of the Inca riches; knowing his colleagues well, he also sent a small quantity of silver to whet their appetites. They declined the offer, sensibly as it emerged, for in late 1525 Garcia and all his companions were murdered by their Indian allies, and their loot was divided among the Indians who lived where they had died, a hundred and fifty miles north of Asunción near a place now called Antequera.

But the story of a great and rich city ruled by a white king, somewhere in the interior, continued to obsess European explorers, and from time to time it killed them. It came with many names, this lost civilisation, this Eldorado: the City of the Caesars, Meta, Omagua, Manoa. For some it was the Empire Puytita, near the Laguna de los Xarayes. At night, around a fire of bones, gauchos still talk of mystic Trapalanda; the Indians call it Tapua Guazu, the great city. Even Bernhard Förster reported rumours of a wild Aryan race, the Guana-qui:

> I know not whether to believe the accounts, widespread but perhaps exaggerated, of a race consisting of wasted, blonde individuals, uncivilised in the extreme, whose different language has prevented contact with the Guaraní. They are said to live in trees, and with the help of sticks are able to walk upright, rather like monkeys. I am not in a position to say

> what truth there may be in these reports, which I have heard from many sides, but the existence of such a racially distinct group seems indisputable. It would surely be of anthropological interest to study their physical form, language etc.

Förster came to South America to escape the Jews; but they had got there almost four hundred years before he did. The Jews of Portugal were forcibly converted to Christianity in 1497; thousands of these 'New Christians' subsequently emigrated to the New World, to avoid the continued persecution. It was their financial know-how that made the New World operate: they formed the backbone of the trading class. An ungrateful Inquisition soon followed them, of course, and 400 New Christians were tried in Brazil alone on charges of Judaising, a crime punishable by burning; merely being Portuguese was usually enough to arouse the Inquisition's suspicion of crypto-Jewry. Even so, Portuguese Jews, converted or otherwise, headed to South America in numbers and some of the Portuguese explorers were New Christians. It is quite possible, for example, that Alejio Garcia, the man who opened up the interior of the New World for a prolonged burst of European missionary activity among the Indians, the 'hidden Jews', was Jewish himself.

RAMIREZ said that we should make Antequera before nightfall. The sound of Roberto stabbing his knife into the rotting woodwork, a cloud of silent black bugs (the jejen, perhaps) and thoughts of Ector's paltry death combined to make me wonder again why I was doing this ridiculous trip. I dozed grimly, grimy with sweat and breathing diesel fumes.

It was beginning to dawn on me that most of the history of Paraguay revolved around white men chasing after other white men in the jungle, or else trying to turn the brown ones white. In Asunción I had met Jim Woodman, an American amateur explorer and epigraphicist: he said that the Europeans had been in Paraguay long before Garcia and the conquistadors. Jim keeps a house in Asunción which doubles as a museum; he stays there when not running a watersports business in Coconut Grove, Florida. When I met him he wore exceptionally tight jeans and cowboy boots with heels so large that he had to bend his knees to avoid toppling forward. He was very earnest. 'The Celts were here ages ago, way back in the fourth, fifth century, and the Vikings and the Irish and the Africans. They were all here.' His pamphlet said: 'I'm also convinced the trail crossed America years ago. It, perhaps, was one taken by the bearded white gods South America's shadowy legends say brought knowledge and culture to Andean tribes.' The walls of Jim's house were covered with photographs of fertility symbols and inscriptions he had found in caves around Paraguay, some not far from Nueva Germania. Most were in Celtic Ogham, which supposedly has an alphabet something like this:

b L F S N   H D T C Q   M G NG Z R   A O U E I

The first of Jim's inscriptions read:

From which he deduced:

(f)-s -g b m-l s-nr q and g—r-ui-m

Which, somehow, he translated as 'A cave shelter: enjoy it, be good cheer. [signed] Grim.' There is a lot of guesswork involved in epigraphy, he said. To me they looked more like the sort of notches bored prisoners make to count off the days, similar to the marks Roberto, the gaucho, had been making in the wheelhouse door with his *machette*.

A LOUD hooting made me sit bolt upright, banging my head painfully on the low roof. Ramirez was sounding the ship's horn repeatedly, urgently. Dazed, I staggered out into the sunlight, thinking that the impossible had happened, and miraculously Ector had been found alive. The crew had

Elisabeth and Friedrich Nietzsche, posing for their confirmation photographs.
'... he always laid stress upon his being much older than I was and used to call me a "little girl", although there was only two years difference between us,' Elisabeth later wrote.

The composer Richard Wagner and his wife Cosima, on whose life Elisabeth modelled her own. Nietzsche visited the Wagners' home at Tribschen on Lake Lucerne twenty-three times and declared 'at no price would I relinquish from my life the Tribschen days'.

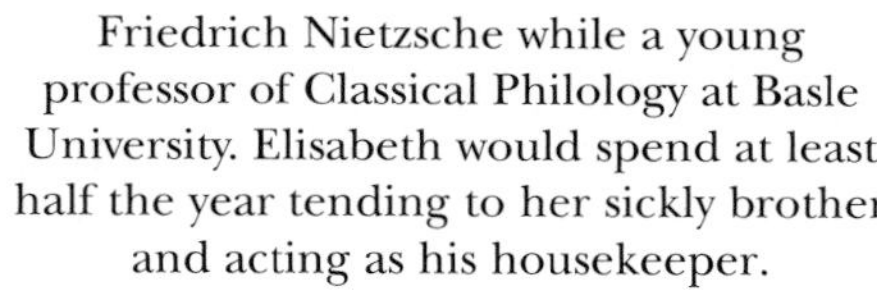

Friedrich Nietzsche while a young professor of Classical Philology at Basle University. Elisabeth would spend at least half the year tending to her sickly brother and acting as his housekeeper.

Bernhard Förster, a professional anti-semite and devoted follower of Richard Wagner, who married Elisabeth Nietzsche on 22 May 1885, Wagner's birthday. Elisabeth was captivated by his views on race, vegetarianism and culture, and helped him to collect signatures for an anti-semitic petition they presented to Bismarck.

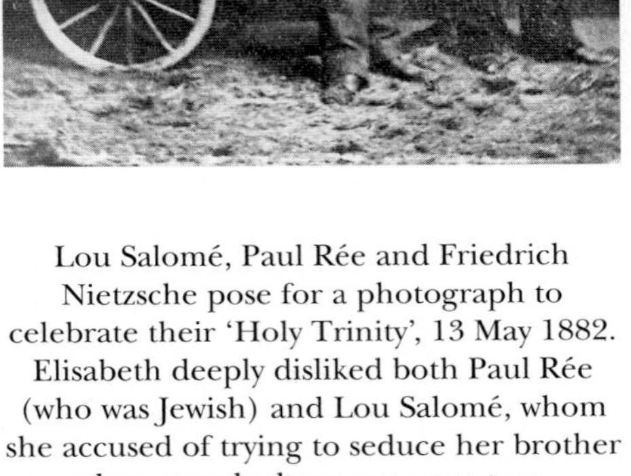

Lou Salomé, Paul Rée and Friedrich Nietzsche pose for a photograph to celebrate their 'Holy Trinity', 13 May 1882. Elisabeth deeply disliked both Paul Rée (who was Jewish) and Lou Salomé, whom she accused of trying to seduce her brother when exactly the reverse was true.

Elisabeth Nietzsche at around the time she left for Paraguay.

The Rio Aguarya-umí, the larger of the two rivers marking the boundaries of the Germany colony.

The *Blanca Doña* (White Lady) stopped regularly on the journey upriver to take on more cargo including an oil tanker, a gas-powered fridge and a live puma.

The first colonists of Nueva Germania, *c.* 1886. 'Our mission is the purification and rebirth of humanity, and the preservation of human culture,' they were told.

Elisabeth (second from left) at a morning meeting with the chief colonists. With her husband sinking deeper into depression and debt, she increasingly took over the running of what she referred to as 'her' colony.

Main Street, Nueva Germania, 1890.

Main Street, Nueva Germania, 1991.

Försterhof, the large colonial mansion which Förster built for Elisabeth in 1888. 'I never imagined it to be half so magnificent,' she told her mother.

The ruins of Försterhof, 1991, with a street sign in memory of the colony's founder. What remains of the building is used as a pig sty.

gathered at the side of the boat and were pointing excitedly into the undergrowth. From somewhere Roberto had produced a rifle. *Mborebi,* a tapir, had come down to the water's edge and had narrowly escaped being turned into supper. I was pleased it had escaped, although I would have liked a close look at one of those extraordinary animals. Having that professional animal-killer Roberto on board was already enough of an affront to the Guaraní goddess, Caaguy Pora, the guardian of the animals, birds and streams. She was the protector of the ecology, the main Green god of the Guaraní pantheon. The man who killed for pleasure or profit incurred her implacable wrath. It was thanks to her that the streams continued to flow when man dammed them, and that the animals continued to reproduce when man killed them without reason. Caaguy Pora could take the form of any animal; if you killed an animal for food, she forgave, but if you killed or captured wantonly her punishment was grave.

I went over to where the puma was panting in her cage. As I approached she hissed demonically; perhaps that was Caaguy Pora's fury in her eyes. I hoped she would devour the first Asunción millionairess she came across. They are unreliable household pets, on the whole. The Rev. William Barbrooke Grubb was almost killed by one in 1891. This leathery missionary was lying asleep in a hut in his mission at Waikthlantingmangyalwa, about one hundred and twenty miles due west of Antequera in the heart of the Chaco, when the incident happened.

> A tame tiger cat had also gone to sleep on one of the beams overhead. What really happened to it I do not know. At any rate, it lost its balance and fell down from the beam, unfortunately right on my chest, and I woke up with a great fright, to find it viciously spitting in my face. In my weak and nervous condition I sustained a great shock, and the cat was made to pay the penalty of death for its unintentional fall, the owner being afraid it might annoy me again.

The good man was in a febrile state because he had just had to crawl about a hundred and ten miles through the jungle after being shot in the back with a seven-inch poisoned arrow, fired by a disgruntled convert. The man responsible for this attempted murder suffered a similar fate to the puma, and had his brains ritually removed with a machete by the elders of his tribe. Which was odd, and a sign of the changing times, because as Barbrooke Grubb admitted, 'an Indian who killed a foreigner was looked on by his people as a hero, and worthy of all respect'.

Barbrooke Grubb arrived in Paraguay in 1886, within a few months of Elisabeth and Bernhard Förster. In addition to being brave to the point of insanity, pious and chaste, Barbrooke Grubb was a gifted amateur anthropologist. His portrayal of the life of the Lengua Indians, of whom now only a few thousand remain, is a rare in-depth study of indigenous peoples in Paraguay. Yet his assumptions of racial superiority were little different from those of many other white men who came to Paraguay. For twenty years he survived among the Indian tribes, by following a simple set of rules:

> That attitude was briefly this: to assume at all times and under all circumstances superiority and authority . . . perhaps a few general instances given here will best illustrate the way in which I carried out this policy. On arriving at a village, I insisted, as far as possible, upon all the people ministering to my personal comfort. I ordered one to prepare my resting place, another to make a fire, a third to bring me water, and another to pull off my knee boots. When the heat was great or the flies troublesome, I made two sit by me with a fan. When on foot and having to cross a swampy patch, I made one of them carry me across – in fact, I avoided doing anything myself that I could persuade them to do for me. . . .

Under the circumstances, it is amazing that someone didn't try to shoot him earlier, but his attitude was echoed by almost every European traveller to the country. The early Jesuit missionaries professed amazement at the weak but biddable Indian character: 'They had', wrote the feisty French missionary François-Xavier de Charlevoix of the indigenous tribes, 'extraordinarily small intelligence, more or less stupidity and ferocity, an indolence and distaste for work, and absence of provision for the future, that had no bounds.' As further evidence of their cultural inferiority, early travellers gave lurid details of the Indians' loose morality, licentiousness and cannibalism.

A Dutch mercenary, Hulderilke Schnirdel, who was present at the founding of Asunción in 1537, is typical of the combination of moral disapproval and straightforward titillation:

> The men and women both in this Countrie goe all naked, as they were created of God. Amongst these Indians the Father sels the Daughter, the Husband the wife. Sometimes the Brother doth either sell or change the Sister. They value a Woman at a Shirt, a Knife, a Hatchet, or some other thing of this kinde. These Carios also eate mans flesh, if they can get it. For when they take any in the warres, whether they be men or women, young or old, they fatten them, no otherwise than wee doe Hogges. But they keepe a woman some yeeres, if she be yong, and of a commendable beautie, but if in the meane time, she apply not herselfe to all their desires, they kill and eate her, making a solemne banquet, as marriages are wont to be celebrated with us.

Only later does Schnirdel coyly admit that 'I for mine owne person did possesse about fiftie men, women, and children.'

In fact, if the Guaraní *did* indulge in cannibalism, they seem to have made it as pleasant an experience as possible for the intended victim. According to Pero Hernandez, in Cabeza de Vaca's *Commentarios*,

> they eat the flesh of their enemies whom they take captive in war, bringing them to their settlements and making great merriment and rejoicing with them, dancing and singing till the captive grows fat. They give him their wives and daughters, in order that he may have every pleasure. It is these wives who take the trouble to fatten him. Those held in the greatest honour among them admit him to their couches, adorn him in various ways according to their custom, and bedeck him with feathers and necklaces of white beads and stones, which are much prized among them. When he begins

> to grow fat they redouble their efforts; the dancing, singing and pleasures of all kinds increase. Then the men come; they adorn and make ready three boys of the age of six or seven, placing a little hatchet in their hands. . . .

The infants then dice up the fattened, contented captive and the women cook him in earthenware pots. Even the babes in arms had a little broth.

Early arrivals to the *Terra Incognita* ignored, or more often demolished, the subtle social structures of Indian tribal life; in Guaraní religion, rich with natural myth, they saw only heathen superstition. A German Jesuit who travelled the wilderness in the second half of the eighteenth century left a remarkable account of one foray to convert the 'hidden Jews'. From his mission at San Estanislao, Father Martin Dobrizhoffer set out barefoot to convert the Indians of the M'baevera forest, the very area that Elisabeth Nietzsche later colonised. It look twenty days of wandering before the priest found some convertible material. Cunninghame Graham described this Indian tribe as 'a community of seemingly quite happy sylvans, whom he proceeded to convert. . . . hapless, harmless folk, as innocent of God and devil, right and wrong, and all the things which by rights they should have known, as they are said to be implanted in the mind of man, no matter what his state, seem to have lived quite happily in their involuntary sin'. Father Dobrizhoffer, touched or possibly infuriated by 'their unregenerate state', burst into tears. 'My friends,' he said in Guaraní, 'my mission is to make you happy.' He played the viol d'amore, as they sat in a circle around him, and then he berated them for their nudity, their savagery and their ignorance of God's word. He told them of heaven and hell, salvation and damnation. The Indians seem to have thought it was all terribly funny, and sat around smoking long cigars and giggling. Then Father Dobrizhoffer took the expedient of presenting the tribe with knives, glass beads, axes, mirrors and fish hooks, which more or less instantly converted them to Christianity. 'I seem to have borne down all before me because I mingled my oration with a copious largesse,' he admitted. In return the *cacique* of the tribe offered his hilarious and generous guest his prettiest daughter and invited him to stay in the forest for ever. The priest declined, but managed to persuade one of the tribe to return to the mission with him, where he was baptised.

Nietzsche thought that 'for youthful, vigorous barbarians Christianity is *poison*; to implant the teaching of sinfulness and damnation into the heroic, childish and animal soul . . . is nothing other than to poison it'. For even the most enthusiastic Indian convert, life in the missions could be a slow death. 'They died like plants,' admits another Jesuit, 'which, grown in the shade, will not bear the sun.' It was the fallacy of every white person who came to the New World correctly to identify the people they found as different, and incorrectly identify this as wrong. It was what Nietzsche again would have called the will to power, 'which was in former times inflamed by the belief that one was in possession of the truth and which bore such beautiful names that one could thenceforth venture to be inhuman *with a good conscience* (to burn Jews, heretics and good books and exterminate higher cultures such as those of Peru and Mexico). . . . what one formerly did "for the sake of God" one now does for the sake of money'.

Bernhard's and Elisabeth's racism and cultural superiority were little different from the ideas of earlier European arrivals in Paraguay, except that their racism was blended with notions of biological purity. They found their Paraguayan neighbours feckless, idolatrous and deceitful, of use only as domestic servants. In Förster's view:

> The principal characteristics of the Guaraní are indolence, sluggishness and indifference. The Paraguayan is content with little, but this contentment is a vice rather than a virtue. A paradisical situation, of living without labour, which might seem ideal to the workshy Jew, is achievable in these tropical and semi-tropical zones. The Indians exist without doing any real work . . . and the excessive use of alcohol will gradually ruin the country and the population. . . . The Paraguayan is passive and without initiative; he is perhaps the most biddable man on earth, even more so than the German, whose patience and governability is exemplary in Europe . . . but you can't trust the word of a Paraguayan.

Elisabeth agreed. Paraguayans she described as 'a harmless race with certain childlike traits that one must never forget in dealing with them. ... the best method of keeping Paraguayan servants is to treat them firmly, but kindly, like children, to let them keep their own ways in eating, drinking and working, and to give them little presents from time to time . . .'

Actually Elisabeth was not content to let people get away with eating whatever they wanted, and they were both scornful of the Paraguayans' carnivorous habits. According to Förster, 'Throughout Paraguay, there is the belief that so long as meat is available, every other sort of food is unnecessary. "Give us today our meat for tomorrow." Just as a German farmer will roast a pig for a party, and want no other food than this anti-semitic dish, so a dish of beef is a meal in itself for the Paraguayans.' Elisabeth echoed this fanatical vegetarianism and backed it up with some bogus medical theorising. Meat-eating is a mistake, she wrote, 'for it heats the blood, which must be avoided in this country. ... my husband, myself and all our vegetarian servants have escaped acclimatisation illness, an ailment which consists of sores on the hands and feet. ... in every case a vegetarian diet would be beneficial and bring about a speedy recovery.'

IT WAS late afternoon when we reached Antequera, the point at which I would leave the *Blanca Doña* and head east to Nueva Germania. It was hardly a port, as Elisabeth had described it, merely a row of one-storey houses made from adobe bricks, lining the river bank. Some of the houses had been painted pink; a sign hung outside one, with *Yerba* painted on it. We made fast at a dilapidated pier as the sun was setting an angry red over the river.

The *Blanca Doña* and her crew planned to spend the night before going on. I shook hands with each in turn. 'I hope you find lots of Germans,' said Captain Ramirez, slapping my back and joggling a farewell eyebrow. 'If you want to go back downriver we'll be back in a week.' Francisco had said I would find a *hospedaje* on the front. 'Just ask for Yolanda.'

In the gloom I dragged my equipment up the hill, pink

mosquito net dragging in the dust. Two heroically fat women were sitting on the porch of one of the huts, eating nuts. Both appeared to be called Yolanda, and both agreed that the mosquito net was the funniest thing to happen in Antequera for about a decade. 'Yolanda will put it up for you,' said Yolanda, and her namesake grabbed it and rolled off into the inner recesses of the house, laughing heartily.

Yolanda I, who appeared to be in charge by virtue of being marginally more obese than her partner, went off to cook, leaving me to sit in front of the house with a warm beer, Bremen again. Antequera seemed to be deserted. In the heavy dusk, an anorexic chicken plucked absent-mindedly at the dirt road around my feet; after about a quarter of an hour, a gloomy-looking cow wandered down the street. I knew how it felt.

The clank of the *Blanca Doña*'s diesel still buzzed in my head, joined now by a great orchestra of cicadas, fizzing and popping overhead, but the beer began to relax me. Yolanda II returned with a plate of *bori-bori*, chicken stew, and *chipa*, small flour pancakes. She cantilevered from side to side as she walked, like a Sumo wrestler. I ate it fast, under the beady eye of the chicken, possibly a close relation of my meal, and certainly a potential cannibal. I watched the river change colour and a fishing canoe steering gently towards the Chaco side.

SEBASTIAN CABOT, the famous chief pilot of Spain, had heard the story of Alejio Garcia, the first conquistador in Paraguay, and of *el Rey Blanco* from Portuguese in Pernambuco and from Garcia's companions left on Santa Catharina. In 1526 he decided to find out what had become of Garcia and to make another assault on the wealth of the white city. In 1526 he headed up the Paraguay with four ships and six hundred men. Some hundred and fifty miles upriver from Asunción near the spot where I was eating my *bori-bori*, he came on a Guaraní tribe by the river who had quantities of silver in their possession, the remains of Alejio Garcia's treasure. Cabot stole it back and named the Rio Paraguay, Rio de la Plata, the river of silver, but he didn't find the City of the Caesars or *el Rey Blanco*.

There is one more chapter of the story of Alejio Garcia. It was rumoured that when the Indians of Antequera had killed Garcia and stolen the silver he had previously stolen from the Incas, one Spaniard had survived: Alejio Garcia's son. The Governor of Asunción in 1543, Alvar Nuñez Cabeza de Vaca, heard reports of a white captive held by the tribe that had killed the Portuguese adventurer, and he decided to liberate him. Cabeza de Vaca had good reason to feel sympathy for the plight of the younger Garcia, having himself spent ten years a captive of American Indians in Florida. When he heard of Garcia's plight, he sent messengers to the tribe, ordering them to relinquish their captive. But the leader of the tribe, whose name was Tabaré, killed all the Governor's emissaries except one, whom he sent back to the Governor with the message not to despatch any more.

So Cabeza de Vaca sent a huge army north with three hundred Spanish soldiers and over a thousand Guaraní warriors. Tabaré's tribe was massacred; three thousand were slain and four thousand returned to Asunción as slaves, but they found no trace of Garcia's kidnapped son. Perhaps the Indians had hidden him in the forest or killed him. Or perhaps he had decided to stay, mixing his own white blood with the brown forest maidens. Cabeza de Vaca was an anti-semite. I fell asleep wondering if he would have gone to the trouble of massacring all those Indians if he had thought Garcia was Jewish.

I AWOKE to the sound of someone playing Guaraní pop music on a radio. It was a peculiar sound, gurgling and repetitive, a sort of cleft-palate Cajun. In the mud-floored kitchen an unspecified Yolanda was frying tortillas.

During the night my right hand had slipped outside the mosquito net. A symmetrical row of white dots ran along my knuckles, each one of which had been bitten with pinpoint precision. 'No one who has become acquainted with the Paraguayan mosquito in all its industriousness,' wrote Förster, 'and suffered its attentions on a hot, still summer night on the Rio Paraguay, will ever forget the experience.'

The pain was spectacular, and I could barely bend my fingers.

The path through the forest from Antequera to Nueva Germania and beyond was made by the soldiers of Lopez's army as they retreated from Las Lomas. By the time of the colony's foundation it was little more than a mud track, barely negotiable by oxcart and liable to surprise flooding. When the band of German pioneers led by Elisabeth and Bernhard Förster arrived here in 1886, the men rode on horseback, and the women, children and furniture were taken in oxcarts, *carreteras*, painfully slow, jolting and impossible to stop. In order to put the brakes on an oxcart, it is necessary to run to the front and wave your arms, by which time you have almost certainly run over or hit whatever you were stopping for. I decided to go by horse.

For two hours I wandered around the tiny village trying to borrow one. The fact that I wanted to go to Nueva Germania was already well known: the Yolandas had seen to that. But, perhaps not unreasonably, no one wanted to see a complete stranger wander away with their horses. I even tried a bit of Barbrooke Grubbing, by simply ordering them to lend me a horse but they just laughed, and so did I. I ate a lunch of stringy meat in broth and lay in the shade of the porch, trying to calculate how long it would take me to walk to Nueva Germania. Yolanda said there was one person left who could help, who was known to have lots of horses: Castellano, the town butcher in San Pedro. Why did a butcher have so many horses, I wondered; put more precisely, what had I eaten for lunch?

In the mid-afternoon, a man stumped into the *hospedaje*, dressed in leather riding chaps and with one withered foot sticking out at right angles. His black T-shirt was rolled up over a swelling stomach covered in dense black hair, and an unlit cheroot was wedged between a gap in his teeth. Castellano looked like a caricature bandito. Except he spoke no English and precious little Spanish. His cuticles were caked with dried blood.

Nueva Germania, he said, was about seventy kilometres along the track towards Santa Rosa between the Aguarya-umí and Aguarya-guazu rivers; three days' ride, two if we rode hard. He patted his stomach gravely with one hand and scratched his testicles with the other. It could be done, but, he shook his head, it would be expensive. We negotiated over Bremen in a cloud of cheroot smoke. Castellano explained that he needed the horses to work his *chacra*, the little farm he kept out of town; if they were away for several days he would be losing money. And then what about his family? What if they needed to get stores from the town? They would have to walk. Also it was very hot, he said, taking off his large straw hat and fanning himself by way of explanation; the horses would need to rest often. And I would need a guide because you never knew who was out there, he waved vaguely. 'The *montes* can be dangerous at night.' He was too busy to come himself.

He peered doubtfully at my knees, which were turning a delicate salmon pink in the sun. 'Do you know how to ride a horse?' I had ridden as a child in Scotland, I said, and was sure I could remember how. Castellano took out his cheroot and narrowed his eyes. 'I could take you for a ride around my house,' he said, brightening. 'How about that instead?' I explained that I was trying to find the remains of a German colony, not improve my dressage. He nodded and ran his tongue over the gums where his front teeth should have been. '*Las rubias*, the blondes, eh?' Then he laughed, a great booming guffaw. 'I get it, you like blonde girls.'

Once Castellano had decided that my motives were basically sexual, the deal was as good as done: 'My nephew will be your guide. He knows how to get to Nueva Germania, and he can bring the horses back. Four thousand Guaraní dollars per horse per day and food for Roberto. And if you fall off and die it's not my fault. You can pay me now.' Castellano folded the notes, a vast quantity of money, into the pocket of his T-shirt and hitched up his breeches. 'Good luck.' We shook hands. 'I hope you find lots of blonde girls,' he shouted over his shoulder as he stumped off down the street.

Yolanda and Yolanda, who had been standing in the doorway pretending not to listen, looked happily scandalised.

*

CASTELLANO's nephew, Roberto, arrived at dawn the next day, mounted on a beautiful bay mare; being pulled along behind it was an animal which, if it wasn't actually a mule, could certainly claim a bit of mule (or possibly hinny) in its ancestry. One of Cunninghame Graham's favourite sayings was from *Kim*: 'The wise man knows that horses are good.' All very well if you have a good horse; mine seemed to have distemper, and a rash of leprosy on its bottom.

Roberto took my luggage, which on Castellano's orders I had packed into *bolsas* made out of two grain bags, and loaded them on to the back of the beast in front of the saddle. The animal already had a fairly serious hunchback; with my luggage on top it looked like an equine Quasimodo, or a shrunken camel. My guide sensibly pointed out, in Spanish, that if I put the bags in front of the saddle there would be no room for my legs, and I would have to ride facing backwards. It was a good point; while I was tying my bags on to its rump my horse shat violently and extensively. Clearly a case of too much Rio Paraguay water. I empathised.

Roberto was about seventeen, with a sharp Indian face under a baseball cap. He was clearly unhappy at having to spend several days taking an obvious lunatic on a pointless riding trip. I wondered what tiny percentage of Castellano's fee he had been promised, as I gingerly mounted the horse and waved goodbye to the Yolandas, who suddenly seemed to have lost interest and didn't wave back. With a languid flick of his leather whip, Roberto jerked his horse into a trot and we left town at a jangling clip; it was immediately painful. Roberto rode ahead, not looking behind.

The forest closed in almost at once, a great bank of creepers on either side. It was silent in the cool dawn air. For the first few miles, the wall of trees was broken occasionally by a small house, often with goats and a cow grazing outside. Paraguayan faces peered out of the doorways into the bright sunlight as we passed. A few fields had been carved out, which became fewer as we rode. At a bend in the track a little child ran after the horses, dressed in nothing but a t-shirt. Unsmiling she reached up to hand me a gift of a chicken's egg and ran away before I could say anything. Flocks of bright-red birds shrieked out of the bushes at the sound of the horses.

My nag appeared to be waking up, presumably relieved to have escaped from certain death at Castellano's hands, and so did Roberto. 'You like *las rubias*, eh?' he said, expertly reining in his horse alongside mine.

'Are there many Germans in the town?' I asked.

'Some,' he said with a frown, 'but they are shy. They live mostly in the forest.'

'Are they friendly though?' I sounded like something out of Rider Haggard.

Roberto laughed, and clicked his horse on. 'They will talk to *you*, I think, *el Rubio*.'

By ten it was getting hot again. A pair of gauchos appeared ahead, whipping on a herd of cattle with shrill whistles and flailing whips. They turned their horses at sharp angles, riding one-handed. We pulled off the track to let them pass at a dusty gallop. I noticed for the first time that our horses seemed to be sweating almost as much as me. Roberto, on the other hand, seemed bone-dry. The horses and I plunged our faces into a little stream.

'We will stop and rest.' Roberto thrashed the long grass by the track with his whip, before throwing his saddle down and lying back on it, with a traditional pre-siesta groan. 'In Paraguay there are many snakes,' he said.

I asked him if he knew of the *macaguá* bird, which attacks poisonous snakes. It is said to use one wing as shield, while attacking the snake with its long beak. If it is bitten, it searches out and eats the seed of a particular forest plant called the *macaguá*. It soon recovers. The Indians followed the bird's example and found an antidote for snakebite.

From behind his hat Roberto said that birds were, on the whole, not stupid enough to attack snakes – at least he had never heard of it; he had, however, heard of Madonna and hummed 'Like a Virgin' as he dropped off.

Bernhard and Elisabeth advised their colonists: 'The snakes are dangerous, and there is no shortage of poisonous species. You are advised to keep an antidote with you at all times, failing that immediately suck the wound and burn it.'

I leafed through my *History of Paraguay*, much of which is about snakes. Most poisonous of all is the *nandurie*, which kills quickly unless an antidote is made from a liana, *icipo*. Then there is the coral snake, and the *frailesca*, a grey viper about a foot long, and its sister snake, which wears a crimson badge at its throat. The one that I was most unenthusiastic about meeting was the *cinqo minuto*, the five-minute snake, so called because that is exactly how long you have to think up some really terrific last words.

At about five that afternoon, we descended into a wide valley. The forest had been cleared, and the red-earth track wandered across a broad expanse of plain. The sight lifted my spirits after the forest gloom, and Roberto cranked his Madonna recital up a notch. Weaver birds flitted in and out of dangling nests in the long grasses. For the first time we crossed a tributary of the Rio Jejui, the river into which the Aguarya-umí and the Aguarya-guazu flow. We splashed water on our heads. It was tepid, but refreshing. Even here in the shallows it flowed fast, winking and rippling in the weakening sun.

Roberto became almost talkative. 'You came on the *Blanca Doña*?'

'Yes.'

'Ector was killed.'

'Yes.'

'*Qué tristeza.*'

As soon as we were out of the water, the sweat began to prick my scalp again. Back in the saddle, I could feel a trickle of sweat moving slowly down my back; on reflection, it felt more like an insect, probably the dreaded *picá*. I hit myself very hard on the back with my whip and fell off my horse. It was the first time I had seen Roberto laugh.

The path was steeper now, twisting up into another patch of forest. Behind, the little valley was cross-hatched with tiny streams, all leading back eventually to the Rio Paraguay. Somewhere in the lattice-work of waterways, as intricate as Naunduti lace, is the final resting place of *los tresorios escondidos del mariscal Lopez y su Concubina*, the cartloads of looted gold and silver, precious jewels and baubles that Lopez and Eliza Lynch took with them on the final march. Between Las

Lomas and the last stand at Cerro Corá, the first couple of Paraguay decided they could move faster without their spoils; like the Pleydel earlier, the cartloads of treasure were pushed off the bank of a river and allowed to sink to the bottom to be retrieved when the war was won. Fourteen witnesses to the hiding place were executed.

By February 1870 Lopez and his ragged army (numbering 409 old men, children and women) were finally surrounded in the woods of Cerro Corá, a few miles from the Brazilian frontier. For several weeks the Brazilians built up their forces for the final assault, and Lopez too kept himself busy: he had a special medal designed to commemorate the imminent victory, tried and executed a number of his leading officers and signed a death warrant for his mother. They had never really got on since Eliza Lynch had come to Paraguay.

On 1 March the Brazilian cavalry attacked in force. Lopez tried to escape on his cream-coloured charger, but the horse stuck fast in a bog and the President was overtaken by a unit of enemy horse. They called on him to surrender, and Lopez replied by shooting at them with his revolver, wounding one. He was unhorsed by a lance thrust and wounded in the stomach, but he still managed to stagger to the far bank before a rifle volley twisted him into the mud. It was a long way from County Cork to Cerro Corá, but Eliza Lynch was always thorough. She buried Lopez on the riverbank, scraping a shallow hole in the earth with her finely manicured fingers; then, under courteous Brazilian escort, she returned to Europe and exile.

On the profits from her stolen jewellery, she lived in London's Thurloe Square and sent Lopez's sons to boarding school in Croydon. She gave some terrific parties, but eventually the money ran out. She went back to Paris; malicious gossips said that, her looks barely impared by middle age and the horrors she had witnessed, she took up where she had left off, as a courtesan.

Her life ended as obscurely as it had begun. She died on 24 July 1886, on what would have been Lopez's sixtieth birthday, in a rooming house for impoverished but genteel ladies in the Boulevard Pereire; and the secret of where, in which of Paraguay's myriad rivers, lies her stolen fortune died with her. The Paraguayans say it is guarded by the *espíritus* of her victims. Elisabeth was unconvinced. She told prospective colonists, 'In a lagoon near the path through the forest, the fleeing Lopez is said to have left behind his gold-filled war chests, although the Germans are sceptical of this story. Certainly treasures are buried in New Germany, but no one need search for them secretly. The fertility of this wonderful red earth is our treasure. . . .'

THE track topped another ridge above a smaller valley. On the horizon a light flickered through the dusk.

'We will stay there. I have friends.'

After journeying for nearly twelve hours, the horses were exhausted, their coats matted with sweat and dead flies. I felt little sympathy. They would probably recover. I, on the other hand, would not. My horse had developed an extraordinary knack of trotting, in a violent and irregular way, at all times, even when standing still. In order to ease some of the astonishing pain in my buttocks, I had tried sitting side-saddle and immediately fell off again, this time crushing the egg in my breast pocket. Most of it I had scraped out with a twig, but the remains had stiffened unpleasantly in the heat.

It was dark when we reached a small cluster of huts. A group of men sat in a circle outside, talking in low voices, and a single kerosene lamp cast their lumpish shadows across the road. The talking stopped abruptly at the sound of our horses and Roberto called out a greeting in Guaraní before dismounting and handing me his reins. He seemed suddenly tense.

One man got unsteadily to his feet, and they spoke earnestly in Guaraní. Roberto walked back. '*Caña*,' he said, 'they are drunk. But we can stay here.' I couldn't see the men's faces, but I could feel their eyes as we unsaddled and tied the horses to a tree. The air fizzed with cicadas, and fireflies flickered luminously through the grass. A radio was playing from somewhere inside the main hut.

I approached the circle and ventured a warbling '*Buenas tardes*.' The man who had spoken to Roberto muttered something and looked away. A couple of the other men grunted.

One, I saw, was staring dead ahead in a stupor. They had the same taut, faraway expressions as Roberto the puma-catcher; not quite unfriendly, but fierce. Some wore riding boots and one had a pistol holstered to his waist. A single glass of *caña* was being passed around, *maté* fashion, from drinker to drinker. They seemed embarrassed, angry almost, to have been disturbed in their cups, which were, I noticed, strewn on the ground around them. I decided not to buy a round.

I walked over to the hut, which Roberto had already entered. An older man, very drunk, swayed out of the door and, seeing me, thrust a whiskery face into mine and breathed something loudly in Guaraní. He repeated it and cocked his head to one side, then staggered off into the gloom. I sat on the porch and tried to massage some life back into my aching legs; the insides of my knees were raw, clearly damaged beyond repair. Roberto re-emerged with some food, cold beans and a lump of meat in batter. While we ate, the group went back to their hushed conversation. Every ten minutes or so one would lurch to his feet and dive inside the hut, to return with another brimming cup full of *caña*. Why didn't they bring out the bottle? Perhaps they were drinking it straight from the still.

Caña is a drink of terrifying alcoholic properties, made from distilled sugar-cane syrup, a sort of nuclear rum. Elisabeth Förster was sniffy about it, arguing that it compounded the Paraguayans' already manifest racial inadequacies and even threatened to disrupt the strict moral code she had imbued in her colonists. Roberto brought me a glass, and I drained the viscous yellow liquid with my eyes closed. It was like swallowing the bar on an electric fire. When I stopped weeping, I saw that Roberto and the old man had dragged an entire bed out of the hut, complete with straw mattress and a rough blanket. Presumably the owner of the *caña* shop had decided that the hundred Guaraní dollars I had given him to pay our board and lodging included giving up his bed. I felt a flood of gratitude and collapsed on it. Roberto erected a hammock for himself.

'Tomorrow we will find the Germans,' he whispered.

The *caña* drinkers carried on through the night. The

hum of their conversation, and the occasional raucous shout, wafted in and out of my sleep.

I woke, cold and stiff, in the early dawn. The drinkers had gone, leaving behind a small hillock of glasses. Roberto too had disappeared. A fine mist hung above the ground and among the boughs of the surrounding forest, the tears of the *izapi* tree. Izapi was the beautiful but stony-hearted daughter of a great Indian *cacique*. Nothing made her weep; she could watch devastation and death without emotion. The tribe was plagued by a series of dreadful calamities, floods and storms and disease, and still Izapi watched it all dry-eyed and austere. The tribe dwindled, and only a few were left alive. 'It is Izapi,' said the remaining elders. 'Our sorrows will continue until she learns to cry.' The tribe's witch doctor, the *cuña-tai*, called on Aña, the moon dweller, to help them. Aña turned Izapi into a tree, which weeps all night, its leaves producing a fine, refreshing vapour that suckles the cracked earth and makes the streams run clear. Izapi was not unlike Elisabeth Nietzsche; she never cried unless she needed to.

Roberto returned with a gourd of *yerba maté* and a flask of hot water. The scalding, musty liquid was immediately refreshing. Roberto sang under his breath as he saddled the horses.

'What is the song?'

'It's a song about the morning,' he said. 'The morning is the best time. Come, we must ride before the heat comes.'

Even with the pain of remounting, the first few hours' ride was glorious. A sweet air cooled my lungs and made me want to shout. In the brightening morning the forest seemed crazily welcoming; tiny humming birds hovered over the bushes by the track and the horses' hoofs made a soft sound in the damp earth.

The landscape can hardly have changed since Förster described it over a century before: 'We travelled through fertile areas, interspersed with woods and waters. Occasionally one would come cross large herds of cattle grazing, or a lone *ñandu*, the South American ostrich, in the cultivated land that cropped up between the forest and the swamps. The indescribable rural charm of the magnificent scenery is lit by the clear atmosphere.' There were fewer dwellings now, although every few miles a shack would peer out from the forest. Even Roberto seemed less saturnine, urging his horse along with affectionate clicks and shouting out the names of the trees. 'That is the *quebracho*,' he said, pointing to a towering specimen, 'the hardest wood in the forest. It means breaking axe.' Boiled, the bark of the *quebracho* is said to cure VD; it was used to build the best houses and could last hundreds of years.

Elisabeth had built herself a vast house in Nueva Germania, the most magnificent house in the colony. She called it Försterhof and described it in a letter to her mother: 'It is grand, with high ceilings, spacious and cool. You have no idea how hot it is here. . . . the roof reaches far down, which keeps it pleasantly cool at all times of day. The three rooms in the centre are very large and almost eighteen feet high. . . . We own a magnificent property.' I wondered if it still stood. And her furniture, which came from the house of her grandfather Superintendent Dr Nietzsche in Eilenburg. 'Clearly the carpenter used excellent wood for the esteemed Superintendent,' she boasted, 'and it is just as solid now as it was eighty years ago.' And her piano, on which she had played Wagner's music – had that, like Eliza's, been unceremoniously abandoned?

Late in the afternoon, we stopped at a roadside store-hut underneath a huge spreading tree, selling sugar, *yerba*, key-rings and warm Coca Cola. Roberto said that we were now just ten miles from Nueva Germania. It was cooler in the shade of the tree. The owner was haggling with two Paraguayan girls over some maize flour and shaking her head vigorously from side to side. The girls were pretty, thin and taut, with dark, thick hair and high cheekbones. Until they smiled. One had no front teeth, and the other merely one blackened stump and two shiny gold incisors.

A chicken hurtled out from behind the hut and ran squawking off down the road, pursued by a boy of four or five. He stopped dead in front of where I sat and stared at me. He had ash-blonde hair and deep-blue eyes. His skin was so pale it seemed almost translucent in the bright sunlight; a Milky Bar Kid in mid-jungle. I felt my pulse racing. He ran for cover in the skirts of the laughing Paraguayan girls. Roberto was laughing too. 'There you are, *el Rubio*, a blonde one.' Roberto talked to the girls in Guaraní, and I took photograph after photograph of the little white face, peering out from behind a swathe of patterned skirt.

Elisabeth had observed with pride 'the radiant German children as they walk to their German school', and added that 'the climate is so excellent, men and animals blossom in it. One could easily send the children born here to a baby competition . . . they delight everyone with their freshness and health. . . .' The little white face did look healthy enough, except for his nose, which was raw from sunburn. 'He is not the child of these people,' Roberto explained unnecessarily. 'They are just looking after him for another family. They say there are many Germans further on. Come, we must go, before it gets late.' We trotted away, and the blue eyes of the little boy and the still-merry brown eyes of the Paraguayan girls watched us intently down the track.

The heat was beginning to recede when, half a dozen miles further on, we descended into a small, fertile valley dotted with houses, but still with patches of forest on the high ground. Beside each house was a patch of neatly cultivated ground, with oranges, mandioca and sugar cane. A river ran through the middle of the valley, and Roberto pointed to a cluster of houses on the opposite ridge, behind which the clouds were gathering.

'That is Nueva Germania.'

I put *The Ride of the Valkyries* on my Walkman, full volume, just to get myself in the right mood. We cantered down the slope past the ruins of what must once have been a brick factory, and splashed through the shallow Aguarya-umí. As we clattered past, some Paraguayan women washing clothes in the stream shouted and waved. At the entrance to the village was a large house, with a mule and cart standing outside. Someone had painted in red and yellow, with elaborate care, a large sign which read, in English: 'GERMANY POP DISCOTEC.'

Twenty yards further on was another: 'Gustav Neumann. *Yerba maté* purveyors. Nueva Germania, Paraguay.' We dismounted outside the village shop, a whitewashed building with a tin roof. My knees buckled at once and I sat down heavily, and narrowly avoided crushing a duck.

The woman who emerged from the shop could not have been less German. She was round and olive-skinned, with thick glasses and a bright pink shirt with bows on it; her face was creased from her siesta. She was screaming quietly and volubly in Guaraní. Roberto kissed her politely on the forehead and introduced his 'auntie' Gregoria. While I dusted myself off, she and Roberto talked. I heard the word '*rubio*' repeated several times.

'You are hungry,' she turned to me, 'and thirsty.' Roberto had disappeared and Gregoria arranged a plastic table under the orange tree in her yard, returning within minutes with a plate of food, meat in breadcrumbs and a potato salad.

'Wiener Schnitzel?' I asked hopefully.

'Milanesa.'

'Where are all the Germans?'

'No no, but he will come,' she said reassuringly and settled back in a plastic chair to watch me eat.

Gregoria's was the largest of a row of perhaps a dozen single-storey houses. Most were whitewashed adobe. New Germany seemed deserted. As I wiped potato salad off my chin, I heard the sound of a horse. A tall, fair-haired man reined in an enormous chestnut stallion at Gregoria's gate and dismounted. He wore high black riding boots and carried a leather riding whip. He smiled broadly and strode up to the table and inclined his head, bringing his heels together. In English with a heavy German accent he announced, 'My name is Christoph Schubert, and I am the doctor.'

Gregoria, beaming, produced another chair and some cold beer. '*Es alëman*,' she said proudly. Dr Schubert drained his beer in three great gulps.

How do you begin a conversation with a representative of a lost tribe of Aryans? I chose the traditional approach.

'What are you doing here?'

Dr Schubert sighed and motioned to Gregoria for another beer. 'Well, you see,' he looked around at the forest trees and the tall palms swaying in the evening breeze on the other side of the road, 'the thing is, I love Nietzsche.'

A large diaphanous insect flapped hard in the pit of my

stomach and for a moment I thought I might faint. This was it. Here, in the middle of the Paraguayan jungle, was a Nietzschean, whose ancestors had been brought here by the great philosopher's sister. Perhaps in this wilderness there had grown up a Nietzschean cult, based on his writings. But, if that was the case, he could know nothing of what Elisabeth had done to her brother's philosophy, how she had linked his name to the fascists and encouraged men like Hitler and Mussolini to use his poetic, arcane brilliance to back up their evil creed. It was my duty to put this original Nietzschean Man right. I took a deep breath and hit him with everything I had in the Nietzsche armoury. How did he interpret the idea of the *Übermensch*? Did everybody in the colony believe in Nietzsche's ideas? How did they reconcile Nietzsche's proclamation about the death of God with the Lutheranism they had believed in back in 1886? What about Nietzsche's 'blonde beast'?

He looked blank.

Of course, I was talking about Nietzsche's later works, which Elisabeth could not have brought with her and which he, therefore, must never have heard of. I would have to limit the discussion to Nietzsche before 1886. 'What do you think of *Thus Spoke Zarathustra*?'

Dr Schubert laid a calming hand on my forearm. 'I don't think you heard me correctly, *mein Herr*.' He pointed towards the forest. 'I love *nature*.'

Dr Schubert, it transpired, was an amateur naturalist; he had left the Munich suburbs for Nueva Germania three years before, to grow plants in the Paraguayan jungle. We talked late into the evening. Gregoria and her tiny, ferrety little husband Avalo brought beer and *caña*, and the fireflies blinked in the orange tree.

Dr Schubert had heard about Elisabeth and Bernhard Förster from talking to his patients. Many of the early settlers had apparently died, he said, worn out by the climate and the parasites and the unyielding clay-like earth; some had just moved away, south to Argentina, where the land was more fertile and the life easier. Some had married Paraguayans and adapted to the local way of life. Here in the village, he said, you could see the German genes reflected in the children, whose skin was usually dark, but whose eyes were blue. Other families, mostly German, had moved into the area after the war. But many of the descendants of the original settlers, the fourteen mostly peasant families that had come with Bernhard and Elisabeth in 1886, had refused to mix with the Paraguayans. They lived in the forest, away from the village, in an area called Tacarutý, which meant 'place of the anthills'.

'They tend to keep to themselves, marrying only Germans and sticking to the old ways,' said the doctor. He was almost the only person apart from the parson who ever went there. 'They speak an old Saxon dialect, which even I don't really understand,' said Dr Schubert. 'To hear them talk, it gives me goose pimples . . .'

'What are they like?' I pressed him.

'You will see for yourself.'

We shook hands in the deepening dusk, and Dr Schubert swung himself into the saddle and trotted away.

As it grew darker I sat under the orange tree trying to collect my thoughts, while a variety of farm animals, ducks, chickens, cats, a dog and a balding goat, wandered around the floor of Gregoria's house, which also turned out to be Nueva Germania's bar. One by one, or in small groups, the of the town came to drink *caña*, eyeing me carefully and talking in hushed voices. An older man with heavier European features and popping blue eyes with red rims came in and stood by the bar.

'Deutsch?' he asked after staring at me intently for several minutes.

'Nein.'

He turned back to his *caña*, shaking his head when I began to talk.

'*Es loco*,' explained Gregoria in a whisper, 'too much *caña*.'

I was too tired to pursue it. In fact I could barely keep my eyes open. Gregoria had made a bedroom for me by clearing out the chickens from a straw-roofed building at the back of her house, part hen coop, part shrine; one wall was covered by a gaudy poster depicting the Ascension. On a wooden shelf, above the reach of the hens, was a shelf with four small tin crosses. The names of Gregoria's dead relatives had been imprinted on them with the point of a nail.

'*Buenas noches*, Jasmine,' said Gregoria. 'Keep the door bolted or the chickens will come back.' Gregoria had decided to call me Jasmine. We had tried Ben, but the pronunciation proved too much, and then Benjamin (which isn't my name). She could get her tongue around the Jamin bit, but decided Jasmine sounded nicer. I collapsed on the straw mattress and fell asleep smelling the scent of oranges and chicken feathers, and dreamed about a tribe of white savages with distended blue eyes.

WAITING for Dr Schubert at dawn, I ate a meal of bread and bitter instant coffee, turning down Gregoria's offer of a special *yerba maté* pick-me-up. I had decided to cut down on the stuff, which I was beginning to crave and which was clearly affecting my subconscious. Breakfast was only slightly marred by the rooster apparently attempting to make love to an irritated duck under the table. So much for racial purity.

The winding six-mile track to Tacarutý was far narrower than the one from the river, with thick foliage on either side. We passed only one building, apparently deserted. An armadillo hurtled across the path, an armour-plated rat. 'They are good to eat,' said Dr Schubert. I asked him if the Germans were still vegetarians and he shook his head. 'No, they mostly eat meat, but they eat more vegetables than the Paraguayans. The constipation in Paraguay, it's amazing.'

It had rained in the night, and bright-blue butterflies swooped and feinted over the muddy puddles. We turned off to the right, through a patch of dense forest. Someone had been clearing *quebracho*, logs were carefully cut and stacked by the track. We came out of the trees on to a plateau, looking out over a small valley; the sun was blinding after the gloom of the trees. A small brown house with a thatched roof peered out of the forest's edge.

Heinrich Schütte, myopic and seventy-four, was attending to his neat garden surrounded with a wooden fence. '*Guten Morgen*,' he said, straightening with difficulty and adjusting his pistol holster. We drank cold *yerba*, *tereré*, in the shade of a vine arbour. His wife Marta, her hair in a tight grey bun, folded her loose-skinned white arms in disapproval as her husband talked. Their clothes, shapeless and baggy, were made from the same blue material. A parrot screamed in the trees behind the house. 'Elisabeth Nietzsche, yes, she was a fine woman.' Heini spoke as if he had known her personally, even intimately. His reverence made me shudder, this friendly old man with the photographic inherited memory. 'Wait here.'

He tottered inside and returned with a dusty etching of Bernhard Förster, the one I had seen in the front of his book, all bristles and bigotry. 'This was Förster, the husband. He was a rude man. My grandfather was a locksmith, he came here from Chemnitz in 1886 on a boat from Hamburg. I have the very squeeze box he brought from Chemnitz, although doesn't really work now.' I wondered if he knew that Chemnitz had been changed to Karl Marxstadt and back again in the intervening years. Marta refilled the maté gourd.

Elisabeth and Bernhard (he called them Luisa and Bernardo) were still remembered by the German families. 'The older ones that is. My grandfather and his friends came to found a new Germany,' said Heini, spitting extravagantly and wiping the picture with his sleeve. He tapped it with an ancient forefinger and added, 'It was very sad about Bernardo, but Luisa, she was always the real leader.'

CHAPTER V

Knights and Devils

WHEN Friedrich Nietzsche was twenty years old and his sister was eighteen, they had the sort of argument over religion that takes place, sooner or later, in almost every family. Elisabeth was devout to the point of sanctimony; Friedrich, though hitherto pious, had begun to have doubts and refused, with maximum bolshiness, to take Communion, Easter 1864.

Elisabeth was scandalised and tearful, enlisting the theological help of her uncles to support her in the bitter row that ensued, which was broken up only when their dogmatic Aunt Rosalie (perhaps remembering the experiences of the founder of Christianity) told Elisabeth 'in the life of every great theologian there had been moments of doubt'. But the dispute had long-lasting implications: it revealed an ideological chasm between brother and sister that was never bridged. At the time Nietzsche wrote to his sister, 'Do you desire spiritual peace and happiness? – very well, then, believe! Do you wish to be a disciple of truth? – so be it; investigate!' Her view was: 'It is much easier not to believe than the reverse.' Nietzsche never accepted that argument, and he dedicated his life to exposing faith as fraud. He never found another credo, after that first crisis of conscience, unless it was faithlessness itself. He rejected Christian morality and all other ideologies with moral imperatives, and for most of his life he wandered Europe searching for something to put in place of a morality he thought was moribund, for a truth, as he defined it. He was seldom happy, and never enjoyed spiritual peace of mind. He had no permanent home, few friends and even fewer satisfying emotional relationships. He never married. From the age of thirty-five he was usually ill and depressed, and shortly after his forty-fourth birthday he went permanently insane.

His sister's life was a perfect contrast. Elisabeth was healthy and happy for every one of her eighty-nine years. Her peace of mind was based on a clutch of rigid religious, political and racial beliefs and an unswerving faith in her own moral rectitude. Those beliefs led her to Paraguay, where they were tempered into an ideology; later she would impose them on her brother, the disciple of truth.

And, as for truth itself, Elisabeth used it when convenient.

CARL LUDWIG NIETZSCHE, the pastor of Röcken, a tiny Saxon village south-west of Leipzig, was overjoyed when his young wife gave birth to a boy on 15 October 1844. The child shared a birthday with the reigning King of Prussia, and Pastor Nietzsche, a dedicated monarchist, named the boy Friedrich Wilhelm after the king. Less than two years later, on 10 July 1846, the Nietzsches had a girl, and christened her Therese Elisabeth Alexandra after the Princesses of Alte-Saxenburg whom Pastor Nietzsche had tutored as a young man. And two years after that a second son, named Joseph, after the Duke of Alte-Saxenburg. Carl Ludwig was a consistent sort.

The parsonage was surrounded by flat green fields and orchards. The children played around the fish ponds and in the woods, and in the bell tower of the twelfth-century village church. Röcken was a sleepy place – idyllic and rather dull. In 1848, cartloads of rebels waving revolutionary banners passed the parsonage on the road to Leipzig. Carl Ludwig was livid at the ingratitude of a rebellion against his beloved monarch and patron, and when he heard that the King had appeased the rebels he burst into tears and locked himself in his study. Otherwise, the revolutions of 1848 and 1849 had no effect whatever on the lives of the Nietzsche family.

Friedrich was four, Elisabeth two when Pastor Nietzsche died of 'softening of the brain'. He was followed to the grave within six months by the child Joseph. It was a devastating blow, particularly when the family had to move to Naumburg on the Saale to make way for the new pastor. Henceforth Elisabeth and Friedrich Nietzsche were brought up in a house containing several very old, pious women and one very young one, their mother: there was Aunt Rosalie, devout, dotty and opposed to Shakespeare; Aunt Augusta, who insisted on doing the housekeeping in spite of her digestive problems; Grandmother Erdmuthe, who couldn't stand noise and habitually wore a frilly lace bonnet, and an ancient maid called Mina.

Franziska Nietzsche was widowed at twenty-three: she was a kind, nervous, unsophisticated woman, and she never came close to understanding her children, though she played a pivotal role in their lives. Perhaps because she was so close to them in age, her relationships with her children tended to be stormy. Later, Elisabeth had few words of praise for her more generous than 'the wonderful way she used to toboggan'. The house in Naumburg was a stifling and precious place. The continual presence of so many old and rather peculiar females throughout their childhood affected both children: they both grew up with a firm dislike of women: in Nietzsche's case this sometimes expressed itself in blistering mysogyny, but in Elisabeth the effect was more complex. Friedrich was the undisputed centre of the family's attention, and Elisabeth seems to have accepted the notion that men, like her brother, were superior beings, the makers of history. Throughout her life she attacked the idea of women's suffrage ('Feminism is a movement of spinsters,' she wrote, 'and its adherents are generally childless women') and she habitually valued the attention and opinions of men above those of her own sex, partly perhaps because she found them easier to manipulate. Much later she would ascribe to Nietzsche an ideal of womanhood which was actually her own: 'My brother's ideal of women was in fact the ideal cherished by every man of high character: the brave woman, who by her cheerful, loving personality tries to lighten her husband's burdens, to refresh him after his dreary hours of work and of wrestling with difficult problems, who relieves him of the petty worries of daily life, and shows some understanding for his higher aspirations....' That was how she believed women ought to behave; it was not how *she* behaved. Elisabeth lived a life that was, in the context of the times, thoroughly emancipated. She might defer to men in theory, but in practice she was adept at getting them to do exactly what she wanted, alternately beguiling and bludgeoning them into co-operation. Elisabeth achieved her ends through and in spite of the men she claimed to defer to. She was at least partially ignored as a child. In later life, people reacted to her in a variety of ways: some admired her, others despised her and almost everyone feared her. But she made quite sure that no one ignored her.

The two fatherless children grew extremely close. Elisabeth idolised her Fritz, and, *in loco parentis* beyond his years, he seems to have returned her affection with a distinct edge of superiority. The children had found a picture of a llama in a story book, detailing its stubborn as well as its lovable qualities; Fritz nicknamed his sister after the animal and called her Llama (with different degrees of affection) all his life.

Friedrich was a nervous child, shy, introverted and precocious. He wrote his first autobiography at the age of fourteen, disguised as a memoir to his father. It is painful to read, the expressions of romantic piety jarring with genuine anguish. They both learned to play the piano; she competently, he with real virtuosity, developing a love of music that is reflected in his more melodious writing. By the age of eight he was writing poems and plays and his devoted sister was collecting them, stashing them in her 'treasure drawer' for posterity. With good reason, he sometimes wanted to destroy his efforts, but she would, where possible, prevent him. It was a dangerous precedent. His passionate reading and writing damaged his already poor eyesight. Both children had inherited myopia, and Elisabeth had a pronounced squint. But she was a pretty child, with long, curly fair hair.

There were Lutheran pastors on both sides of the families, going back several generations, and it was assumed by all that Friedrich would go into the Church. To this end Aunt Rosalie gave him extra religious tuition. He showed religious zeal extraordinary even for a child. At fourteen he wrote: 'In everything God has led me safely as a father leads his weak little child. . . . I have firmly resolved to dedicate myself for ever to his service.' The earliest photographs show a serious little boy, with long hair and mournful eyes, his face set in a dour line. In fact there is only one photograph of Friedrich Nietzsche with anything other than an expression of deep seriousness. Elisabeth, by contrast, either grins at the camera, full of merriment and devilry, or pouts. Friedrich won a place at Schulpforta, the famous Protestant boarding school where the Schlegel brothers, Fichte, and Ranke had all been educated. The school combined academic excellence with strict Prussian discipline, and he thrived in the pressurised atmosphere; he set up his own literary society, Germania, with two friends and became obsessed with Nordic saga; he read Byron, Shakespeare, Goethe and Hölderlin, composed poetry and music. He also began to doubt the Christian mores he had been infused with throughout his upbringing.

Elisabeth lacked her brother's early intellectual promise, but she was no dunce. Her records from the private Naumburg school for young ladies show that she was an excellent pupil in all subjects except English. Her academic determination partly reflected a sibling rivalry; later she recalled an occasion when a school inspector had visited both the girls' and boys' schools in Naumburg, before Nietzsche left for Schulpforta. The man had been struck by Friedrich's precocity, but she added, fifty years after the event, that 'the inspector of the girls' school took a great interest in me and also inquired my name'. Both children were somewhat arrogant in manner, and outside her brother's company Elisabeth was distinctly bossy. Friedrich wrote: 'I have a pleasant and varied circle of friends, but there can be no question of influence. First I would have to meet someone I considered to be my superior.'

Once a week, Friedrich would meet his mother and sister at an inn between Naumburg and Schulpforta, and between times the children wrote to each other constantly. Both were avid letter-writers all their lives. In Elisabeth's case it was pure habit; she would often write whether or not she had anything to say. Nietzsche himself was disparaging about receiving letters: 'A letter is an unannounced visit, the postman the agent of rude surprises. One ought to reserve an hour a week for receiving letters and afterwards take a bath.' But he relied utterly on sending and receiving letters, which too often took the place of real human contact. He needed to write as others needed air; often he would write letters but never post them.

When it was decided that Elisabeth should finish her education in Dresden, Nietzsche wrote to their mother: 'Dresden will be quite adequate for E's spiritual education and in some ways I envy her. . . . I have plenty of confidence in Elisabeth – if only she would learn to write better. And when she tells a story, you cannot believe how splendid, wonderful and enchanting it would be if she could manage not to keep exclaiming "Oh" and "Ach".' This from a brother less than two years her senior. He instructed Elisabeth to visit art galleries and to send him written descriptions of one or two paintings every week; he told her what to read and, often, what to think about what she read. The fact that Elisabeth, who was more than capable of thinking for herself, did not tell him what he could do with his advice was a sign of the unhealthy reverence she already seems to have felt for her brother. Her jealousy of him grew stronger as she grew older, and Nietzsche seems to have exploited it. When he developed a crush on the sister of a school friend, he asked Elisabeth to send some Schumann scores to the object of his new infatuation, and she refused huffily. So he sent some poems. He seems to have enjoyed comparing his sister to other girls he met; of the sister of a friend he wrote to her, 'Marie Deussen is, despite her youth, a quite splendid, spiritual girl, who really, dear Lisbeth, occasionally reminds me of you.' The gently taunting tone is unmistakable.

Was there something incestuous in their relationship? Something, perhaps, certainly nothing provable, but enough for at least some people to go to remarkable lengths to establish this as fact. In 1951, a book was published in New York under the title *My Sister and I*, which purported to be the last book written by Friedrich Nietzsche, and containing the 'confessions' of 'the boy who grew up in a house full of manless women'. A 1953 advertisement called it 'the story of a Famous Brother and a terrifyingly ambitious younger Sister, who grew to love each other physically as children and continued to do so into maturity. . . . the 19th century's greatest philosopher tells how he was gradually led into this extraordinarily dangerous love-trap. . . .' It is steamy in the extreme:

> It first happened between Elisabeth and me the night our young brother Joseph died, though we had no idea that he was dying when she crept into my bed. ... suddenly I felt Elisabeth's warm little hands in mine, her hissing little voice in my ear, and I began feeling warm all over. ... I was usually in the midst of a sound sleep when she got into my bed, and thrilling as I found the ministrations of her fat little fingers, it also meant my being kept awake for hours and hours.

My Sister and I is full of such soft-core pornography and would radically affect any consideration of Nietzsche's relationship with his sister if there was any reason to believe that Nietzsche wrote a single word of it.

The book was said to have come to light through a young American journalist who had been given it in exchange for a favour done for an English ex-clergyman on a transatlantic crossing in 1920. It then passed, supposedly, into the hands of Oscar Levy, an English Nietzsche scholar who allegedly translated it and wrote the introduction. His family vehemently deny that he did either. Then, the story goes, it ended up in the hands of Samuel Roth, a New York publisher of a reputation so dubious that in 1927 a protest was mounted against him signed by 176 literary figures, including Einstein, Hemingway, Eliot, D. H. Lawrence, Thomas Mann and Yeats. Roth later claimed that although he had planned to publish the book in the 1920s, his offices were raided by the Society for the Suppression of Vice, looking for an edition of *Ulysses*, and they carried off everything – including the original German manuscript of *My Sister and I*. It was not until 1951, he claimed, that a moth-eaten copy of Levy's translation miraculously reappeared in the bottom of a trunk. He promptly published it as Nietzsche's lost manuscript. Levy, by this time, was conveniently dead. Years later, a man called George Plotkin, a professional forger, admitted to Walter Kaufmann, one of the greatest Nietzsche scholars, that he had written the book 'for a flat fee'.

My Sister and I is almost certainly a rather poor hoax: it is full of anachronisms, Anglicisms and references to events that Nietzsche could not have known about. Its language, though it copies Nietzsche's aphoristic style, is a pale pastiche, and it is philosophically void. The book proves nothing – except, perhaps, that Nietzsche is still prey to people who would change him posthumously, even if they must stoop to forgery. There is no evidence to suggest that links between Elisabeth and Friedrich Nietzsche were sexual; but there is copious proof that their relationship was as emotionally charged, as possessive and as destructive as any sexual relationship.

At university in Bonn, away from home at Christmas for the first time in his life, Friedrich composed eight songs as a present for his sister and sent them to her, bound in lilac-coloured morocco leather and bearing a silhouette of himself. He also sent precise instructions on how they were to be played.

The young Nietzsche attempted, somewhat half-heartedly, to join in the bibulous buffoonery of his university contemporaries. He got drunk and joined the Bürschenschaft Frankonia, a student union dedicated to duelling and hard drinking. He even contrived to get the requisite duelling scar, which he carried on his nose for the rest of his life. But his mind was some way away from the childish, beery superficiality of university life. Despite periods of self-doubt, he was already convinced of his own potential. This was more than youthful ambition; he felt destiny pressing hard on him, reinforced by the effects of a spoiled childhood, but there was something else too. He had written about it when a child, a vague, shapeless dread looming outside his conscious mind: 'What I fear is not the terrifying shape behind my chair, but its voice; not the words so much as the horrifying, inarticulate and inhuman tone of that shape. If it only spoke as humans speak.' This may be no more than a childish nightmare, but it is horribly prescient. Increasing doubts caused him to abandon theology and Bonn. He moved to Leipzig (along with his philology professor, F. W. Ritschel) after deciding to devote himself to classical scholarship. There he studied the great pessimist Schopenhauer and found in him an echo of his own coalescing philosophy. Pessimist though he might be, Nietzsche needed something to believe in, to replace his decaying Christianity, and on the evening of 28 October 1868 he found it.

He had heard Wagner's music before but had been unimpressed; yet when he heard extracts from *Tristan* and *Die Meistersinger* that evening he was enraptured: 'I am quivering in every fibre with excitement and ecstasy.' Less than two weeks later, he met the *Meister* himself. Wagner was staying incognito in Leipzig, but, having heard of a young student who raved about his music and never being one to shy away from a possible plaudit, he asked his hostess to arrange a meeting. Wagner held court that night, playing parts of the *Meistersinger* and reading aloud, as only one so self-obsessed as he could, parts of his own unfinished autobiography. Nietzsche was enchanted with this 'wonderfully lively and animated man who speaks very fast, is very witty and makes a private gathering of this private sort very cheerful'. Wagner and Nietzsche discussed their shared passion for Schopenhauer, and at the end of the evening Wagner invited Nietzsche to visit him.

Nietzsche later described their encounter as a 'fairy tale', and it initiated a relationship that was to have dramatic and far-reaching consequences for both Friedrich and Elisabeth Nietzsche. Wagner was thirty-one years older than Nietzsche, the same age as Pastor Carl Ludwig would have been, whom he oddly resembled. Through their mothers, Wagner and Nietzsche were, in fact, distantly related. Whether or not Nietzsche found in Wagner a father-figure, his obsession with the older man and his works was as passionate as his later rejection of him. 'Together we could march to the bold, indeed giddying rhythm of his revolutionary and constructive aesthetic,' he wrote to his friend and fellow student Erwin Rohde.

But while at Leipzig Nietzsche made another, far more awful discovery: he had contracted syphilis. Two Leipzig doctors treated him for the infection in 1867; much later he himself stated he had caught the disease in 1866. He had certainly visited a brothel in Cologne in 1865, but had been embarrassed and played the piano to cover his shame before fleeing into the night. Thomas Mann believed he later went back to the brothel; Freud and Jung helped to spread a rumour that he had caught the disease in a Genoese male brothel, for which there is no evidence. Elisabeth claimed he had never had syphilis, and another friend that he had never had sex. The progressive paralysis which killed him and drove him mad may, conceivably, have been contracted some other way, but the point is that he *thought* he had syphilis, which is not something you tend to think without good reason, still less if you are a virgin.

In 1869, at the age of twenty-four, through an astonishing stroke of good fortune and the good offices of his Professor Ritschel, Nietzsche took up the chair of philosophy at Basle University. Elisabeth, still in Naumburg, was delighted by her brother's rapid rise to fame. 'I know that they are all talking about it in the Ratskeller,' she said. 'They will say "How happy his mother must be, and his sister," and they are right, they are right, says your tenderly, ardently, eternally loving sister.' Basle had the added attraction of being close to Tribschen, Wagner's house on Lake Lucerne. When Nietzsche left to take up his new post, Elisabeth, twenty-three years old and, thanks to the timely demise of Grandmother Nietzsche, financially independent, decided to study in Leipzig as her brother had done. (Her private income was regularly topped up as, one by one, her many aunts and uncles passed away.) She attended a number of lectures and concerts, took lessons to improve her English and immersed herself in the town's social life. When the Franco-Prussian war broke out Nietzsche volunteered as a nursing orderly. He served for a month, but collapsed at Erlangen in September 1870 having contracted dysentery and diphtheria from some of the soldiers he was looking after. Elisabeth helped to nurse him back to fitness, but his health was seriously impaired. Safely in Basle he sent his sister a bound copy of his inaugural address, 'The Personality of Homer', with a dedication to 'my dear and only sister Elisabeth'. Nietzsche cut a dandyish figure around the town, with his grey top hat and erect bearing. The characteristic moustache had yet to reach the remarkable proportions of later life, but it was well on the way, already blossoming on his upper lip, six inches long and gently curved.

Within a month of arriving at his new university and in

spite of bouts of ill-health which could leave him prostrate for days, Nietzsche went to visit the Wagners. So far from forgetting the Leipzig student, as Nietzsche feared, Wagner had formed a good impression of the intense young man who had talked so earnestly of Schopenhauer; he perhaps sensed, too, a man who craved a mentor, a father-figure, as much as Wagner himself needed disciples. Almost overnight. Nietzsche was adopted into the intoxicating atmosphere of Wagner's home.

With Wagner, Nietzsche formed, next to Elisabeth, the most intense relationship of his life. The composer was already the pre-eminent artistic personality of his age, a figure whose musical genius was matched only by his consuming egotism; from the distance of a century, his cultural and in particular his racial ideas, his crude Teutonic nationalism and verbose theorising seem dubious in the extreme, but his capacity to inspire was astonishing. Nietzsche considered him 'divine', and in return Wagner put him in the centre of the dazzling spotlight that was his personality. The fact that Wagner considered most of his relationships, that with Nietzsche included, in terms of his own needs cannot detract from the many kindnesses he showed Nietzsche in these early years. Nietzsche was entranced by Tribschen and the Wagner family circle, which combined, he thought, artistic brilliance with an intellectual freedom that could not have been further removed from the bourgeois banalities of Naumberg. Later, in *Ecce Homo*, he would write: 'I offer all my other personal relationships cheap, but at no price would I relinquish from my life the Tribschen days, those days of mutual confidences, of cheerfulness, of sublime incidents – of *profound* moments. . . . I do not know what others may have experienced with Wagner: over *our* sky no cloud ever passed.' It wasn't true, of course, and eventually a cloud so large and black passed over the relationship that the light went out of it.

The house at Tribschen, a pretty four-square building on the lakeside, was an elaborate testament to the composer's vanity. Its plush interior reflected Wagner's taste for the grandiose, complete with busts of himself. Nietzsche came to know Wagner when the composer was at the height of his creative powers: *Die Meistersinger*, *Siegfried*, *Götterdämmerung* were all products of the Tribschen years. He visited the Wagners, in total, twenty-three times before they left Switzerland; a room was set aside for the young professor, who repaid the honour by bringing toys for the Wagner children and carrying out small commissions for the family – buying Christmas presents, procuring a painting of Wagner's uncle and helping him proof-read his memoirs. At the second Christmas spent with the family, he presented Wagner with a gift of Dürer's engraving *Knight, Death and the Devil*, which shows a gallant knight overcoming all obstacles – Wagner in armour.

His gift, however, was overshadowed by Wagner's gift to his wife. As she woke on Christmas Day, which was also her birthday, she heard music playing: 'Richard came in with the five children to put the score of his symphonic birthday greeting into my hands. I was in tears, but so was the whole household. Richard had put his whole orchestra on the stairs, and thus consecrated our Tribschen for ever.' That description, with its lush sentimentality and exhibitionism, might make one's flesh crawl; but the episode produced the lovely 'Siegfried Idyll'. Wagner's bold talk of cultural renewal, indeed of artistic revolution, drew Nietzsche to him. But there was another reason why Nietzsche found Tribschen so alluring: he seems to have been in love, although perhaps subconsciously, with Wagner's wife.

Cosima Wagner played an extraordinary role in the composer's life: she was lover, companion, mother, diarist, administrator and co-creator of the Wagner myth. Franz Liszt's daughter, she had left her husband, Wagner's friend the composer Hans von Bülow, to live daringly 'in sin' with Wagner, bearing him three children and finally marrying him. She was haughty, prejudiced and, particularly when seen side by side with the diminutive composer, exceptionally tall. In the depths of his later madness Nietzsche was to write to her, 'Ariadne, I love you', and sign himself 'Dionysus'. When he was finally taken to the lunatic asylum at Jena, years after his rift with the Wagners, he informed the warders that 'My wife, Cosima Wagner, brought me here.' He almost certainly never declared his love to Cosima when sane. Her own attitude to the young man was relentlessly platonic and often rather patronising.

So far from objecting to Nietzsche's new attachment, Elisabeth luxuriated in it. Nietzsche introduced her into the charmed circle of Tribschen at the end of July 1870. Soon she was acting as babysitter to the Wagner brood, who called her 'Aunt Elisabeth'. If she resented being treated as a child-minder while her brother played official philosopher at Wagner's court, she didn't show it; she was too busy absorbing the example Cosima set as the doyenne of a cultural Utopia. Later she described her impressions: 'The whole of Tribschen, together with its inmates, was a charming idyll; at the head, the ideal couple, then the beautiful children with all their wealth of imagination and resource . . . and the old angular house which, with its simple garden and grounds, took its place so unpretentiously and naturally in the glorious landscape.' Her only objection was to the lavish Parisian interior of the house; otherwise, she was hooked. More than thirty years later she wrote:

> I can still remember the last evening I spent there; the sun was just setting, but the moon already stood full and bright over the luminous snowfields of Mount Titlis. . . . in front walked Frau Cosima Wagner and my brother – the former dressed in a pink cashmere gown with broad revers of red lace which reached down to the hem of the garment; on her arm there hung a large Tuscan hat trimmed with a crown of pink roses. . . . then followed Wagner and myself – Wagner being attired in a Flemish painter's costume, consisting of a black velvet coat, black satin knickers, black silk stockings, a light-blue satin cravat tied in a rich bow, with a piece of his fine linen and lace shirt showing below, and a painter's tam-o'-shanter on his head, which at that time was covered in luxuriant brown hair. . . . Yes, Tribschen was a blessed isle, and whoever has known it, thinks of it with a profound regret.

Nietzsche was overwhelmed by Wagner's ideas and his music, Elisabeth was as yet more concerned with the colour of his knickers and the shape of his wife's hat, but for both of them knowing Wagner was the most exhilarating experience of their lives so far.

Nietzsche's first major work, *The Birth of Tragedy* (1872), was partly an academic study of Greek drama; but it was also an undisguised paean of praise to Wagner. It was roundly, perhaps rightly, denounced by many scholars; newspapers began to label Nietzsche, Wagner's 'literary lackey'. But Wagner, naturally enough, was delighted with the book and claimed to have read 'nothing more beautiful'. He would read it after breakfast to put him in the right mood. Wagner's was the sort of constitution that cannot digest without a dose of flattery.

At the beginning of 1871, Nietzsche's health had hit a new low, with painful haemorrhoids, insomnia, headaches and vomiting. He sent a telegram to his sister, asking her to come to Basle urgently to tend to him. When Franziska said she was unwilling to see her daughter set off in bad weather, Nietzsche was so enraged he vomited with anger and blazed back: 'I am in no mood for such jokes.' Elisabeth arrived shortly afterwards; gradually they fell into a pattern: for about half the year Elisabeth would tend her brother and keep house for him (and visit Tribschen), spending the rest of her time in Naumburg, where she helped to found the Naumburg Wagner Society. Nietzsche was content with the new arrangement 'because of my sister's cheerful manner, which fits my temperament excellently'. Neither brother nor sister showed any inclination to marry, to Franziska's consternation: at twenty-five Elisabeth, after all, was nearing the age when women in Naumburg became spinsters for life. Her daughter seems to have worried about it from time to time, but more because of what her brother might think than on her own account: at one point, after she claimed to have rejected three suitors, she wrote to her brother that if she should end up 'as an old maid . . . then, my dear Fritz, do not think badly of me and love me also in my old age'.

On Wagner's behalf Nietzsche wrote an *Exhortation to the German People* in an (unsuccessful) effort to raise new funds for Wagner's Festival Hall project at Bayreuth; perhaps it was just as well that it was never published, since it plumbed new depths of sycophantic Wagnerian rhetoric, calling on

German citizens to dig deep for the 'great, brave and indomitable champion of German culture: Richard Wagner'. Long before he finished the great four-opera cycle, *The Ring of the Nibelung*, Wagner had conceived of building a grand opera house, on a scale way beyond anything currently on offer, in the Bavarian town of Bayreuth, a place uncontaminated by Jews where pure German culture could flourish unimpeded. There would assemble Germany's musical elite, and only there could Wagner be properly appreciated. Nietzsche rode in Wagner's carriage when he laid the foundation stone in 1872.

By now Nietzsche's enthusiasm for the 'mole-like' activity of philology, never very strong, was waning. In 1871 he had applied for the chair of philosophy, where his thoughts increasingly strayed, but was turned down. He needed a claim to fame of his own, and he settled on the idea of a school for scholars, an ideal colony or, as he called it, a 'cultural sect' or community where like-minded men could converse on elevated intellectual matters, where 'we shall love, work and enjoy for each other'. It was Tribschen on a grander, more academic scale. He asked Elisabeth to act as administrator of this fantasy and, flattered, she accepted. The plan was shelved shortly afterwards, on account of Nietzsche's poor health, but it remained lodged in Elisabeth's memory.

The first Bayreuth festival was planned for 13 August 1876. Both brother and sister decided to attend the grand opening of Wagner's crowning achievement. Elisabeth's enthusiasm for all things Wagnerian had swelled, but Nietzsche's had begun to wane. In April he had published his fourth *Untimely Meditation: Richard Wagner in Bayreuth*. It contained much of the old devotion, but by now it was, it seems, beginning to jar with Nietzsche's true feelings. It is almost impossible to date the moment at which love of Wagner ceased to be the ruling element of his life. In June 1874, he had (perhaps deliberately) left a Brahms score on the piano at Bayreuth, to Wagner's fury, who found it insulting that anyone should play music other than his own, particularly in Bayreuth. There had been an ugly scene between the two friends. What seems certain is that by the time the festival began Nietzsche had become frustrated with playing second fiddle to Wagner's entire orchestra. He was also extremely ill. Naturally, with such a grandiose operation, technical hitches marred the first performance. The dragon for *Siegfried*, constructed in London at fantastic expense, appeared without the neck, which had accidentally been shipped to Beirut. The curtain rose at the wrong moment, and there were so many people packed into the small Bavarian town that the food ran out.

Nietzsche loathed the whole occasion, partly because he was again struck down with shattering headaches, but also, perhaps, because he saw the Wagner dream suddenly thrown into tawdry relief. Wagner strutted about, happily absorbing the flattery that lapped about him. Later Nietzsche wrote: 'Truly a hair-raising crowd! . . . Not a single abortion was missing, not even the anti-semite. – Poor Wagner! To what a pass he had come! – Better for him to have gone among swine! But among Germans!' Bayreuth showed what Nietzsche would later call Wagner's 'histrionic self-deception'; now, his eyes cleared by pain, he saw him clearly. At least, that is what he saw in retrospect. He fled to the Bohemian forest to recuperate in the company of Paul Rée, a talented and cynical psychologist who had attended some of Nietzsche's lectures in Basel. It did not go unnoticed in Bayreuth that Nietzsche's new friend was also Jewish.

Where Nietzsche saw Bayreuth as awash with 'the whole idle riff-raff' of Europe, Elisabeth saw only vast expanses of social advancement. Later she would claim that, like her brother, she had been disappointed with the festival, attended by 'philistines and housewives'; in fact she adored it. As the sister of Wagner's greatest friend, she was allowed to visit Wahnfried, Wagner's home, where she 'peeped into the room and saw that at least forty orchestra conductors, young artists and authors, were waiting for an audience with Wagner . . . in that rapid glance I saw only interesting, artistic heads and fine intellectual faces; the more elderly men in the crowd spoke in gentle undertones, and the younger men listened with becoming reverence. Indeed, a serious, reverent and devout spirit seemed to prevail among the small throng of men waiting to see the Master.' She was privileged to attend the royal performance of *Rheingold*; she paid court to the Wagners, and the Wagnerites, including a number of highly presentable young men, paid court to her. One of these was a handsome racist fanatic of thirty-two called Bernhard Förster.

THE anti-semitism and crude nationalism that had helped to drive Nietzsche away from Bayreuth were exactly what had attracted Förster. A Berlin schoolmaster and natural pedagogue, Förster stood on the fringes of Wagner's circle but over the years he made repeated attempts to gain the *Meister*'s support for a variety of anti-semitic ventures. Wagner, to his credit, did his best to ignore him – which may explain Förster's eagerness to cultivate Elisabeth, as a possible passport to Bayreuth acceptance. He was certainly in no hurry to marry her, but he told her that he had read her brother's book, *Richard Wagner in Bayreuth*, and had found it enthralling.

Wagner apart, the two had much in common. Förster was also the child of a Protestant pastor; his widowed mother lived in Naumberg and moved in the same circles as Frau Nietzsche. In January, following the Bayreuth festival, the Försters, mother and son, paid a visit to Elisabeth and her mother at home in Naumburg. Again Förster enthused about Nietzsche's work, and the two talked avidly together about the rebirth of the German spirit and the Jews, whom Förster said were destroying Germany. 'It was really a feast for me to listen to someone who talks our language,' Elisabeth wrote to her brother. Förster's language, laced as it was with anti-semitic bile and Wagnerian pretension, could not have been further removed from Nietzsche's. Though they both dreamed of the regeneration of German culture, Förster's approach was racial, while Nietzsche's was cultural. Nietzsche had already met Förster's brother Paul, another well-known anti-semite, and had disliked him thoroughly; he had no wish to make the acquaintance of another Förster, and, indeed, it was almost a decade before the two would meet for the first and only time. In the interim, Förster introduced Elisabeth to a new and exciting set of moral certainties to an ideology she never lost.

Förster had fought in the Franco-Prussian war in which he had won the Iron Cross, and on his return to Berlin had taken up schoolteaching. But he believed he was destined for better things and thought he had found in Wagner a kindred spirit in the personal war he waged against Jews.

In 1878 Nietzsche wrote the first part of *Human All Too Human*. It marked the definitive break with Wagner; indeed it was overtly anti-Wagnerian in tone. The letter which accompanied the copy he sent to Richard Wagner was the last he ever wrote to the man who had once been his inspiration. Why did Nietzsche turn against Wagner? The answer to that question depends at least partly on who is asking it. For some Wagnerians, Nietzsche's attitude was that of a 'pint-pot capacity railing peevishly at the impermissible magnitude of quarts'; for the Nietzscheans, the break was evidence of Nietzsche's disillusionment with Wagner's pomposity, and proof of the independence of his own ideas. That, certainly, was the impression Nietzsche himself sought to give, and which Elisabeth, while stressing the genius of Wagner, faithfully reproduced in her biographies. Partly it *was* a growing disillusionment on Nietzsche's part with what Bayreuth had come to represent: the *Reichsdeutsch* element in Wagner, his theatrical vanity, his nationalism and crude racial theorising. More specifically, Nietzsche objected to what he saw as the hypocritically Christian tone of *Parsifal*. But it was an emotional as well as an intellectual parting of the ways; perhaps it was simply that two such tremendous egos could never have survived together in such a restricted cultural space. Neither forgave the other for his deficiencies, real or imagined; but Nietzsche never stopped loving Wagner's music, while Wagner, until he died, spoke of his former disciple with the peevish tones of an abused parent.

Cosima Wagner did not look far to find an explanation for Nietzsche's new hostility; she blamed Paul Rée, the Jew, for the insulting tenor of *Human All Too Human*: 'Finally Israel intervened in the form of Dr Rée, very sleek, very cool, at the same time as being wrapped up in Nietzsche and dominated by him, though actually outwitting him – the relationship between Judea and Germany in miniature.' Elisabeth concurred in Cosima's assessment, particularly since she was now a thoroughgoing convert to Försterian anti-semitism: the atheist Rée was responsible for the sickeningly cynical tone of the book. But it was the book's openly anti-Christian polemic that upset her most, and the fact that its publication might affect her popularity at Bayreuth. She was right: the name Nietzsche was no longer mentioned in Wagnerian circles, and *Human All Too Human* was effectively banned. Wagner wrote a damning article in the *Bayreuther Blätter*, the official organ of the Wagner movement, in which he poured scorn on professors who 'criticise everything, human and inhuman'. With over-arching arrogance he later concluded that the only explanation for Nietzsche's hostility was that he was mad – a view that is still held among some Wagnerians today. He even took it upon himself to write to Nietzsche's own doctor, telling him he believed the cause of his erstwhile friend's illness was excessive masturbation.

The strain of the controversy was certainly telling on Nietzsche's health, which deteriorated progressively until, in May 1879, he resigned from Basle. Henceforth he lived the life of an intellectual gypsy, wandering through Europe, alternating between moods of blissful ecstasy and deep depression; when in the grip of the former, he was a new Columbus, discovering new worlds of thought; as he slid into the latter, he longed for his own death. Much as she might resent this new opposition to Wagner, Elisabeth did not abandon her brother. She came to Switzerland to collect him and was appalled by his appearance, now so ravaged by pain that she hardly recognised him. That Christmas he nearly died.

While Nietzsche distanced himself from the Wagnerites, Elisabeth's new friend Bernhard Förster was strenuously attempting to do the opposite. On 8 November 1880, after a prolonged session in a Berlin wine tavern with some like-minded colleagues, Förster had caused a public disturbance by throwing what amounted to an anti-semitic fit on a horse-drawn tram in Charlotten Strasse at half-past four in the afternoon. Picking out the passengers he thought were Jews, Förster had railed about Jewish impudence in mock Yiddish, cursed the Jewish press and praised his friend, the ex-preacher and well known Jew-baiter Adolph Stöcker. The passengers did not react well; although Förster noticed this, he thought that changing the subject (or just shutting up) might be seen as cowardice. Finally a group of passengers, led by a Jewish businessman, forced him and his friend off the tram and a heated dispute took place on the pavement. The businessman started to take down names with a view to reporting the pair for agitation. 'But you're only a Jew,' said Förster's friend. At which point the businessman punched him in the face, knocking his hat off. A brawl ensued, which ended only with the arrival of a passing policeman. A rather battered Förster was hauled off to the police station. When he gave his particulars, Förster stated that his father was an Aryan, implying that this was more than could be said for his accusers. As far as he was concerned, that was excuse enough for his actions.

News of the incident reached Bayreuth, where Cosima noted in her diary: 'When we hear that Herr Förster has been maltreated by some Israelites, R says, "The Germans have never thrashed reviewers, but the Jews thrash Germans."' Berlin buzzed with 'the latest Jewish scandal'. Förster was reprimanded for 'unfitting and undignified behaviour', and fined ninety marks. If anything, it intensified his hatred of Jews, and in racist circles his stock rose dramatically. He followed up his notoriety by launching, with some Berlin colleagues who shared his bigotry, an anti-semitic petition which they planned to present to Bismarck. This demanded that Jewish immigration be suspended, that Jews be barred from the Stock Exchange, that their activities in the press and financial world be restricted and that a census be taken of their numbers.

Germany of the late 1870s and 1880s was fertile ground for the spread of anti-semitism, and an economic crisis combined with anti-clericalism to provide Förster with a growing audience. While he considered himself an intellectual, Förster was always a lightweight, adhering to each of the fashionable causes that Wagner espoused at one time or another: he opposed innoculation and vivisection, and supported homoeopathy, vegetarianism and the sanctity of the soil; many of these ideas would later reappear among the more peculiar tenets of Nazism. He wrote long, rambling discourses on art theory, national education and opera, many of which found their way into the *Bayreuther Blätter*. But his verbose pronouncements boiled down to one central belief: that the Jews were engaged in a single-minded attempt to destroy German culture through their corrupt capitalist business practices. Echoing Wagner's anti-semitic 'Jews in Music', he wrote a long and repetitive discourse on 'Modern Jewry and German Art', using the engraving by Dürer of *Knight, Death and the Devil* as a symbol of German art under threat – the picture that Nietzsche had given Wagner. It ended with a call to arms, and a sinister threat to those who refused to co-operate: 'Either we rid ourselves of these Jews and the honouring of the Golden Calf, or we are lost and deserve to be lost. Anyone who permits the smearing of German culture with vile gold, betrays his Fatherland and becomes a traitor to the most holy German people. . . . as we read in the old law books of the Ostrogoths, whoever betrays the Fatherland was hanged on a bare tree.' By contrast 'the true German is a fighter, a brooder and a poet', who would rather 'let that most lamentable of all nature's products, *Homo sapiens judeo progrediens communis*, die in its own void.'

He made every effort to enlist Wagner's support for the petition, but the composer was adamant: he wouldn't sign *any* petitions, particularly ones containing such 'ridiculously servile phrases and anxiously expressed concern'. He told Cosima 'how embarrassing he finds such relationships, when he is obliged to write to untruthful, narrow-minded, phrase-making people who are none the less devotees'. But in Elisabeth Nietzsche, Förster found a partner only too willing to support him. Elisabeth canvassed Naumberg, enthusiastically collecting signatures for the anti-semitic cause. The petition was finally signed by 267,000 people and ceremoniously carried to the Chancellor's palace by horse and cart on 13 April 1881. Bismarck studiously ignored it, but Förster was undeterred. He had preceded the presentation of the petition with the foundation of the Deutscher Volksverein, the German People's Party, in March 1881, a specifically anti-semitic group which attracted 6,000 people to its first meeting.

And, while Förster's fame was growing, Nietzsche, the prematurely pensioned philology professor from Basle, sank into peripatetic obscurity. He wandered from spa to mountain top, from Sorrento to Stresa, Venice, Marienbad, Messina and Genoa, searching for his lost health, burdened and elated by the growing conviction that he carried in his mind the seeds of a revolutionary philosophy. Usually he was alone; sometimes Paul Rée would accompany him, sometimes Peter Gast, a bad composer but a loyal friend from the Basel days. He found some peace in Sils Maria, a tiny town high in the Engadine mountains, where long walks in the clear air invigorated him; the solitude alternately inspired him and drove him to fits of loneliness. Sometimes he would live for days off nothing but dried fruit in his usually unheated room.

He found some solace in Bizet's opera *Carmen*, which he heard for the first time in November 1881; it was a good antidote to what he now saw as the grand pomposity of Wagner's music: 'I almost think *Carmen* is the best opera there is.' The next year in Genoa with Rée, he saw Sarah Bernhardt in *La Dame aux Camélias*, but the performance ended when she burst a blood vessel on stage: she reminded him of Cosima Wagner. Nietzsche was now thirty-seven and had never experienced a woman's love.

From time to time he had expressed a wish to marry, using the same tone that one might employ to suggest a change of wallpaper. But the insulting insouciance of his writings surely belied a real need for affection and a fear of women: 'The true man wants two things: danger and play. For that reason he wants woman, as the most dangerous plaything.' His own emotional immaturity was remarkable. In 1876 he had met Mathilde Trampedach in Geneva, a twenty-three-year-old Dutch beauty of refined tastes. They discussed poetry. Five days after being introduced he proposed, by letter, and was politely but firmly rejected. Perhaps reacting to the over-attentive women of his childhood, he saw women as accoutrements, and intelligent women as threatening. He later wrote that 'man should be trained for war and woman for the recreation of the warrior'. Women should provide love and housekeeping; and Elisabeth had hitherto been prepared to do both. It was through Paul Rée that he met a woman, intelligent, beautiful, calculating and in absolutely no danger of agreeing to do his housework; and he immediately fell in love with her.

Lou Salomé was the daughter of a Russian general of Huguenot and Baltic German origin. She had left St Petersburg at the age of nineteen with her mother to study in Zurich. When Nietzsche met her in 1882 she was twenty-one, sixteen years his junior, but already far older than her years. Lou was to become one of the most brilliant and stylish women of the nineteenth century. Intellectual and artistic men tended to ask her to marry them within hours of meeting her, and she became adept at turning them down. Finally, many years later, she consented to marry one, Frederick Carl Andreas, a rather peculiar professor of oriental literature, and eventually became Rilke's mistress. Rée had met her in Rome at the home of Malwida von Meysenbug, a middle-aged woman of emancipated views and large fortune who made it her mission to cultivate artists and writers, in particular independent young women. Rée proposed to her almost immediately, but she declined and suggested instead that they should live together as 'brother and sister', with an older man for company; it was a revolutionary idea and, by the morality of the time, totally unacceptable. Rée agreed at once, and suggested that Nietzsche join them. Nietzsche and Lou met in St Peter's. She recalled that his first words were 'What stars have sent us orbiting towards each other?' A few days later, in spite of the obvious deficiencies of this chat-up line, Rée made a marriage proposal to Lou on Nietzsche's behalf, which was turned down. A little later Nietzsche tried again, this time in person, and got the same response.

The three continued to discuss the idea of a sexless *ménage à trois*, in which they would live and study together, although neither man had given up hope of winning her over. Lou was later to become a close friend of Sigmund Freud and an important psychologist in her own right; you didn't need to be Freud to realise that this particular plan, which they called the 'Holy Trinity', was likely to end in the devil's own fracas. The threesome arranged to meet up again later in the year, but before parting they agreed to commission a photograph to commemorate their triple alliance. A Swiss photographer, Jules Bonnet, was chosen for the job and Nietzsche arranged the pose. The resulting picture is hilarious, and a sexual minefield.

Nietzsche and Rée are harnessed to a small cart by lengths of rope. In the cart, kneeling down and brandishing a small whip, is Lou Salomé. Nietzsche appears serene, Rée embarrassed and Lou, well, demonic. On his return to Naumburg, Nietzsche told his family about Lou, whom he described merely as a potential disciple. He was careful not to tell his mother or sister the full extent of his feelings for her, or the details of their plan. Had he done so, Elisabeth would certainly not have agreed to accompany Lou to Bayreuth that summer, where *Parsifal* was to be performed for the first time. It was planned that the Nietzsche siblings and Lou would all meet in Tautenburg in the Thuringian forests, after the festival. Nietzsche, his hostility now public, was *persona non grata* at Bayreuth; indeed, when Wagner heard his name mentioned, he stormed out of the room. But Elisabeth was still determined to go, and agreed to accompany the young Russian woman. Although their characters differed in almost every respect, the first encounter between Lou and Elisabeth was friendly enough. By the end of the journey from Leipzig to Bayreuth they were calling each other *Du*.

Lou was fêted at Bayreuth, much as Elisabeth had been six years earlier. She was introduced to Wagner and Cosima, and the men, young and old, flocked around her. In particular she formed an alliance with Count Paul von Joukowsky, a rich young Russian designer and Wagner's new favourite; they were seen together constantly and it was even rumoured that the young Count had persuaded Lou to take off her dress so that he could design another around her. It probably wasn't true, but Lou wouldn't have cared one way or the other. There was added irony in the flirtatious friendship between the young Count and Lou; Joukowsky had become the disciple that Nietzsche had not, faithful to Wagner until death. Elisabeth was scandalised, and almost certainly extremely jealous of all the attention being lavished on a mere girl. Her anger redoubled when she found that

Lou was showing off a grotesque picture of her brother and his Jewish friend tethered to a cart. But she finally exploded when she discovered the immoral plan, confirmed by Malwida von Meysenbug, that Nietzsche planned to live with Lou and Rée in Paris.

When Elisabeth returned to Naumburg and told him what she thought of Lou, Nietzsche was initially angry and embarrassed. He wrote to Lou calling off the Tautenburg rendezvous, and then relented and asked her to come anyway. When Lou and Elisabeth met again in Jena, prior to departing for Tautenburg, a slanging match ensued. Lou responded to Elisabeth's haughty moralising with ballistic self-defence: 'Don't get the idea that I am interested in your brother or in love with him,' she shouted. 'I could spend a whole night with him in one room without getting excited. It was your brother who first soiled our study plan with the lowest intentions.'

Elisabeth was not used to that sort of talk and seems to have decided, if she had not decided already, that Nietzsche would be better off without this Russian hussy. Nobody contradicted her, and nobody talked about her brother like that. She had not liked the blasphemous tone of her brother's latest philosophy as it was, and Lou personified it, 'that rabid egotism which tramples on everything in its way, and that complete indifference to morality'. The month in Tautenburg, intended as relaxation for Nietzsche's ailing body and mind, was tense in the extreme. Elisabeth was tearful, Lou was strained and distant (taking to her bed at one point) and Nietzsche alternated between asking Lou to leave (which she wouldn't) and trying to declare his love for her. When the time came to go home Elisabeth stayed behind, molten and unwilling to let their mother see her fury. When Nietzsche explained the situation to Franziska, she took Elisabeth's side and called her son 'a disgrace to his father's grave'. Nietzsche, furious himself, left in high dudgeon.

'I have the Naumburg virtue against me,' he wrote. That was an understatement. Elisabeth now launched herself into a one-woman campaign of character-assassination against Lou Salomé, who she was convinced was trying to ensnare her brother, although exactly the reverse was true. She bombarded Nietzsche's friends and acquaintances with letters detailing Lou's crimes. 'I warn Miss Salomé to watch out,' she screeched. 'If she should ever dare again to come near Fritz alone with Rée or quite alone without her mother or some other worthy chaperone and ruin poor Fritz's reputation by her compromising presence – but I will say nothing more. . . .'

She did say more, a lot more, about the 'low, sensuous, cruel and dirty creature' that was Lou; she even attempted to have her sent back to Russia as an immoral woman. But by now the trinity was already breaking up under the weight of its own triangular jealousies. The three met again in Leipzig in October; it gradually seems to have dawned on Nietzsche that he was being squeezed out of the arrangement and that Lou was beyond his reach.

Deserted by his best friend and the woman he wanted, and now the object of his sister's caustic moral hectoring, he fled to Italy. He wrote to Rée and Lou, long reproachful testaments of pain, wounded pride and loneliness: 'I am a headache-plagued half-lunatic, crazed by too much solitude.' He even threatened suicide: 'I have suffered from the disgraceful and anguishing recollections of this past summer as from a kind of madness. . . . Sometimes I think . . . of driving my solitude and resignation to the ultimate limit and –' Soon his reproaches turned to anger; he called Lou a 'dried-up, dirty, evil-smelling monkey with false breasts'. In his philosophical writing too, his misogynistic imagery took on new vehemence: 'How rudely the bitch sensuality knows how to beg for a piece of spirit, when a piece of flesh is denied her.' Perhaps remembering the grotesque photograph, he would later write, 'Are you visiting women? Do not forget your whip!' Paul Rée, once his closest friend, was now 'a sneaking, slanderous, mendacious rogue . . . who dares to speak contemptuously of my intellect, as if I were a lunatic who doesn't know what he is doing'. He began to take doses of sleeping pills, chloral hydrate, in large quantities: 'I am being broken as no one else could be on the wheel of my own passions.'

His relationship with a sister he now called 'morally bloated' was also in tatters. 'It is painful,' he said, 'for me to hear my sister's voice.' Although they were eventually reconciled, Nietzsche never forgave Elisabeth for her unwarranted intrusion into his affairs; perhaps rightly, he thought she had, by her interference, destroyed his one opportunity to be loved; that was certainly her intention. 'For a year now she has cheated me out of my greatest self-conquest,' he wrote, 'by talking at the wrong time and being silent at the wrong time, so that in the end I am the victim of her merciless desire for vengeance.' 'There can be no question of reconciliation with a vengeful anti-semitic goose,' he wrote in May 1884. It is doubtful whether Elisabeth felt the slightest remorse for her actions; she had, after all, taken what she saw as an irreproachable moral line. Elisabeth thought all moral lines were irreproachable, so long as they were hers. Although she regretted her brother's animosity, she was increasingly preoccupied with the other man in her life.

Bernhard Förster's career as an anti-semitic Siegfried had reached something of an impasse. His new party and 'The German Seven', an anti-semitic group of which he was member, were attacked in liberal newspapers for what they were: a bunch of rabble-rousing opportunists fuelled by race-hatred. Förster had called his anti-semitic petition 'A cry for help from the conscience of the German peoples, and later generations will not understand how it could remain unnoticed by the leaders of the state'. But ignored it was, if not unnoticed. Förster's racist activities, and in particular his active agitation among his own pupils, had led to another series of inquiries, forcing Förster to resign his teaching post at the end of 1882. One paper put it pithily: 'The ferocity with which he waged war with one portion of society rendered it impossible for him to be any longer entrusted with the education of another.'

ELISABETH had grown closer to Förster, whom she had seen again at the Bayreuth festival; unlike her irascible brother, here was a man of action and one whose views coincided with her own. She wrote: 'He is filled with magnificent enthusiasm for Wagner's efforts to regenerate our country. We feast on compassion, heroic self-denial,

Christianity, vegetarianism, Aryanism, southern colonies. . . .' The latter craze, Förster's latest, came directly, as usual, from Wagner's most unedifying writing. In *Religion and Art*, published in 1880, Wagner railed against the emancipation of the Jews in 1871, and repeated his belief that the miscegenation of noble and ignoble races was destroying the best human traits. Only by retaining the purity of the Teutonic race could one bring about 'a real rebirth of racial feeling'. Moreover, 'the degeneration of the human race has come about through its departure from its natural [that is, vegetarian] food' – this from the man who had once excoriated Nietzsche for a brief dalliance with vegetarianism. His solution was a simple one: 'What is to prevent our carrying out a rationally conducted migration of these peoples to those quarters of the globe whose enormous fertility is sufficient to maintain the entire present population of the earth, as is claimed for the South American peninsula itself?' Colonising South America would have the added advantage of preventing 'the English traders' from getting their hands on any new colonies. Förster leaped at the idea; here was an opportunity both to prove his Wagnerian mettle and to escape the pernicious influence of the Jews. He was also unemployed. 'The national anti-semitic movement began with the petition,' he wrote, 'and it moves ever onwards.' This wasn't quite true; although Förster and his like represented the first bloom of an anti-semitic plague, the day when racial hatred could galvanise a nation was still some way off; Förster enjoyed some table-thumping support among beery and disgruntled racists in the countryside, but in metropolitan political circles he was not taken very seriously.

Colonisation fever had gripped Germany, itself caught in the depths of economic depression; colonial societies mushroomed, catering to thousands of disillusioned and often poverty-stricken would-be emigrants. By the early 1880s several hundred thousand Germans had taken ship for South America, usually destined for Brazil and Argentina. Förster adopted Wagner's ill-considered notion and elaborated on it. Not only would he found a colony in South America, but he would create a new Fatherland, the mirror image of the old Germany which had become a 'step-fatherland' through the evil effects of Jewry. The colony would be the nucleus of an entire empire in South America. He found enthusiastic supporters in E. Kürbitz, a banker in Naumburg, and Max Schubert, a factory-owner from Chemnitz, both of whom shared his opinions. While Wagner may have thought of the idea, he clearly had not envisaged Förster as the man to carry it out, but the *Bayreuther Blätter* and its editor Freiherr Hans Paul von Wolzogen espoused Förster's *judenreine* cause with a will. Förster chose Paraguay for a number of reasons: a spectacularly bloody war had left the country depopulated, and the immigration office of the Paraguayan government under Colonel Morgenstern de Wisner seemed ready to grant land on highly advantageous terms; several Germans had travelled to the country already and written enthusiastically about its merits, and a successful German colony had been established at San Bernadino, just outside Asunción. Moreover, just as Germany was waking up to the possibility of overseas empire, the areas of possible colonisation were drying up, particularly for what Förster had in mind. North America, he felt, was inimical to propagating true Germanness, and Russia was 'already being systematically destroyed by Jews and nihilists'. Paraguay was just about the only place left.

Förster left Germany in January 1883 to find a suitable site, but before embarking he made sure his plans were well publicised. News of the project even reached England, where *The Times* called Förster 'the most representative Jew-baiter in all Germany' and described his departure as 'the comedy of the modern Pilgrim Fathers':

> Herr Doctor Förster, one of the ring-leaders of the anti-semitic agitation in Germany, shook the dust of an unappreciative country off his feet and, with a small but devoted band of adherents, left Berlin ... to embark for Paraguay, where they will found a new Germany unpolluted by any of the descendants of Abraham. ... He is a man, like too many of his countrymen, of one idea, and that idea is Germany for the Germans, and not for the Jews. Finding that idea unrealistic in his native country, he, with a few devoted men

> like himself [in fact Förster travelled alone], has sailed to a far country, there to found a new Deutschland, where synagogues shall be forbidden, and Bourses unknown.

Förster read the article and wrote to a friend: 'let them make fun of me, I know what I want'.

For all his bravado Förster, like most racists, was an insecure man. Where Nietzsche had, however briefly, embraced Wagner for the grandeur of his vision and the power of his music, Förster seems to have cottoned on to Bayreuth as a salve for his own inadequacies; there was a place for everyone in Bayreuth, thugs and bullies as well as philosophers and aesthetes. His writings had not sold well and Förster blamed the Jews; not only were they corrupting German art and morals, they were dominating the publishing, journalistic and educational professions as part of their malign conspiracy. They were out to get him. On little pieces of paper, in his elaborate curled handwriting, he would jot down the percentages of Jews at Berlin University: 'Law 60%, Medicine 100%, [etc].' With Elisabeth he shared a profound Lutheran faith. Förster had found his life's work where Martin Luther had written 'Know, Christian, that next to the devil thou hast no enemy more cruel, more venomous and violent than a true Jew'; but Förster went further, reaching the original conclusion that Christ could not be a Jew *because* he was the son of God. *Ipso facto,* God was a gentile.

Förster seems to have been as emotionally immature as he was politically unsophisticated; he had confided to Elisabeth that he did not think he would be able to love again because his heart had been broken by a seven-year affair with a woman who had deceived him. But Elisabeth was not the sort of woman to allow a mere technicality to stand in her way, and anyway it was probably just an excuse. In Förster Elisabeth thought she had found her White Knight. His ideas were fashionable and daringly simple, and she understood them in a way she never understood her brother's philosophy, now or later. 'I find Fritz's views more and more unsympathetic,' she wrote to her mother. 'Do you understand now why I wish Fritz shared Förster's views? Förster has ideals that will make men better and happier if they are promoted and carried out. I laugh at the uproar he causes among stupid people.' But Elisabeth equated love with control, and to an extent her emotions were at the mercy of her vaulting ambition. Cosima Wagner was more than a role model for Elisabeth, she was a symbol of what German womanhood could achieve, since she had found her man of genius and helped him to his destiny. Elisabeth believed she too had found such a man – 'some day Förster will be praised as one of the best Germans and a benefactor of his people', she said, rightly as it turned out. She genuinely admired Förster's ideas, but perhaps she sensed his weakness as well; Elisabeth could dominate Förster as she had never dominated her brother.

Just before he left Hamburg at the beginning of 1883, Förster received a telegram which read: 'Greetings from Wagner. Congratulations on your "Dreams". Have a good trip.' Wagner was referring to Förster's latest turgid emission, a pamphlet called *Dreams of Parsifal.* It was the first and only time that the *Meister* had positively acknowledged his most ardent disciple. Förster was delighted, but he would have been considerably less pleased if he had heard the Wagners discussing his emigration project over breakfast a few days later: 'We hear', reported Cosima, wrongly, 'that numerous people are going, that parents are entrusting their sons to him. This alarms R. greatly since he has no great confidence in it.' Richard Wagner was probably the only person alive who could have dissuaded Förster from his Paraguayan plan; but four days later he was dead.

Förster got the news when he arrived in Asunción for the first time, and wrote to a fellow devotee: 'What a thunderbolt it is to hear that Wagner has gone to Nirvana ... but it is a consolation that we lived through the greatest and most productive part of his sumptuous career. ... much as I search, I can find no greater man and none to whom I owe more; my hard work here is dedicated to the service of his ideas.' Five thousand miles away Nietzsche was both moved and relieved by the news that the man he had once loved and later so bitterly opposed was dead. It had been hard, he said, for six years to be the enemy of 'the man one most reveres'. He took to his bed for several days and then wrote to

Cosima: 'I regard you today, even from far away, as I have always regarded you – as the woman my heart most honours.'

THAT year Nietzsche wrote the first part of *Thus Spoke Zarathustra*, the bleakly brilliant summation of his apocalyptic philosophy. For the first time Nietzsche introduced the Superman, a figure of the future who could survive the end of morality and recreate himself by overcoming *Ressentiment*, a concept intended to inspire but one which would develop sinister overtones in the wrong hands. With the completion of *Zarathustra*, Nietzsche believed he had brought the German languge to perfection and created at the same time a philosophy that could alter the world: 'My son Zarathustra may have betrayed to you what is going on within me; and if I achieve all I desire to achieve I shall die in the knowledge that future millennia will take their highest vows in my name.' But the world wasn't listening. More than that, it seemed to be studiously ignoring him.

Elisabeth, temporarily reconciled with her brother, was initially enthusiastic about the book – she may even have the dubious honour of being the first person thoroughly to misconstrue the notion of the Superman. She promised to send a copy to Förster, whom she thought had taken the first step towards superman status. But the conciliatory tone was short-lived. Nietzsche was still upset by Elisabeth's part in the Lou affair, and a week spent with his mother and sister in September led to bitter arguments. Elisabeth wrote to Förster, 'My brother's goal is not my goal, his entire philosophy goes against my grain. . . .' In that she was entirely accurate, for the source of their disagreements was now less her disapproval of his philosophy than his contempt for hers, as evidenced by her new alliance with Förster. Nietzsche never sought to disguise the fact that he considered Förster intellectually and politically reprehensible. His feelings were partly emotional, since he would have made life difficult for any prospective suitor for his sister, but his objections were primarily ideological.

In the 1887 edition of *The Gay Science*, Nietzsche wrote a

description of the type of man he most despised. It was, and perhaps was even intended to be, an accurate character-portrait of Bernhard Förster:

> Here is a man who has turned out a failure, a man who possesses too little spirit to be able to enjoy it and just enough culture to realise that fact; bored, weary, a self-despiser . . . such a one as is fundamentally ashamed of his existence – perhaps he harbours a couple of little vices as well – and on the other hand cannot help over-indulging himself and exacerbating his vanity worse and worse with books to which he has no right or more intelligent company than he can digest: such a man poisoned through and through . . . falls finally into an habitual condition of revengefulness, of the will to revenge.

Specifically it was Förster's nationalist trumpeting and crude anti-semitism that appalled Nietzsche and, by association, threatened his own reputation. 'This accursed anti-semitism', he wrote, 'is the cause of a radical breach between me and my sister.' He believed Förster's vegetarianism would make him gloomy and depressed, in contrast to the British taste for roast beef which had made them such effective colonists, and as for Förster's notions of Aryan purity, they were nonsense. 'To enthusiasm for the "German national character" I have indeed attained very little,' he declared, 'but even less to the wish to keep this "glorious" race *pure*. On the contrary, on the contrary . . .'; and finally snobbery made the idea of living on the same level as twenty peasant families distinctly unappealing. Even Franziska Nietzsche, desperate as she was to see her daughter married off, had serious reservations about this bearded agitator and his wild schemes.

Elisabeth, however, was determined. She wrote regularly to Förster as he wandered Paraguay (usually alone) in the two years he took to find a site for his colony. She told him that pioneers would flock to his standard, that he should build himself a large house and that the project was a certain success. She even sent him money to engage a servant, since she worried that he should have to look after himself. Under that kind of pressure a man as weak as Förster was putty. He decided he was in love with Elisabeth and told her he would return to Germany and marry her. Then they would voyage to Paraguay together, the joint leaders of a glorious colonial mission. Elisabeth was delighted, although she worried about her brother and his failing health: 'Is it right to leave my brother? Is it not my duty to remain here and take care of him?'

Förster returned to Germany in March 1885 and married Elisabeth in Naumburg on 22 May, Wagner's birthday, a date which might have been calculated to annoy Nietzsche. The day, wrote Förster, 'shall bind the hearts of two people who are inextricably entwined not only by nature and also by the shared spirit of Richard Wagner'. Nietzsche refused to give her away or even to attend the ceremony, and went for a picnic on the Lido instead. But he did send a gift, one which Elisabeth had specifically requested; it was, of course, the engraving of Dürer's *Knight, Death and the Devil.* Of all Dürer's great works, it is perhaps the most powerful, yet in the circumstances it seems grotesque; no doubt the couple saw themselves as the brave Aryan and Christian knight, death and the devil as Jewish intrigue. Nietzsche said gloomily, and probably untruthfully, that he hoped their marriage would be happier than the picture. Later that month he wrote to his mother: 'From my own point of view it is impossible to have closer contact with such an agitator. He seems to have the same feeling.'

Elisabeth and Förster toured the country, lecturing about Paraguay to Wagnerian societies, in beer halls and colonial clubs, recruiting Aryan disciples for their colony and riding what Nietzsche called 'two horses, anti-semitism and Paraguay.' The response was less ecstatic than they had hoped, but gradually they assembled a corps of pioneers: the poverty-stricken, the racist and the merely gullible. Together the couple produced Förster's book, *German Colonisation in the Upper La Plata*. Nietzsche was almost certainly galled that a mere travel book should attract more attention than his own works; he thought that putting Förster's picture in the front was an act of supreme vanity and told Elisabeth so. The philosopher steadfastly refused to join in his sister's project, despite her entreaties, and he provided numerous reasons:

the climate was alien, he said, and there were no large libraries, he might be seasick, and he was anyway unwell. In fact the climate was murderous, there were no libraries and he was more ill than he knew, but Nietzsche seems to have been trying to tone down his objections to a project he now couldn't prevent. He even agreed to a meeting with his new brother-in-law. They met for the first and last time in Naumburg on Nietzsche's forty-first birthday. Elisabeth later recalled that they talked about sex, and how great men have no need of physical solace. 'My husband', recalled Elisabeth, 'told how [Heinrich Freiherr von] Stein had complained to him of feeling so lonely among the young men of the great city, who really knew no other problem but the sexual problem, and paraded their disgusting, overheated sensuality as a state of health. My brother spoke of similar complaints he had heard from Stein. . . . "Perhaps we are alike," said my brother, "at any rate we are masters of our senses, and know more important problems than that of sex."' This was male bonding of a sort, I suppose, although rather tactless given Förster's newly married status. After the meeting Nietzsche was moderately forgiving about his new relative. There was something noble in his character, he said, he was a man of action if impetuous, sincere if misguided. Privately he wondered whether his sister and brother-in-law were the stuff colonists are made of.

Elisabeth and Förster and their band of Aryan pioneers boarded the steamer *Uruguay* at Hamburg on 15 February. Förster made a short speech: 'I am in the company of a small number of friends and companions whom others will shortly follow,' then the steamer pulled out of the harbour. The couple had sent Nietzsche a ring as a parting gift, inscribed with the injunction 'Think lovingly of B and E'. His attitude to Elisabeth was still ambivalent, and about Förster he thought anything but lovingly. He was glad Förster had gone, he said, and hoped every other anti-semitic agitator in the country would do likewise. But the departure of his sister affected him deeply for, though she irritated him beyond words, she had always loved him, as no other woman had. 'How lonely your Fritz now feels,' he wrote to her, 'for I have lost *all* my friends in the last few years without exception. . . .

he is living in a remoter, stranger, more unapproachable land than all the Paraguays could be.' And in another letter he told a friend: 'I have lost my sister . . . not through real death but by an irreversible separation. She has gone to South America with her husband to found a colony. There is every prospect that it will succeed, but the more it prospers, the less chance there is that she will return. But then, the opinions of my brother-in-law, by which he is prepared to live and die, are far more alien to me than Paraguay.' In a last letter before her departure he pleaded with Elisabeth not to desert him: 'I would give everything I possess if it would help to bring you back.'

CHAPTER VI

Elisabeth in Llamaland

IN HIS parting speech to the small crowd which assembled to bid the colonists farewell at Hamburg docks, Förster had announced that he was going to Paraguay 'partly to complete and partly to prepare the purchase of land for colonial purposes': he was being, strictly speaking, honest, because the first, last and most crucial problem with the planned colonisation of Paraguayan lands was that neither Bernhard nor Elisabeth Förster owned any.

An area had been chosen for the colony about 150 miles north of Asunción covering some 600 square kilometres. The locals called the area Campo Cassaccia, and it had once been sparsely populated. But now, thanks to the war, it was all but deserted: two-thirds was forest but one-third, said Förster, was fertile farming land. Most of Campo Cassacia seems to have been the property of a rich, flamboyant Paraguayan called Cirilio Solalinde, and his asking price was steep – 175,000 Marks, way beyond anything Förster or Elisabeth could raise. It took months of negotiations, during which the fourteen peasant families they had brought from Germany idled their time away in Asunción, before the Försters managed to strike a triangular land deal involving Förster, Solalinde and the Paraguayan government. The government would pay 80,000 Marks to Solalinde, who would then hand over 40,000 acres to Förster; in return Förster had to make a down-payment to the government of just 2,000 Marks. It seemed a simple and, from the Försters' point of view, excellent arrangement. But, as with every Paraguayan deal, there was a snag: at least 140 German families had to be settled on the property within two years, or the money must be paid back and the land forfeited. Förster, convinced that people would arrive in droves once the colony had been established, happily signed his life away on 23 November, fully eight months after the colonists had disembarked. He began selling off parcels of land, despite the fact that the Paraguayan government still had legal title to it. Förster, who had always excoriated the Jews for using credit to finagle honest Germans into buying things they didn't own, now started doing exactly that.

To raise still more cash, Förster and Elisabeth set about soliciting donations and loans from friends and relatives in Europe. One supporter was Julius Cyriax, a committed German Wagnerian known to Förster from the Bayreuth days, now resident in London. A chemist by profession, he made a living by dealing in 'surgical instruments and appliances, glassware, confectionery, patent medicines, medical books and shop fittings and every description of druggist's sundries'. As the sole proprietor of Rossiter's Hair Restorer and author of such best-selling titles as *Deep Petrissage of the Abdomen as an Aid to the Diagnosis of Tapeworm* and *Mechanical Stimulation of the Coccygeal Ganglion*, Cyriax seems to have been a man of means; at any rate, he was generous when it came to sending money to Förster. 'I shall have to remain in your debt for a while,' wrote Förster, 'but in a few years' time I hope to be able to pay you back.' He never did. Other contributors to Nueva Germania included Förster's four siblings and Franziska Nietzsche, two of Elisabeth's girl friends from Naumburg and even her elderly nurse-maid Alwine. The only close relative who steadfastly refused to invest in the colony was Friedrich Nietzsche. Before the couple left for Paraguay, he had responded amusingly to his sister's 'jolly suggestion' that he put up some money, 'if it would encourage your husband to come round to a good opinion of your hopeless, loafer brother and the good European and the anti-anti-semites'. To his sister's suggestion that a portion of land be named Friedrichshein after him he responded that it should be called 'Llamaland' instead.

Once in Paraguay, Elisabeth made further attempts to tap into her brother's minimal resources. Nietzsche felt guilty at the repeated demands or, rather, angry for being made to feel guilty when he turned them down. Knowing his views on anti-semitism, she now tried to play down the colony's racism, but her brother was rightly unconvinced. In June he wrote to her:

> You say that New Germany is not anti-semitic, but I know for certain that the colonisation project has a decidedly anti-semitic character from seeing the 'correspondence sheet' that is sent out in secret and only to reliable members of the party. (I hope my brother-in-law does not give it to you to read! It becomes ever more unpleasant.) . . . Oh, my good Llama, how have you come to fall into such a misadventure . . . for if I know my dear sister, she would rather die than leave her project in the lurch. But that is Nietzschean!

He also feared his Basle pension might be cut off by the 'economic and skilful' university authorities if they discovered he was a South American landowner, and he cited the advice of his old friend from Basle, Franz Overbeck, who considered the whole project a dangerous gamble. Elisabeth was furious and promptly revealed her true colours: she decided that Overbeck, who was an atheist church historian, but a Protestant by birth, was in actuality a Jew. His race explained everything. Later she wrote to her mother: 'I hear that Overbeck is a Jew; that speaks volumes and I believe it.'

While Elisabeth stayed in Asunción, fulminating against her brother's stinginess and his inability to make his mind up without deferring to a Jew, Förster and an advance band of settlers had taken the journey north and began to clear the forest to make way for a town, to be christened Försterröde. Throughout 1887 work went ahead on Elisabeth's mansion. From the beginning she had dreamed of a large house of her own. 'Just think how grand it would sound,' she had written to Förster, 'Förster of Försterhof.'

The effort of constructing a building on the scale Elisabeth had in mind was clearly considerable. It began to tell on Förster, who (though he was only forty-three) wrote to Cyriax, 'I am getting old and very tired. Once the house is finished, then the continuation of our work will be assured. Then I too will be able to rest.' The strain and the climate were affecting the resilient Elisabeth too: 'the few years I have been married have aged me by ten years', she told her mother. 'If the last few years haven't given me grey hairs then I won't ever get them.' Elisabeth suffered from homesickness, and Förster from some seriously bad temper. 'I hope that unquiet Bernhard is not making life too hard for our Lissen,' Franziska Nietzsche wrote to her son. But they could not have returned to Germany, even if they had wanted to. Before leaving, it seems, Förster had publicly accused a government minister of having Jewish ancestry and had been sued *in absentia*. If he set foot in Germany, Franziska reported, he would probably be arrested.

In March 1888, a grand inauguration ceremony was held at the colony and the Försters finally took possession of their mansion. The occasion swelled equally Elisabeth's head and her prose style, and she wrote an effusive letter to her mother:

> In front of every farm house we passed, people stood festively dressed, presented me with flowers and cigars, and handed me their babies for my benediction. Suddenly, eight splendid horsemen appeared. They were our New Germans who had come to greet us; among them were Herr Erck and other leading colonists. They brought Bern's favourite horse, beautifully decorated with black, white and red rosettes, which he mounted at once. That was only the first reception and we were still not in our own country. You ought to have seen the procession: first the wagon, then the riders, and then the long train of people. Now we reached the Aguarya-umí, which borders on our property. We were not received with a cannon salute, but cheerful gunshots rang out as we approached and a charming small wagon appeared, decorated with palm leaves like a green arbour and carrying a small red throne. All very pretty. Here I embraced my dear Frau Erck and Herr Erck made a solemn speech of welcome since I had never been here before. Then the procession moved to the port of Aguarya-guazu, the commercial centre of the colony with the store and immigrant house.
>
> Here the first triumphal arch had been erected and the official reception took place. We sat in the centre of a marvellously shady square, and three very beautiful girls appeared,

> the oldest, about 15, was almost a lady; she was pretty as a picture and the beauty of the colony. She recited a charming poem of welcome that her father had written and gave us flowers. Then we ate breakfast while the populace feasted on wine and cumin.

In fact one of the colonists became so drunk that he fell in the river and drowned. The Paraguayans unsentimentally named the harbour Kaú, Guaraní for drunkard. That incident Elisabeth omitted, but her breathless description went on:

> The wives of the colonists who had been brought together brewed coffee, and our New Germans sat together under a beautifully shady tree. . . . they all had such open and honest German faces. Then Herr Enzweiler, a very industrious and capable colonist, made a speech of welcome, raised his glass and shouted 'Long live the Mother of the Colony,' which pleased my heart. . . . accompanied by the sounds of '*Deutschland, Deutschland über alles*' we drove and rode to our house.

There then followed another series of triumphal arches, flowers, solemn good wishes and thanks to God for her good fortune and the size of her domestic staff – twenty peons, cooks and servants. Leaving aside Elisabeth's impressive capacity for exaggeration and her understandable desire to dispel her mother's reservations about the whole project, one thing is certain: at the age of forty-two, Elisabeth was finally someone to be reckoned with in her own right, the wife of a brave pioneer, mistress of a large mansion, mother of an Aryan colony and Queen of a potential new Germany. The descriptions are all her own.

Back in Europe, Nietzsche made no attempt to hide what he felt about Germany, old or new: 'I have no respect left for present-day Germany. . . . it represents the most stupid, the most depraved, the most mendacious form of the "German spirit" that ever was.' And he was more convinced than ever that he wanted 'nothing whatever to do with this anti-semitic undertaking' by his sister, let alone underwrite his brother-in-law's growing overdraft at a Naumburg bank. He repeatedly told her that ten horses would not drag him to Paraguay, adding sadly, 'indeed, I'm already a sort of immigrant, I also have my Gran' Chaco . . .'. Once again he felt his own psychological wilderness closing in.

He drafted a letter to his sister suggesting that every anti-semite be packed off to Paraguay and outlining his reasons for refusing to invest in the scheme: 'My position is financially insecure, and yours has not been proven. But above all our wishes and our interests do not coincide insofar as your project is an anti-semitic one. If Dr Förster's project succeeds, then I will be happy on your behalf and as far as I can, I will ignore the fact that it is the triumph of a movement which I reject. If it fails I shall rejoice in the death of an anti-semitic project. . . .' But he was none the less impressed when he heard Elisabeth's inflated description of her own eminence, and he boasted to his friends that Elisabeth's house had become a social centre of the country, and that his relations were now among the largest landowners in Paraguay with property the size of a small princedom. Her reception was worthy of a priest, he told her – a somewhat back-handed compliment in his case.

He could afford to be generous, because he too had achieved a breakthrough. At the beginning of 1888, Nietzsche received a letter from Georg Brandes, a prominent Danish scholar who admired his work for its 'aristocratic radicalism'. Nietzsche, delighted, wrote back saying it was 'the shrewdest comment on me I have so far read'. It was also practically the only comment for many years. Since Nietzsche had abandoned Bayreuth, he had written the greatest part of his oeuvre: *Dawn*, *The Gay Science*, *Zarathustra*, *Beyond Good and Evil* and *Genealogy of Morals*. The works had attracted little or no attention, and some had seen the public light of day only because he had published them at his own expense. But when Brandes began to lecture in Copenhagen on him, it gave rise to a renewed burst of self-confidence in the forty-three-year-old philosopher, confidence which, as his mind began to disintegrate under the strain of disease, found expression in a combination of astonishing hubris, euphoria and, for a time, apparently improved health. He confided to friends: 'Between ourselves

. . . it is not inconceivable that I am the foremost philosopher of the era, perhaps even more than that, a bridge between two millennia, decisive and doom-laden.' To Elisabeth he wrote as 'Your brother, now quite a famous person'.

Elisabeth, as was her wont, promptly put him in his place. 'Personally I would have wished you another apostle than Mr Brandes; he has peeked in too many pots and eaten from too many plates. . . . I cannot suppress a well-meant piece of advice. Avoid a personal meeting, exchange pleasantries with him by correspondence, but do not look at him too closely.' Brandes, of course, was Jewish. Nietzsche was enraged. Once again Elisabeth was trying to bring him down at the moment of his greatest triumph. He drafted but never sent a letter breaking off all contact with his sister: 'It is time we said goodbye. I see every word you ever said to me ten times more clearly now. . . . You have no conception of what it means to be closely related to the man and the destiny in whom the question of millennia has been resolved – quite literally I hold the future of humanity in the palm of my hand.'

Elisabeth had little time for her brother's delusions of grandeur since she had plenty of her own. She and Förster bombarded Germany with reports of the colony's excellent progress; their thinly veiled propaganda found a willing home in the pages of Hans von Wolzogen's *Bayreuther Blätter* and a variety of other colonial newspapers. Förster wrote: 'We are dreaming of a rebirth of our race . . . when the axe resounds in the primordial forest, when we clear the underbrush with the sweat of our brow to prepare the fertile soil for cultivation, when we dig trenches to drain stagnant water – how far all these activities seem from the sacred hill of Bayreuth. But we feel in our hearts that it is precisely this kind of work that makes us the spiritual heirs of Richard Wagner.' Elisabeth's declarations were still more plangent. A piece entitled 'A Sunday in Nueva Germania' appeared in the *Bayreuther Blätter* in late 1888:

> After supper we sit in the garden and look into the distance. . . . there are fields, gilded with red from the evening sun on both sides of the river, interspersed with fields of lowing

> cattle. What a peaceful, happy picture this affords, nothing is alien. No, everything is homely ... you dear Bayreuth friends, have you perhaps solved the puzzle in your way? Do you realise that the only fruitful spirit of colonisation has emanated from Bayreuth? ... but now, other noises reach us on the soft currents of the evening breeze; the singing of German men reaches us from a garden a little way off. How the jungle trees must wonder at these strange new sounds wafting through the tree-tops. For twenty years deep silence has ruled here [Elisabeth seemed to have assumed that the Indians were not only biologically inferior, but mute], but now there is this strange new life. The song is 'I don't know why, but I'm so sad', which the German sings when he is particularly happy. They are singing in the distance with love and pride and yearning. Up into the star-studded southern night sky, into the mysterious gloom of the jungle: '*Deutschland, Deutschland über alles, über alles in der Welt*'.

Both Elisabeth and Förster spoke of the triumphant first sailing of the ship *Hermann*, which would transport colonists from the river to the colony, and of the railway that would surely soon be built, connecting Nueva Germania to the outside world. It was a place were simple Paraguayan servants rushed to do a white man's bidding, where the food fell from the trees and where Germans, tired of the economic vicissitudes of life in the Fatherland, could find 'a healthy climate, cheap food and pleasant surroundings'.

This was, of course, the purest fantasy. The climate was usually roasting, the heat broken only by the irregular but torrential rain which drowned animals, ripped up fences, poured through straw roofs and made travel all but impossible. The downpours brought with them swarms of fat malarial mosquitos. The burrowing sandfly, the *picá*, was a constant menace; it bored into your feet and, if left untreated, the wound rapidly went septic. The earth was thick and glutinous, virtually unploughable and resistant to most kinds of crops. Every mouthful had to be fought for.

Förster had insisted that the colony's buildings, except in

the tiny town of Försterröde, be built at least a mile apart, the better to cultivate homely German virtues in solitude. The result was crushing depression, made worse by Förster's over-bearing attitude. He would ride around the colony on a white horse and insisted that other colonists dismount when he passed. If the German workers sang 'I'm so sad', that was because they had every reason to be: two years after arriving in Paraguay, many were still living in communal mudbrick houses, little more than shacks, sodden, smelly and unhygienic. The only completed house was Elisabeth's beloved Försterhof. At first the settlers ignored the siesta, working all day; but when they began to drop from heat exhaustion, they quickly adopted the Paraguayan habit, refined over centuries, of sleeping through the afternoon when the sun was overhead. Roads were left unbuilt since every available hour was spent trying to coax crops from the red earth or to fatten up the few livestock; in spite of the torrential rain, clean water was in short supply. Wells had to be dug to depths of 100 feet before reaching water, and they quickly ran dry. While Elisabeth opined on the childlike, biddable qualities of her Paraguayan peons, many of the other colonists found them lazy and disrespectful. Fights began to break out between the races which Elisabeth had to break up, though she would 'rather have spent time on ideological matters'.

She was well aware that discontent was brewing, but for the time being she was content to enjoy her newfound eminence. When an aristocratic Mecklenburg family, the von Maltzans, responded to the propaganda barrage and agreed to join the enterprise, she was delighted. Baron Hermann von Maltzan was a well-known African explorer and colonial figure, and persuading his family to come to Paraguay had been a remarkable coup. Elisabeth shared her brother's reservations regarding the peasant stock of New Germany, but with the Maltzans she could hold tea parties and coffee mornings on the verandah of her large house – Naumburg on the Aguarya-umí.

Early in 1887, the Försters had met General Osborne, the former American Ambassador to Argentina, an entrepreneur and optimist. He was negotiating with the Paraguayan government to build a railway line which would run from the mouth of the Rio de la Plata to Panama, through Bolivia and Peru. If it was ever built, he assured the Försters, it would pass through or very near to New Germany. When he left, the courteous general expressed a profound hope that he would one day travel by train to visit 'the little queen of Nueva Germania'. Elisabeth was delighted with the title, and began to assume an ever more regal air. Even in later life she always referred to New Germany as her 'princedom'. Her husband was also dreaming ever larger and more impossible dreams. As Nietzsche reported, he had become so important in the affairs of the country that he thought he might even become the next President of the Paraguayan Republic; 'you can imagine what a strain it is for Förster and me not to deal with each other as enemies', he added. Förster's stock at home appeared to be rising too, as a result of his fictional descriptions of life in the colony. By October 1888, he claimed that the colony contained a baker, a shoemaker, three carpenters, two smiths and a sawmill owner. Opportunities remained, he said, for a tailor, a tanner, a plumber, a brewer and a cigar maker. A school was being built, and plans were being made to raise funds to pay for a pastor. Although some Germans had been tempted by his glowing descriptions and had come to join the original fourteen families that had travelled on the *Uruguay*, others had actually left. 'There have been settlers who didn't realise what it would be like here,' Förster admitted cautiously. They didn't realise because he hadn't told them. He assured his readers that most of the settlers were German, and that the majority were Protestant. The full complement of settlers should be in place by the end of 1888: 'If we make a start here, the truly German way, we are going to expand our colony in this propitious climate for hundreds of miles in every direction, justifying the prophetic name we have chosen for it.'

In the first two years, forty families made the trip to Nueva Germania. Of these, a quarter had quit by July 1888, leaving seventy of the hundred town plots unsold. Title to the land depended on finding 110 families in less than a year. Förster wrote to General Bernardino Caballero, the man whom he sought to replace as President of Paraguay, on 24 September 1888 to ask for help. Stressing the President's reputation as a defender of progressive ideas and citing a number of witnesses to the colony's progress, he admitted that: 'The colony's management is in a little difficulty since it has spent more than was previously calculated. It was impossible, of course, to calculate exact expenditure beforehand for such a great and important work and it is well known, from experience in the colony of San Bernadino, that expenses are high in a new colony.' Thousands of pesos had already been spent, he said, on providing for the new colonists' needs and still more on 'literary propaganda in Europe in support of Paraguayan colonisation'. But he maintained an optimistic tone: 'For all this, my colony is doing well and there is no doubt I will be paid back for all my work and expenses . . . A well-led colony will always be a good business and the capital spent on such a project will yield a considerable profit after the third year. In order to allow others to share in these profits, I'm thinking of forming a union or company with sufficient capital to broaden the base of the business . . . I have already spoken to some important men in Asunción who have assured me they will go into this enterprise with me and share in the profits. This is the reason why I come to you, General, to ask your advice and invite you to participate in this venture.' The letter did not, apparently, elicit a reply.

If Elisabeth realised the dangers of the situation, she did not say so. Förster certainly did realise. He had promised to refund the price of their land to any colonists who chose to leave, as well as to pay compensation for any improvements to it. Since the only capital he had was what he had collected from the colonists in the first place (which had now been spent), the only alternative was to borrow. He spent more and more time away in Asunción, searching for creditors, or feverishly writing to Germany for more funds and in particular to Max Schubert, the industrialist who ran the Chemnitz Colonial Society, and who had supported Förster from the start.

In 1888 Förster's nemesis arrived in the small and rather unprepossessing shape of one Julius Klingbeil. Elisabeth was later to accuse this man of being a 'filthy little egotist', a possible kidnapper, a liar, a smuggler and a lunatic probably sent by the Jesuits to destroy her colony. He was, of course, nothing of the sort but in reality a barely literate Antwerp tailor of German peasant origin, who came to Paraguay to improve his health. He had read Förster's descriptions of Paraguay in his advertising pamphlet and found the idea irresistible, particularly as he shared Förster's anti-semitism. He arrived in March with his wife and ten companions, having already made a down-payment on a plot of land. Klingbeil may have been a simple man, but it took him no time at all to realise that he, along with every other colonist, was the victim of a major fraud.

When he appeared to pay his respects at Försterhof he was led into a large salon, equipped with expensive furniture. Nothing was missing to make life comfortable: a large couch, comfortable chairs, a piano, stone floors and curtained doors. On the wall was Förster's favourite Goethean motto in gilt lettering: 'Over all obstacles, stand your ground.' At dinner the nominally abstemious Försters provided a large selection of excellent wines and copious liqueurs. Having seen Förster's picture, Klingbeil had expected to meet a man of action, full of good intentions and heroic ideals. What he found was a bundle of nerves. Förster could not sit still, but shifted around continually, speaking only rarely and then in monosyllables. The eyes that had stared forcefully from Förster's portrait trembled constantly and he could never look you in the eye. He seemed, thought Klingbeil, quite insane; but cunning too. Could this be the same man who had written such uplifting books, and who enjoyed such a reputation at home in Germany? But if Förster was a pathetic mixture of cowardice and ambition, his wife was worse. She was just as ambitious, but with quite extraordinary energy. She would have been admirable, he later reflected, had she not used her heroic talents for such evil ends. It was horrible to see her dominating her husband, who seemed to have no idea about the colony's future at all and deferred to her constantly. She spoke for both of them, like a queen, and even referred to communal Nueva Germania as 'their' principality. She was a tiny woman in expensive and elegant clothes; it was almost amusing to see her twittering around the room, hands, mouth and feet all moving at once. Time and again she steered the conversation back to money, boasting of the colony's success and pretending that the plots of land were selling fast.

Klingbeil and his wife went to bed, exhausted and infuriated by Frau Förster's interminable and mostly nonsensical chatter. They realised they would never make their fortunes here, but perhaps they could enjoy a modest life in Nueva Germania, even if Förster himself was so disappointing. They almost felt sorry for him – what a miserable life he must lead with that dreadful woman. But pity soon turned to scorn. The Försters complemented each other perfectly, her bravado compensated for his weakness. She did all the administrative work, bullying and cajoling the colonists into submission, while Förster did little except travel to Asuncíon and write long, mendacious reports for colonial newspapers in an attempt to gather yet more gullible recruits. Over the ensuing months, Klingbeil gradually realised the extent of the deception. The Försters lived in a large mansion, while the colonists survived in pathetic huts living off strange and horrible food, more degraded than the lowest peasant in Germany. A vegetarian, Klingbeil had been attracted to the colony by Förster's descriptions of a beautiful land bursting with fruit and vegetables. He was shocked to discover that the Försters now ate meat, though Förster had stated clearly that 'the people of New Germany will not indulge in the foul and disease-inducing consumption of meat . . .'. The unfortunate colonists who had believed him and stuck to their dietary principles found themselves surviving on corn, rice and beans. Milk and cheese were sold, but at extortionate prices from the colony's only shop – which belonged, of course, to Förster. In fact, trade of every type was monopolised by the founder and his wife to prevent any capitalist 'Jewish customs' from creeping into the community, and every colonist had to sign a contract saying they would do no business within the boundaries of the colony. Klingbeil complained bitterly about the climate, which was the opposite of what had been promised. It was constantly hot and very humid; when it rained it was impossible either to work or to leave the settlement for weeks on end.

Förster claimed to speak French and Greek, but could not speak either. He had even lied about the 'remarkable industry' of the Paraguayan women. The men did all the work, Klingbeil complained, including cooking and cleaning, and the women never washed but lay around smoking cigars and eating the lice off their bodies. As if to prove the point, Frau Förster had tried to enlist Klingbeil's wife to do *her* housekeeping. Klingbeil had refused, saying they were a large group with only one woman to cook, and they needed her themselves, whereupon Frau Förster became extremely angry and accused the new arrival of being unhelpful. Klingbeil was outraged.

Himself a volatile character, the little Antwerp tailor lasted only a few months before he came into terminal conflict with the domineering self-styled Queen of the colony. He went to complain about the state of their housing and announced his decision to leave. Elisabeth was furious, weeping with rage, and accusing Klingbeil of causing all the colony's problems. 'There have been enough lies,' he replied, before he remounted and rode home to his miserable shack. That day, he packed his few belongings and rode out of the colony for ever.

Klingbeil's fury lasted all the way back to Germany, where he heaped his resentment and a catalogue of the Försters' dubious activities into a 160-page book. Apologising for his lack of literary style, he said his motives were to act as a warning against fraudulent demagogues like Förster, who pretended to be patriotic but were just rogues and exploiters of the poor. 'I have been reproached for trusting too much to Bernhard Förster, but his propaganda for the colony in Paraguay led me into misery,' he wrote. 'My experiences and the experiences of other German emigrants to Paraguay are so sad and such a bad example that I feel obliged, for reasons of conscience, to tell the whole truth to the people.' No other nation would even consider colonising such a pitiful country, he concluded, and the government should intervene immediately.

Julius Klingbeil's *Revelations Concerning Bernhard Förster's Colony New Germany* was published in Leipzig at the end of

1889. It demonstrated to the whole of Germany what had been known only to a few lost and bewildered German peasants in the heart of the Paraguayan jungle: that the new Aryan republic was a sham, and the Försters were arrogant swindlers. It raised a storm.

Nietzsche had already written with some glee to Overbeck that 'in Paraguay things are as bad as they can be. The Germans, who were lured over there, are in rebellion and demand their money back – and there is none. Acts of violence have already occurred. I fear the worst.' The news that, instead of being thought of as Aryan champions, they were being reviled in the liberal press as rank criminals affected Elisabeth and Bernhard Förster in different ways. She had no intention of reading such a dreadful book, she said, and immediately went on the offensive, attacking Klingbeil in the pages of the *Bayreuther Blätter*, which still remained open to her. She alternated between flattering her husband's old anti-semitic allies and criticising them for their lack of support.

> Oh you anti-semites, is that your loyalty, your courage, shamefully to abandon one of your most ideal leaders? ... Anti-semitism has above all a positive aspect: the urge to deepen and ennoble the true German characteristics; it is motivated by the urge to create or renew institutions which strengthen true Germanness in an idealistic or economic sense and protect it from foreign influences. ... What is my husband fighting for here and now? Is it not true Germanness? And the goal? Is it not to create a new German place as a substitute for the old? ... Let anti-semitism prove through action, here in Nueva Germania, that it aims to create something in the true German tradition.

The situation in New Germany was improving rapidly, she claimed: the railway was sure to be built soon, and the steamship *Hermann* was opening the colony to the outside world and 'bringing the German flag to new territories'. (She neglected to mention that the *Hermann* was far too small for regular commercial use and had had to be sold, or that another expensive boat, the *Esperanza*, had been too large to get up the Aguarya-umí in the first place.)

A few 'loyal' colonists were persuaded, or more probably browbeaten, into writing letters in support of the colony's founders: Bernhard Förster was honest and reliable, they said, and Elisabeth had baked cakes for the children at Christmas. Some attacked Klingbeil on the founders' behalf: he had ripped off the Indians by selling them bad wooden carvings; he was lazy; he had tried to get through customs without paying duty on equipment for distilling schnapps; he was a Catholic or, worse, a Jesuit. But next to Klingbeil's denunciations, the counter-accusations looked pale, and the whole unedifying rumpus was having a bad effect both in the colony and in Germany. The hitherto solid Max Schubert of the Chemnitz Colonial Society began having doubts about the Försters' honesty; he threatened to withhold in Germany funds which had been donated to the colony until the situation was clarified. Even the faithful Cyriax seems to have stopped sending money; his contribution to helping the colony was the advice that Förster should try manufacturing chocolate and exporting it to London, or selling Paraguayan handicrafts to the South Kensington Museum. Meanwhile Förster was already paying crippling interest on loans from Paraguayan banks, while casting around for a way to pay off the debts incurred on the *Hermann*.

Although Förster had roundly denounced Klingbeil and had called for an official investigation to clear his name, psychologically fragile at the best of times he had started to crack. He spent almost no time in New Germany, but became a regular at the Hotel del Lago in San Bernadino, the German colony just outside Asunción. He began to drink heavily, in an attempt to calm his nerves and the crippling headaches they brought on, while he sent ever more desperate entreaties back to Germany.

Elisabeth, now running the colony single-handed, sent him encouraging letters as he languished in deepening gloom, miles downriver in the comfort of a brand-new hotel. 'My dear heart-Bern,' she wrote, 'Your depression worries me. Please calm yourself. Although I admit the situation is precarious, I don't think Max Schubert is such a crook. . . . if they are honourable, everything will be all right and you have no cause to worry. . . . many problems are coming to a head now: the Klingbeil book and the Chemnitz affair. But things will get better.' To add to her woes, Elisabeth was now suffering from a serious eye infection, and in April one of Paraguay's periodic revolutions broke out, with fighting near by at San Pedro. She made light of it, saying that Paraguayans would never dare attack a group of Germans and she gave short shrift to a couple of government officers who asked permission to take their troops through New Germany in pursuit of the rebels. The colony, she told them, was under the protection of the German flag, and she was proud when they said they had heard of Bismarck. Her fortitude would have been remarkable in any event; it was the more so because news had reached her some time before of another calamity five thousand miles away in Italy.

Throughout the time Elisabeth was away, Nietzsche's mood swings had become ever more extreme. At times he would long for death, knowing that the dark shadow behind his chair he had felt as a boy was growing longer: 'With me a catastrophe is being prepared. I know its name, but I will not pronounce it.' What he did pronounce, though, was a ringing curse on the house of Wagner. In *The Case of Wagner* (1888) he repudiated all connection with the man he had once adored, calling him 'one of my diseases', whose followers persist in 'chewing the cud of moral and religious absurdities until they choke'. In *Twilight of the Idols* (1889), a study in decadence and decay, he examined 'What the Germans lack.' He wrote: 'The Germans – once they were called the nation of thinkers: do they still think at all? Nowadays the Germans are bored with intellect, politics devours all serious things – *Deutschland, Deutschland über alles* was, I fear, the end of German philosophy . . . nowhere else are the two great European narcotics, alcohol and Christianity, so viciously abused. Lately even a third has been added, one which is capable by itself of completely obstructing all delicate and audacious flexibility of spirit: music, our constipated, constipating German music – How much dreary heaviness, lameness, dampness, sloppiness. How much *beer* there is in the German intellect!'

By the end of 1888 and now living in Turin, his spirits

reached *tempo fortissimo* and the disease took a final grip on his mind. He felt ten years younger as he walked the streets, the people seemed to stare at him in awe. At night in his *pensione* he would play the piano for hours. Mostly he played Wagner. On his forty-fourth birthday he began work on *Ecce Homo*, an autobiography boiling with grand ideas and self-praise. In 'Why I Am Destiny', the results of the death of God, of a world released from the false straitjacket of Christian morality, are laid terrifyingly bare: 'When truth starts battling with the lies of millennia, we shall have convulsions, a spasm of earthquakes, a displacement of mountains and valleys such as no one has dreamed of.' He began to correspond with August Strindberg; the old Swedish and the still-young German philosophers drifted into insanity in tandem.

That Christmas, his mood of elation reached a crescendo. 'In two months' time I shall be the foremost name on earth,' he wrote; his health was excellent, his appetite unimpaired and his fame assured. If his books were still unread except by a few Scandinavian intellectuals, well, that was a sign of other people's (particularly German) stupidity and his own greatness. Suddenly he believed he had political power, and his anti-German feelings came to a head. 'I have ordered a convocation of princes in Rome,' he wrote to Strindberg. 'I want to have the young Kaiser shot.' He signed himself Nietzsche Caesar. Strindberg replied, 'I want, I want to be mad,' and ended, 'Meanwhile it is a joy to be mad.'

On 3 January, Nietzsche took his customary walk through the streets of Turin. At the Piazza Carlo Alberto, he came across a cabman savagely beating his old horse. Nietzsche threw his arms around the animal's neck and collapsed weeping to the ground. A crowd gathered, including his landlord, who had him carried back to his *pensione*; eventually he regained consciousness, but never his sanity. He penned a furious flurry of insane letters, to the King of Italy, the Vatican and various friends. Signing himself Dionysus or 'The Crucified', he inveighed against the Reich, Germany and anti-semites: 'I have just seized possession of my kingdom, and am throwing the pope into prison and having Wilhelm, Bismarck and Stöcker [Förster's friend] shot.' In another letter he finally declared love to Cosima Wagner, addressing her as 'Ariadne'. When Overbeck received a letter saying 'I have just had all anti-semites shot,' he hurried to Turin to find his friend and bring him home.

Elisabeth was understandably upset by the news of her brother's collapse and wondered whether she should go back and tend to him. But in conjunction with her sisterly concern, she also began the long process of reinventing her own relationship with him. 'He never said an unkind word to me,' she decided. Instead of being a bad-tempered burden with a taste for Jewish company, she started to turn him back into the idolised figure of her childhood. The myth-making had begun.

FÖRSTER was too wrapped up in his own problems to spare much of a thought for a brother-in-law he had never liked and who had heartily disliked him. 'Bernhard does not show the slightest sympathy for my grief,' Elisabeth told her mother. While stressing that she was still a good wife, she concluded that her husband was impossibly selfish and that without her help his colonial project would have been a disaster long before. If she only had the money, she would leave Paraguay at once. There had never been much love in their marriage. They shared a set of beliefs: in God, Wagner, Germany and anti-semitism, but both were too egocentric to share much else. Förster had used Elisabeth as a passport to the inner circle of Bayreuth and, perhaps, had recognised in her a character far more robust than his own. Elisabeth believed that the path to success was by hitching her wagon to the right man and following him to glory. In the context of her times, she may have been right. But the sort of man she chose was an accurate reflection of the sort of woman she was. Förster had appeared in her life at the time when her brother had apparently failed her; at some point during her first three years in Paraguay she must have realised that her husband was failing her too. But to the qualities of stubbornness and fortitude should be added loyalty. Elisabeth never withdrew.

Just before their wedding anniversary on 22 May she wrote to Förster, still languishing at the Hotel del Lago and nearing the end of a six-week drinking binge: 'Don't worry about this terrible Klingbeil book, I won't read it if you don't want me to. I don't care a fig for all this, if only our dear Fritz would recover, then he could write a hundred such books in reply. I'm so lonely in the evenings, and I wish you would come back now. . . . Everything will get better. . . . I'm sad that we shall spend our wedding anniversary apart.' He probably never read it. On 2 June he wrote Elisabeth another letter, gravid with self-pity: 'I am in a bad way,' he wailed. 'When will things improve?' At eight o'clock the next morning, a terrified maid discovered Förster lying dead in his room at the Hotel del Lago.

Elisabeth rushed to San Bernadino. Although distraught she acted quickly, persuading a Paraguayan doctor to sign a death certificate confirming her own diagnosis: that her forty-six-year-old husband had died of a 'nervous attack' brought on by the slanders of his enemies and the trials of his chosen duty. She later reconstructed the last hours of his life as proof that he had died a martyr for his people, like the Wagnerian heroes he aspired to emulate. A Spanish Evangelical priest, she said, had been talking with Förster the night before his death when her husband 'suddenly rose from his couch saying that he felt faint and unwell, and exclaimed "I think I am getting nerve fever." He sat down on a chair, by the bed, one hand behind his head and the other pressed to his heart. Later he lay down to sleep, having apparently recovered from the feverish attack . . . but on 3 June, the condition of the invalid deteriorated considerably until the fatal attack, which was confirmed as quickly as possible by the doctor.' She agreed with the Director of the San Bernadino colony, one Herr Schaerer, when he pronounced that 'the false friends and the intrigues of enemies have bored into his heart'. Whereas the noble Förster had lived by his Christian beliefs, he had found only doubt, suspicion and human wickedness all around him. 'This one discovery – set against all the hopes and potential success of his ideal – broke the heart of this brave man, and prematurely ended this hopeful, this extraordinarily valuable life.'

What Elisabeth did not know, or chose to ignore, was that her husband had written a letter to Max Schubert the night before he died. Schubert's strange behaviour, he said, had driven him to bankruptcy; as a 'last request' he begged the director of the Colonial Society not to abandon New Germany. His hands were clearly shaking as he wrote: 'My body and mind have reached the stage where I assume I shall shortly be relieved of my heavy burden. . . . perhaps the deserving enterprise I have started will prosper better without me.' After sealing the letter, Förster had poisoned himself, using a deadly cocktail of strychnine and morphine. Elisabeth kept the phial of poison found by his bedside as a grisly souvenir and later made the mistake of showing it to one of the colonists, Herr Chagga. There is further evidence that Elisabeth's story of 'death by nerves' was a lie. Some time before, Förster had confided to a German doctor in Asunción, Dr Jaensch, that 'he and his wife would simply take poison if the colonial project failed'. He had completed half of the threat. His suicide note clearly indicated that it was not remorse or an admission of guilt that drove him to kill himself – any more than it was guilt which caused Hermann Gœring to bite on a cyanide capsule in Nuremberg jail fifty-seven years later. Neither admitted they were wrong, but both accepted they had lost.

In 1881 Förster wrote of Dürer's *Knight, Death and the Devil* in *The Relationship between Modern Jewry and German Art*: 'the artist leaves us in no doubt that he will achieve his aims. . . . when he dies he will submit nobly and gloriously and the philosophical calm will not leave him even in the worst throes of death'. Förster may well have believed his end was a glorious one. He was buried in the German cemetery overlooking San Bernadino and the still blue waters of the Ypacarai Lake; the German proprietor of the hotel reluctantly agreed to accept some land in New Germany as payment for Förster's large bar bill.

The colony's 'loyalists', led by Oscar Erck, wrote Elisabeth a letter of condolence: Förster, they said, 'not only led us to our new home, but was also in every respect a warm friend and adviser. We, the undersigned, offer you, dear lady, our most deeply felt sympathy. The magnanimity of his character and the greatness of the ideals which he realised here will ensure that the noble spirit of the deceased will be honoured for many generations. May the Almighty give you special strength to carry such a loss with resignation.' It was signed by fifty-three people, rather less than half the colony.

The Wagnerite Hans Paul von Wolzogen wrote a poem to the fallen Förster, the hero of Valhalla, which appeared in the *Bayreuther Blätter*. It ended:

> Do not call him defeated
> because German strength is broken,
> an eagle with a broken wing
> under a blue foreign sky;
> at the silent grave
> grieve only for German devotion,
> For joy rules at Valhalla.

He also suggested that Förster's body be returned to New Germany and a memorial be erected to him, representative of his noble ideals. More immediately, he urged his readers to contribute money to a Bernhard Förster Foundation to 'enable colonists without means to settle in the colony' and 'build a little Christian house of God in Försterröde'. Wolzogen's fund-raising talents were on a par with his poetry: in three years, he collected a grand total of 36.30 Marks – approximately enough to buy half a dozen spades.

While Wolzogen's panegyric boosted Elisabeth's reputation in Bayreuth as the widow of a great Wagnerian martyr – an image she encouraged by dressing in black for the rest of her life – it hardly improved her financial position. Elisabeth had admitted there were debts to pay on her husband's estate, but maintained that he had left the colony 'in excellent order'; exactly the reverse was true, and though she valiantly fought off creditors and sued her detractors, she was quite unable to raise more cash; Klingbeil's *Revelations* were still fresh in the memory. Even among the most dedicated colonists there was mounting dissatisfaction that after four years they still had no legal title to the land.

In 1890, the colonising venture was bought out by a hastily formed corporation of businessmen, the Sociedad Colonizadora Nueva Germania en el Paraguay, consisting of two Germans, an Italian, a Spaniard, an Englishman and a

Dane. As far as Elisabeth was concerned it was an interim measure, and the idea that the colony might be under the permanent control of non-Germans was intolerable. New Germany belonged to her, and it was only a matter of time before she made enough money to get it back. At the end of the year she departed for Germany, there to persuade the citizens of the Fatherland to rally to her cause. She would save the colony, build the church that was so urgently needed for the spiritual welfare of her colonists and clear her husband's name. She left Oscar Erck behind as temporary administrator.

Elisabeth's almost pathological concern that Nueva Germania should survive combined with another obsession to persuade her that she must return home. The news of her brother was alarming. It was not the least of Elisabeth's failings that she considered herself conversant with medical matters, although she had no expertise whatever; she had convinced herself that Nietzsche was suffering from chloride poisoning, a result of the heavy sleeping draughts he had taken throughout the latter part of his life; his health, she decided, had also been impaired by a Javanese narcotic he had been given by a Dutchman in 1884. Much later, she was to spin another, still more fantastic explanation for Nietzsche's collapse: someone, she said, had been writing Nietzsche anonymous letters saying that her husband had written a scathing article about *Zarathustra* to appear in an anti-semitic newspaper. A letter from Nietzsche, she said, had been found in her dead husband's effects, in which her brother 'bitterly reproached my husband with having stolen away and corrupted the sister who was his most loyal disciple'. The letter, she claimed, ended with a threat: 'I take one sleeping draught after another to deaden the pain, and for all that I cannot sleep. Today I will take such a dose that I lose my wits.' This letter (which has not been found and almost certainly never existed) thus confirmed Elisabeth's diagnosis and made Elisabeth herself a central, though blameless, factor in his martyrdom. Her description of her brother's mental crisis is a crude reflection of the heroic end she had already invented for her husband, a lonely figure driven to distraction by the intrigues of enemies. 'The whole letter sounded like the last wail of his tortured soul,' she later wrote, 'the bow snapped, the hero broke down – during the last days of 1888 a paralytic stroke overtook our loved one, and crippled that incomparable brain for ever.'

SOON after his dramatic collapse in Turin, Nietzsche was taken to the lunatic asylum at Jena, not far from the Nietzsche home in Naumburg. He strode into the clinic like a nobleman, thanked the startled attendants for the magnificence of his reception and said that his wife, Cosima Wagner, had brought him there.

Although his mother would have preferred to nurse him at home, his state was too unpredictable to be without constant supervision. He was silent much of the time, brooding behind his moustache, now grown to vast proportions, the right side sprouting white hairs; but then he would break into loud lamentations, followed by rage and occasionally violence. His mother lacked the money for the most expensive treatment: he was diagnosed as suffering from 'paralytic psychic disturbance', and registered as 'Patient, second class'. Wearing the demeaning institutional hat of the asylum, he called himself the Kaiser and the Duke of Cumberland; he smashed windows and complained of headaches; the warder he accused of being Bismarck.

In his calmer moments he would play the piano or crouch tearfully in corners. 'I am dead because I am stupid, I am stupid because I am dead,' he would repeat over and over again, a madman's mantra. His endless, meaningless chattering sometimes carried on through the night. It was while he was in this state that he is supposed to have written *My Sister and I*. Occasionally he did seem lucid – so much so that at least two of his friends believed his madness to be feigned – but his memory ended abruptly in 1888: of the previous two years of his life he remembered nothing.

After fourteen months of anxious pressure from his mother, the asylum authorities declared him officially incurable and in May 1890 he was released to return with her to Naumburg. He seemed calmer, but was still unpredictable: he had been at home a short time when a policeman had to prevent him from undressing in the street; after that he went out only rarely; and then always under his mother's watchful eye.

He was waiting at the railway station in Naumburg when Elisabeth's train pulled up, just before Christmas 1890, holding tightly to his mother's arm and standing erect 'like a Prussian soldier'. For perhaps the first time in his life, Nietzsche did as his mother told him. He certainly recognised his sister and seemed content when she read him passages from *Zarathustra*. But, through his madness, a bitter memory of Elisabeth seems to have filtered. Although his handwriting was all but illegible now, he left a few semi-coherent jottings which betray outright hostility towards his sister, evidenced in a cruel mimicry of her self-inflating tendencies. One of these scraps appears to read 'As mother of the colony, I still have so much to do for the country. That is the main pleasure for Fritz I am monstrously good. I do not know whether I am leaving my husband's work in the lurch.' So far from leaving her husband in the lurch, Elisabeth was working hard to turn him into a martyr.

It took her just five months to compile *Bernhard Förster's Colony New Germany in Paraguay*, which was published in the spring of 1891. The book included newspaper articles and reviews written from and about the colony since its founding. It was highly selective and was intended to serve a number of purposes: most importantly it appealed for funds to maintain the colony and build a much-needed church there; it rebutted Klingbeil's accusations and painted Förster (and by association Elisabeth) in a dazzling light. Förster was 'a battling hero worthy of Valhalla, in the image of whose face the true Christ is united with the real German race, who has fallen on a foreign field for his belief in the German spirit'; Elisabeth was a 'broken-hearted woman' fighting to save his reputation from the slanders of liberal (read Jewish) journalists – Elisabeth was careful to play down her anti-semitism, which had, albeit briefly, become rather unfashionable. She even went so far as to claim that her husband had latterly renounced his racism, which was patently untrue.

Desperate to entice more colonists, Elisabeth happily repeated most of the old fictions: 'The climate of Paraguay is like paradise to me, and on this visit to Germany I view the weather here with a shake of my head,' the local food was excellent and cheap ('The palm hearts taste like lobster') and the colonists were uniformly healthy and happy. People had died, it was true, but they were mostly drunks anyway. She poured scorn on the dangers from wild animals. There were virtually no snakes left, she said, and the mosquitos were almost benign. The greatest danger was from the 'colony tiger, which creeps into the huts of new settlers and frightens the poor souls with humming and sniffing, but always turns out to be just a good old ox'. Practically the worst thing she had to say about Paraguay was that the heat sometimes made it hard to stiffen cream adequately and it was advisable to bring a couple of pretty polished commodes, as 'we don't pay much attention to our toilette there and the conventional observances'. It was her most extravagant piece of creative writing so far.

Even Elisabeth can have had few illusions about how the book, with its manifold inaccuracies, would be received by some of the more unhappy colonists she had left behind, many of whom were anything but delighted that she was coming back. Perhaps that was why she delayed her return to Paraguay by six months. But there was another reason too.

At the time of his collapse, Nietzsche's work was known only to a handful of friends and a few far-sighted intellectuals like Georg Brandes. The sane Nietzsche had made great efforts to publicise himself and his work, all of which had failed; but, insane, he was becoming worthy of public attention. 'To vegetate on', wrote Nietzsche, 'in cowardly dependence on physicians and medicaments after the meaning of life, the right to life, has been lost, ought to entail the profound contempt of society.' In Nietzsche's case society did exactly the reverse. Newspaper articles began to appear on the mad philosopher of Naumburg – even Lou (now Andreas-) Salomé, to Elisabeth's intense irritation, began reminiscing in print about the great mind she had known. Ironically, this voyeuristic interest in Nietzsche's disability brought the first stirrings of popular interest in his work. As Nietzsche's friends had feared she might, Elisabeth decided to involve herself, even though she had no legal right to do so.

Nietzsche left behind a vast quantity of unpublished written material, box after box of notes and jottings, aphorisms, laborious copies of excerpts from other books, sayings, ideas and notions. That was how he wrote: incessantly, therapeutically scribbling on loose pieces of paper as his ideas took shape. Nietzsche's *Nachlass*, his unpublished literary legacy, contains both the profound and the mundane, the precious and the pointless; some of it he had no doubt intended to keep or incorporate into later writings, some he had merely not bothered to throw away. There were also a number of completed works which had yet to appear in print.

Elisabeth's first foray into editorialising Nietzsche was an attempt to suppress the publication of *Zarathustra IV*, because it contained passages she considered sacrilegious. She told her mother that she feared they might be prosecuted under the blasphemy laws; in fact, she probably just didn't like what the book said. Eventually she relented; but it was an instructive, and for Nietzsche's more perspicacious friends a jarring, moment. Before finally departing for Paraguay in July 1892, she arranged for the publication of a cheap edition of Nietzsche's works, the first of many. Peter Gast, Nietzsche's faithful friend and the only one who could read his impossible handwriting, was left to start editing the *Nachlass*, while Franziska tended to his physical remains. But it is clear that already Elisabeth had every intention of keeping her own control over both of them.

Elisabeth returned to New Germany in August 1892, to be greeted enthusiastically by Oscar Erck and her other supporters. She told them the good news: the Imperial High Prussian Synod had agreed to send a pastor at its own expense and pay his salary for two years, and they were going, she had decided, to set up a distillery for making sugar-cane spirit for local consumption. Somewhere along the way Elisabeth had forgotten her objections to alcohol. Some viewed her return with foreboding. George Streckfus, a colonist, wrote to Max Schubert of the Chemnitz Colonial Society a few months after Elisabeth had returned: 'I do not think Germany has cured Frau Förster of her sickness, almost amounting to megalomania; on the contrary, she appears to be even more domineering and deluded. . . . equally I do not think a *caña* distillery is a blessing for New Germany.' His remarks were reinforced by a still more hostile report from one Fritz Neumann, a key member of the community. There was neither running water nor roads, he said, those who had tried to settle in the forest had been driven out by nature, and the undergrowth had already suffocated their collapsed huts and abandoned plantations. Förster's project had been an unmitigated disaster. It was sinful to have brought people here in the first place, but trying to persuade others to follow suit was a crime. The Goethean exhortation to 'stand your ground' so beloved of Förster rang hollow after his suicide, of which every colonist was now fully aware.

Disillusionment was widespread and, while Elisabeth continued to claim victory over the forest, the colonists trickled away in ever greater numbers. One wrote: 'if there is not an improvement by next year to the impossible situation here, I will have to think of moving on, though God knows where I will go. The world is large, and it would be madness to stay in this place for years when God seems to have abandoned it. If I sacrifice myself now, I will only regret later that I did not leave sooner. . . . if I had the money, I would go today, but that is the chain which binds so many here to misery.' Elisabeth launched herself, with customary ferocity, into a campaign against Neumann, but this time it was a losing battle. Max Schubert had continued as director of the Chemnitz Colonial Society and now received a steady stream of letters from both sides. On 18 July 1892, another colonist, Walter Glitza, had sent a particularly worrying letter: 'the favourable letters you get are all fabricated,' he said. 'There is not a single colonist who is content with his lot, and who can blame them, for the life is miserable here.' Who, then, was forging the other letters? Suspicion necessarily pointed to Elisabeth and her henchman, Oscar Erck.

The *coup de grâce* was administered by a popular colonist called Paul Ullrichs, whom Elisabeth had slandered in print. Max Schubert printed his riposte in the Colonial Society Newsletter, with an apology for its strong language but the excuse that 'truth and not delicacy of feeling must now guide our actions', and concluded, 'The first condition for any improvement in New Germany is the removal of Frau

Förster'. Elisabeth, one step ahead as always, had already decided to cut her losses. By careful planning, she contrived to turn an undignified rout into a face-saving retreat. Franziska Nietzsche, bovine and biddable as ever, agreed to send her daughter a telegram saying that Nietzsche's illness had worsened and requesting her daughter's immediate return. Elisabeth promptly sold her house and her land and left Paraguay forever. Though a pack of enraged colonists, in lynch mob mood, bayed at her heels, she walked out of New Germany – she did not run.

In August 1893, she sailed from Asunción, which had hardly changed in the intervening years, although now the finishing touches were being put to the Presidential Palace which President Lopez had begun. It was only by a matter of weeks that she missed the grand ceremonial opening by President Gonzalez and an exhibition of Paraguayan national projects. Her valedictory message to the colony appeared much later in, of course, the *Bayreuther Blätter*. She looked back over her time in Paraguay and made a last appeal for financial help. She was delighted to be able to announce that a German colonial company, the Hermann Society, had agreed to buy the land from the Sociedad Colonizadora Nueva Germania, which could not have been expected to maintain its pure German character since it consisted largely of foreigners. She had done her best, she said, to complete the work her dear departed husband had begun, 'but how insignificant is the feeble strength of a woman' in the struggle against 'dishonest individuals who had confused public opinion'. The Hermann Society could be relied on to maintain the colony's essential German character and, having removed undesirable elements, the settlement was now enjoying a new lease of life. She appealed to her supporters to buy shares to ensure that the colony was firmly and finally in German hands. Her motivation was pure love, she said, for the ideals of her husband and for the colony, her adopted child – the 'love of a mother who can no longer care for her child but is deeply concerned to know that it is in truly good hands ... I must now bid farewell to colonial affairs,' the appeal ended, 'another great life's task now commands all my time and energy: the care of my dear and only brother, the philosopher Nietzsche, the protection of his works and the description of his life and thought'.

The article was written in January 1895, and signed Elisabeth Förster-Nietzsche. Elisabeth was known by many names; as a child she had been Lisbeth, Lichen or Llama; in Paraguay and the pages of the *Bayreuther Blätter* she had always been known as Eli Förster. Her brother had even teased her about the name. 'My dear Llama,' he had written in 1885, 'I shall I think have the right to call you by that name because your husband calls you by another name (a Hebrew one) which is quite a miracle for an old anti-semite. Eli means "my God", and probably in a special case, "my Goddess".' By court order she now changed her name, thus linking Nietzsche's name to a man whose views and personality he had despised. And, having grafted Förster's name on to Nietzsche's, she now set about doing the same thing with his ideas.

CHAPTER VII

Will to Power

RETURNING to Naumburg from Paraguay for the second and last time, Elisabeth found her brother more docile, less prone to the terrible rages that had overtaken him in the first flush of madness. He spoke little now and would sit quietly for hours on end staring into space. But he was prone to yawning fits, and his speech began to deteriorate; 'I do not speak prettily,' he would mumble. Creeping paralysis began to envelop his right side. It was this pathetic figure that Elisabeth now sought to turn into the focus of a cult. Germany in the first half of this century was fertile ground for such an enterprise, and Nietzsche, with his emotive, mythical language, his cruel imagery and his veneration for strength, was partly to blame. Perhaps there would have been a Nietzsche cult without Elisabeth; but it would have been, I think, neither so popular nor so dubious without her remarkable talents for propaganda.

How cynical was Elisabeth in her manipulations? She was merely incapable of distinguishing between what *she* wanted and what was actually true; it was inevitable once she had gained control of Nietzsche (first his writings and then his body) that her own attitudes would cast a shadow over his. For Elisabeth there was no contradiction in this: she was her own final court of appeal. If the facts did not fit her own interpretation, then it was the facts which had to be changed, not her opinions; Elisabeth changed her mind often, but her opinions never. Nietzsche once wrote that 'convictions might be more dangerous enemies of truth than lies. . . . I call a lie: wanting *not* to see something one does see, wanting not to see something *as* one sees it.' Elisabeth didn't call that lying; that was having the courage of your convictions. But as Nietzsche himself pointed out, having the courage of one's convictions was 'a popular error; rather it is a matter of having the courage for an *attack* upon one's convictions'. It was probably while still in Paraguay that Elisabeth became convinced she could make her brother famous – thus, in a way, succeeding where he had failed. She decided to turn her brother into a myth, a cause, a symbol (with all the ugly overtones those words suggest), much as she had attempted and failed to do with her husband. Her job was made easier by the fact that the focus of that myth was no longer in a state to contradict her. She genuinely believed she knew her brother better than anyone else including, quite possibly, himself. If he had regained his sanity, as from time to time seemed possible during the ebb and flow of his illness, she would probably have told him just that. Soon after returning from Paraguay she discovered that Peter Gast was planning to write a biography. Her response was categorical: 'His life I am going to write myself,' she told him bluntly, 'no one can do that as well as I.'

The fact that there was money to be made out of her brother had been shown by the speed at which the cheap edition of his works had sold. She set about organising Nietzsche's friends and associates with the same imperious manner she had used towards her colonists in Paraguay. She warned Gast that he could continue as editor of Nietzsche's works, but only with her consent. Strictly speaking, this was nonsense. As his legal guardian since the collapse, Franziska Nietzsche was also the executrix of his written works. Elisabeth began collecting everything Nietzsche had written. The landlord at his writing retreat in Sils Maria had gathered together much of the loose paper left lying in Nietzsche's room, and though Nietzsche had earlier asked him to destroy the jottings, he kept them, occasionally giving away pieces as mementoes to people who asked for them. Elisabeth demanded them all back. She also wrote to Nietzsche's friends and correspondents, asking them to send their letters for collection in a Nietzsche archive. Some complied, others refused, like Cosima Wagner, who promptly destroyed her letters from Nietzsche, leaving only eleven extant and the question of whether he had ever directly declared his love to her while sane for ever open.

The collection of Nietzsche's works was housed in the upper part of the house in Naumburg, Weingarten 18, now christened the Nietzsche Archive and complete with headed notepaper. The official opening was on 2 February 1894. Into the Archive she crammed everything connected with her brother and everything she could find that he had written. To Franziska she left the duty of nursing the invalid, while she made herself responsible for nursing his rise to fame.

Gast was quickly replaced by a new editor, Fritz Koegel, a young, handsome and artistic individual whom Elisabeth had taken a shine to – not least because of his talents as a flatterer. Another important figure in the early years of the Nietzsche Archive was Rudolph Steiner, later the educational reformer and head of the Anthroposophic Movement. Steiner, though young, had already written a book on Nietzsche and was a well-known intellectual figure in Weimar, where he worked at the newly founded Goethe–Schiller Archive. Elisabeth doted on both these young men, so much her junior in years, and so much her senior in intellect. In August 1896, Steiner agreed to undertake the difficult task of teaching her the meaning of her brother's philosophy, but soon gave up in disgust, noting that 'Frau Förster-Nietzsche is a complete laywoman in all that concerns her brother's doctrine. ... [She] lacks any sense for fine, and even for crude, logical distinctions; her thinking is void of even the least logical consistency; and she lacks any sense of objectivity. ... She believes at every moment what she says. She convinces herself today that something was red yesterday that most assuredly was blue.' Yet Steiner too was guilty of contributing to the mythical aura that Elisabeth wove around Nietzsche and his work. 'Whoever saw Nietzsche', he wrote, 'as he reclined in his white, pleated robe, with the glance of a Brahmin in his wide and deep-set eyes beneath bushy eyebrows, with the nobility of his enigmatic, questioning face and the leonine, majestic carriage of his thinker's head – had the feeling that this man could not die, but that his eye would rest for all eternity upon mankind.' Elisabeth was the main culprit in the immortalising of Nietzsche before he was even dead, but she had many willing accomplices.

It was Elisabeth's biographical work that turned Nietzsche into a symbol of something superhuman, rather than merely human, all too human. She made him into a prophet rather than a philosopher. It took Elisabeth more than ten years to write the complete story of her brother's life in two vast volumes (which were later boiled down into two shorter works: *The Young Nietzsche* and *The Lonely Nietzsche*). Her intentions in writing the biography were threefold: she wanted to create an image of her brother that was little short of divine; another of herself as his only true confidante and supporter; and she wanted to put the best possible construction on his philosophy – her own.

The results were gushing, inaccurate and extremely popular. Minute detail was lavished on her brother's 'wonderfully beautiful, large and expressive eyes' and 'his extraordinarily decorous manner'. 'The only female relative', she claimed, 'who, from her earliest days, saw something unique about Fritz, and who gave expression to her conviction was myself, his little sister.' She alone, then, could speak with any real knowledge of her brother's life and philosophy. 'He used not to speak so openly or so confidentially to any one of his friends as he did to me. . . . I always suspected [no doubt she was right] that my brother said more to his friends than to me concerning all that went on in his soul. Many an error arose from this.' It was, she claimed, her duty to correct these. 'I more than anyone am duty bound to repel attacks, to remove errors and to portray the facts and experiences of my brother's life with the most scrupulous accuracy, for no one stood so near to my brother as I did.' And when she was not praising herself, she quoted her brother's praise: '"My sister is not a woman at all," he supposedly said, "she is a friend" – a remark which seemed in laughable contrast to my extremely feminine appearance.' She was a 'helpful trusting soul' and 'his helper and comforter in times of stress', who 'listens not only with her ears and with her understanding, but also with her heart'.

A relationship that had often been stormy, if not straightforwardly hostile, was reduced to a minestrone of mutual adoration, and their serious disagreements were largely ignored. 'Never in our lives, indeed, did we say an unkind word to each other; and if we sometimes wrote unpleasant things, it is because, when apart, we came under the baneful influence of others.' *Ecce Homo*, for example, contained passages which were extremely hostile to Elisabeth; this largely explains why she suppressed its publication for eight years after the death of its author.

The biography was the long-awaited opportunity for revenge on Lou Andreas-Salomé. The Russian littérateuse was nothing but a shallow upstart, 'a forerunner of a certain sector of the modern emancipated woman', with a 'simply revolting' way of expressing herself (Elisabeth never forgot the gloves-off fight at Jena); it was she who had wanted to marry Nietzsche, but he found her 'essentially distasteful'. Paul Rée was simply a weak individual, quite under the thumb of the dominating Salomé. It was also a chance for a second line of defence against critics of her colony in Paraguay, that 'malicious brood of dwarfs who hate everything lofty and superhuman'. Her husband had been 'marked out by nature as leader and ruler of a community' and she believed that 'if Förster had not died so young, the colony of New Germany would have been all that he projected – that with his eminent gifts for colonising he would have attained all that he hoped to attain for the glory of Germany'. The colony, so far from being a swindle, was really a charity: 'it was principally poor people who came to us; they received land from us as a gift and lived on the advances that we made'.

Nietzsche had, after initial doubts, approved of her marriage, since 'he was far too good a psychologist not to see that, apart from all questions of love, a woman with so much desire for action as I needed an area in which her energies would find full scope'. The minor differences between brother and husband had been, she said, the work of 'an intriguing young lady, who wanted to marry Förster herself, [and] thought to achieve this end by secretly setting Nietzsche against Förster'. The only reason her brother had failed to attend her wedding or come to say goodbye was because 'he dreaded the emotional scene of a personal farewell', and as for his 'various adverse and sceptical comments on the colonial enterprise', they had been 'much misunderstood'.

She claimed that he had even considered coming to the colony himself. Her own anti-semitism, in the light of Nietzsche's manifest opposition to it, was blurred; she even claimed that she had never agreed with her husband's views in this regard. And anyway, she blustered, the anti-semitic political movement had not helped to support the colony in any way – as if that made it, or her, any less anti-semitic.

Despite her assertion that she 'had not the slightest intention of advancing any of her own views', those areas of Nietzsche's thinking she found unacceptable were skated over or wilfully misrepresented. The break with Wagner, whose memory she avowedly cherished, had simply been over artistic differences. She dwelt instead on the 'story of a friendship, with all its sorrows and its delights; the romance of two geniuses who were able for a while to walk side by side along cheerful and sunny highways'. As for her brother's opposition to German nationalism, she simply denied it: 'whatever people may say, he loved his German Fatherland. All his passionate reproaches were only the utterances of a loving heart. He wished to see the Germans really great, filled with and transfigured by a genuine culture . . . and this the German can do because he is brave.' According to her recollection he 'often indulged in "a bout of genuine patriotism", when he would say "I love the Germans"'. And if he seemed to criticise the Germans, that was simply because they had failed to recognise his genius. Neither was the author of *The Anti-Christ*, apparently, anti-Christian: 'he cherished a tender love for the founder of Christianity' and he had 'a real liking for serene, pious Christians'. Moreover 'he never forgot to mention what a boon Christianity has always been, and can still be, as a religion of the masses'. This was the man who pronounced in *Ecce Homo* that the 'concept God [was] invented as the antithetical concept to life – everything harmful, noxious, slanderous, the whole mortal enmity against life brought into one terrible unity'.

Elisabeth's hagiography of her brother could be dismissed as fiction (by the generous) and malicious, self-serving, overwritten nonsense (by the realistic) were it not for the fact that she made it virtually impossible to approach the life of Nietzsche, and indeed his works, other than through her own twisted filter. And she knew what she was doing; in perhaps the most revealing passage in the biography she inadvertently gave herself away. From childhood, she says, 'the most difficult task of my life began, the task which, as my brother said, characterised my type – i.e. "to reconcile opposites'".

It took her more than a decade to build up this sanitised, mythical image of her brother. She claimed that Nietzsche had specifically appointed her to be the guardian of his heritage ('this extraordinarily rich collection was made by myself alone') and his biographer. As such, she was prepared to defend her self-appointed territory with all her very considerable strength. The only problem was that, while her mother was alive, she and not Elisabeth was the legal guardian of Nietzsche's work. With the help of Fritz Koegel, Elisabeth worked out a plan to gain full control of the Archive. An anonymous group of donors would offer Franziska a sum of money, with the proviso that all rights to Nietzsche's estate should be handed over to Elisabeth. Relations between mother and daughter had deteriorated since Elisabeth's return from Paraguay, and it was only after a series of acrimonious disputes, including a threat from Elisabeth to have her mother declared incompetent to be Nietzsche's guardian, that she agreed in December 1895 to make Elisabeth and her cousin Adalbert Oehler the sole trustees of Nietzsche's works. Franziska later claimed she had signed only under duress and had immediately regretted it, the more so when she discovered, as she had always suspected, that the money to be paid to her for the care of her son was in the form of a loan guaranteed by anonymous figures, and not a gift at all.

One of the anonymous 'donors' was Count Harry Kessler, a young, debonair aristocrat with aquiline features and a long blonde moustache. On 26 October 1895 he wrote to Elisabeth with a request to send relevant compositions to an art magazine, *Pan*, with which he was involved. He was, henceforth, to play a key role in Elisabeth's life. Kessler was one of the paramount observers of his day: an art patron, literary connoisseur, diplomat and indefatigable diarist. The son of a wealthy Hamburg banker and a celebrated Irish beauty, Alice Lynch (no relation), he was educated at Harrow in England, and in France, later going to university, like Nietzsche, at Bonn and Leipzig. Like so many people, he found Elisabeth's energy and enthusiasm as irresistible as her brother's writing, and he treated her with an old-fashioned gallantry she adored. In politics they could not have been further apart; while Elisabeth was a fanatical conservative nationalist, and a monarchist to boot, Kessler's links with left-wing ideas had earned him the nickname the Red Count. For at least the early part of their acquaintance, Kessler was one of Elisabeth's staunchest supporters; and she doted on him, even offering him the editorship of the Nietzsche papers – which he declined, though he agreed to act as the Archive's 'artistic adviser'. Kessler brought to the Nietzsche cult a cosmopolitan *élan* Elisabeth, now in her sixties, could never muster. The young Count got to know everybody in the course of his extraordinary career: he saw Josephine Baker dance naked in Paris ('apparently she does this for hours on end'), he heard Yehudi Menuhin's debut ('The boy is truly marvellous. His playing has the afflatus of genius and the purity of a child'); at school he had founded a magazine for his schoolmates, one of whom was Winston Churchill; he met Virginia Woolf, Proust, George Bernard Shaw and most of the other prominent intellectuals and artists of his day. On all of them he turned his subtly discerning eye and ready wit. While he provided moral and financial encouragement to Elisabeth Nietzsche, he was also one of the few who managed to penetrate the pseudo-divine mystique she spun around her brother. The description in his diary of his first sight of the insane Nietzsche is moving and rare, perhaps unique for the time, in its lack of pretension and hyperbole:

> He was asleep on the sofa, his mighty head had sunk down and to the right on to his chest, as if it were too heavy for his neck. His forehead was truly colossal; his manelike hair is still dark brown, like his shaggy, protruding moustache. Blurred, black-brown edges underneath his eyes are cut deeply into his cheeks. One can still see in the lifeless, flabby face some deep wrinkles dug in by thought and will but softened, as it were, and getting smoothed out. His expression shows an infinite

> weariness. His hands are waxen, with green and violet veins, and a little swollen as with a corpse. . . . The sultry air of a thunderstorm had fatigued him, and although his sister stroked him several times and fondly called him 'darling, darling' he would not wake up. He did not resemble a sick person or a lunatic, but rather a dead man.

That description was written after Nietzsche's body as well as the Archive which bore his name had been moved to Weimar in July 1897. Franziska Nietzsche had finally died on 20 April of that year, leaving Elisabeth in sole control of the invalid her mother had nursed for seven years. Naumburg, she decided, was not the place to house the fruits of his genius or the remains of his body. Far better would be Weimar, seat of classical learning and home to Goethe, Schiller and Liszt. Elisabeth persuaded one of Nietzsche's richer friends and admirers, Meta von Salis, to pay for an appropriate site for the Archive. Villa Silberblick, on the hill overlooking Weimar, was in some ways a peculiar choice: one might have expected Elisabeth to object to a place which bore the name of an affliction from which she suffered, although Silberblick also means beautiful view. The building itself was large and ugly, so exposed to the elements that the locals called it Villa Sonnenstich – Villa Sunstroke. But it was certainly imposing and grand. On the ground floor was arranged a staggering array of Nietzscheana: letters, diaries, photographs and pictures, not just of Nietzsche's life, but also of Elisabeth's time in Paraguay. There was even a bust of Bernhard Förster. Nietzsche was usually kept out of sight upstairs, viewed only occasionally by the most important guests.

While Elisabeth tended to her brother and his image, Fritz Koegel, followed by a stream of other editors, some more, some less competent, had by 1900 begun to work on a third collected edition of Nietzsche's works. Thanks in part to the popularity of Elisabeth's biographies, they sold extremely well. As Nietzsche's health sank, his fame rose. In 1896, Richard Strauss had completed his dramatic symphonic interpretation of *Thus Spoke Zarathustra*, and in 1899 he visited Elisabeth, a sign of how well established Nietzsche's name had become. Prominent intellectuals from all over Europe began to make the pilgrimage to Weimar, and Nietzsche's works were read by thousands. Elisabeth used some surprisingly modern marketing techniques. In October 1898, Arnold Kramer had completed his studies for a statuette entitled '*Friedrich Nietzsche in His Invalid Chair*'. Elisabeth arranged for replicas of different sizes and prices to go on the market immediately. Inspired by her success, Elisabeth, who had now permitted the publication of *The Anti-Christ*, decided to publish his unfinished work, *The Will to Power: Attempt at a Transvaluation of All Values*. To that end she made contact again with Peter Gast, the only man who could decipher Nietzsche's jottings, and persuaded him to return to Weimar.

Of all this Nietzsche was, perhaps mercifully, unaware. By early 1900, the fawning descriptions of him had moved up a gear: 'How I felt when I saw him in the grandeur of his being, the infinitely deepened beauty of psychic expression,' warbled Isabella von Ungern-Sternberg, who had met the sane Nietzsche just once before, in 1876, 'these deep sad eye-stars, which roam in the distance and yet seem to look inward, radiated a powerful effect, a magnetic intellectual aura which no sensitive nature could resist.' In his maxims Nietzsche had noted that good writers 'prefer to be understood rather than admired', and he would have been astonished at how he had become so greatly admired but so little understood.

In fact Nietzsche, an idol in his own twilight, was dying. On 20 August he caught a cold which settled on his lungs. Four days later he had a seizure, and the next morning he was dead. If life means more than the mere exercise of breathing, then Nietzsche's life had ended in 1889, but, though most other contemporary accounts agree that for the last ten years of his existence he was little more than a human shell, Elisabeth claimed he was still capable of sentient communication, at least to her. In 1891, she claimed,

> he wrote me a touching little letter, containing the following stanza:

The tie that sister binds to brother
Is strongest of all ties, I hold;
They're riveted to one another
More firmly than by ties of gold.

Is it necessary to say that no trace of such a letter survives? Perhaps the real thrust of Elisabeth's character is contained in another recollection, rank with false modesty: 'one day he turned to me and exclaimed, "Why are you so famous, Lisbeth?" The question was so pathetic, yet comic, I threw my arms around him, crying and laughing at once, and said, "I'm not a bit famous! The people only come because they haven't seen me for so long." Yet he shook his head and remarked again and again, "Well, so the Llama is famous too".'

By the time Nietzsche died, the Llama was well on the way to becoming very famous indeed; by her own account, he died with her name on his lips. 'At two o'clock in the morning, when I handed him a refreshing draught and moved the lampshade aside so he could see me, he cried out joyfully, "Elisabeth," so that I thought the crisis was over. But his beloved face changed more and more; the shadows of death began to overspread it, his breathing grew more and more laboured . . . then came a slight tremor, a deep breath – and softly, without a struggle, with a last solemn, inquiring glance he closed his eyes forever.' Was it likely that a man who, for two years had not known where he was, who he was, that his was now a household name and that his mother was dead, would have remembered his sister with his last gasp? Elisabeth thought so.

In the flurry surrounding the funeral arrangements, she entirely forgot a request Nietzsche had once made of her. She remembered it later though, and wrote it down: '"Lisbeth," said my brother solemnly, "promise me that when I die only my friends shall stand about my coffin – no inquisitive crowd. See that no priest or anyone else utters falsehoods at my graveside, when I can no longer defend myself, and let me descend into my tomb an honest pagan."'

Of all the people who clustered around Nietzsche's graveside in the little churchyard at Röcken next to the house where he had been born fifty-six years before, perhaps only

Peter Gast, now an employee of Elisabeth, could really claim to have been his friend; most of the rest had come to know Nietzsche only in the form Elisabeth had presented him, an unseen, mystical being or a silent wraith wrapped in Brahmin's robes. Elisabeth had drawn up a long list of mourners and issued a press release; that was how hard she tried to keep out the inquisitive crowd.

The man who had pronounced a ringing curse on the house of God was buried with full Lutheran rites, his coffin adorned with a silver cross. 'I have a terrible fear that one day I shall be pronounced "holy",' so Nietzsche had written in *Ecce Homo*. 'I do not want to be a saint, rather a buffoon . . . perhaps I am a buffoon.' 'Hallowed be thy name to all future generations,' intoned Peter Gast at his graveside.

AT ABOUT the time that Nietzsche was lowered into the ground at Röcken, five thousand miles away on the banks of the Aguarya-umí in central Paraguay, Fritz Neumann was fishing and watching the *pito-qué* birds slip in and out of the forest undergrowth. Underneath a tall tree, where the birds always congregated in the cool of the evening, a tall copse of *yerba* trees had seeded itself.

In the decade after Elisabeth left Paraguay, New Germany had teetered close to disaster. Since her unlamented departure, it had to be admitted, the ideological heart of the colony had been broken. Those who had stayed were the most dedicated to the founders' ideals, the Ercks, the Schüttes, the Fischers, the hopelessly poor, like the Schuberts and the Schweikharts, and the grimly determined, like Fritz Neumann himself. The pastor they had been promised had never materialised, and no more money had been sent from the colonial Hermann Society. The ships had been sold off, leaving only the track through the forest to Antequera as a means of getting goods to market. Few bothered, and they survived on what little they could grow. Thankfully no one had tried to take their little parcels of land away, but if there had not been a few Paraguayans left to teach them the tricks of survival, they would all have been dead.

Many of the people who, like Neumann, had come with

such grand hopes back in 1887, had trickled away, the richer ones back to Germany, others to the Corrientes in Argentina or to Chile and Brazil, where the life was easier. Those that stayed had clustered around the large house Elisabeth had left behind. Even the richest family was much too poor now to consider returning to a home that was barely a memory; for most there was not enough money to get to Asunción, let alone back to Germany. Some of the poorest had tried to set up on their own in the forest; they were seldom seen, except when they came to town with something to sell, ragged and desperate people. The Paraguayans called them *gente perdita*.

The population of the colony had dwindled. In the two years after Elisabeth left, more than 100 colonists packed their meagre possessions on to carts and headed back down the river; now there were barely seventy people left. Even Oscar Erck, Elisabeth's trusty lieutenant, had begun to wonder whether it would be better to disband the colony. Neumann had decided to give it one more year before he and his family abandoned the place. Mistakes had been made; they had tried to cultivate the wrong crops, concentrating on tobacco, cotton, sugar cane and maize, which were difficult to grow and hard to move. Without river transport, they had to go by cart; when it rained, the journey took weeks. An unexpected frost had killed all the coffee plants one year. But it was good land for *yerba*, the Paraguayan tea to which all the German colonists had become addicted. It grew abundantly in the forest and upriver in the Sierra Amambay, but collecting it was backbreaking work. You had to spend days, sometimes weeks, in the *yerbales*, as the *yerba*-rich parts of the forest were called, harvesting by hand. The Jesuits had known how to cultivate the tea, indeed they had established large plantations, but when they had been thrown out of the country in the eighteenth century, the secret had gone with them. The Indians had never bothered to learn how to plant the crop and had reverted to the old methods of collection. For some reason just planting *yerba* seeds didn't work – they steadfastly refused to germinate.

The birds flickered and darted around the *yerba* trees;

Neumann put another piece of meat on his hook and tossed it into the river. The grey water sucked at the bank and he sucked on his pipe, deep in thought.

WITH Nietzsche's death, Elisabeth's plans for immortalising her brother took on a new impetus. She had long hoped to turn Weimar into another Bayreuth, a cultural capital, with the worship of her brother at its centre. At her urging, the Grand Duke Wilhelm of Sachsen-Weimar appointed Count Harry Kessler as director of the Weimar Art Museum and his friend, the Belgian architect and designer Henry van de Velde, as artistic consultant to the court of Weimar and director of the Weimar Art School. She had another reason for encouraging van de Velde, a prime exponent of the German form of art nouveau, *Jungenstil*, to make his home in Weimar. Soon after his arrival she commissioned him to redesign Villa Silberblick on a scale commensurate with her ambitions for her brother. Försterhof in Paraguay had been her first architectural monument to herself; the redesigned Villa Silberblick, of which she gained complete ownership in 1902, was her second.

Van de Velde excelled himself: the warren of ground-floor rooms was turned into two large reception rooms; a vast marble bust of Nietzsche, carved by Max Klinger and paid for by Count Kessler, glared down from the far end of the room, panelled now in local beechwood, *Buchen*, which glowed when the sun shone through the windows. At the other end was the bust of Förster. Elaborately curved and upholstered in strawberry pink, the furniture and interior decor had none of the French frippery, the lavish use of 'pink satin and little cupids' that Elisabeth had disliked at the Wagners' home in Tribschen. There was to be nothing frilly about this martyr's shrine. The whole was restrained and elegant, and, to make sure no one missed the point, the letter 'N' was reflected in the shape of the front-door handles and a brass plaque, a foot high, above the fireplace. Elisabeth was delighted with van de Velde's work, completed in 1903. The next year Paul Kühn wrote of the Nietzsche Archive as a future 'memorial and symbol' of a new culture. At last she had the right dignified setting in which to entertain, with increasing extravagance, the growing lines of distinguished and influential well-wishers.

One person who did not share Elisabeth's own delight in her new-found fame was the very woman on whom she modelled herself. Even before Nietzsche's death, Cosima Wagner had written archly to her daughter Daniela about her one-time babysitter: 'Did you know Elisabeth Nietzsche is now living a life of luxury, with servants and equipage?' She resented the growing popularity of Nietzsche's ideas, which she claimed had all originated with her husband, and poured scorn on Elisabeth's ambitious self-promotion. 'She seems to have gone a bit loopy since all this fame-madness began,' she wrote to her son-in-law, the English-born race theorist Houston Stewart Chamberlain, 'the new religion or philosophy she is presenting seems to me to be a clear sign of that, and if the whole thing was not so terribly sad, so frighteningly wild in its consequences, then one couldn't but find it funny. The best thing to do is to look away and forget it all.'

In the early years of the century, Elisabeth busied herself with the final part of her biography, in which she would set the seal on her image of Nietzsche as the great 'seer-saint'. She accepted no interpretation but her own: when a Leipzig doctor suggested that Nietzsche's insanity might be the result of a syphilitic infection, she publicly denounced him; when an Italian writer, C. A. Bernoulli, tried to publish the letters belonging to Nietzsche's friend Franz Overbeck (which contained unflattering references to Elisabeth), she took him to court in a series of legal actions that dragged on for years.

She was not above plain forgery, if it would help to burnish the image of her relationship with her brother. On more than one occasion, if she found a particularly complimentary passage in a letter written by Nietzsche to someone else, she would burn their name off the top, insert her own and pretend it had been sent to her. She produced 'copies' of letters she said had been sent to her, but claimed that the originals had been stolen in a box of letters while she was in Paraguay. It is impossible to say how many letters which failed to give the right impression were destroyed. Fearing that Fritz Koegel, when he left her employ, took with him copies of letters in which Nietzsche said what he thought about his sister, she took legal action against his heirs to prevent their publication. But arguably her single greatest act of misrepesentation was the publication of *Will to Power*. This was Nietzsche's supposed masterwork, a grand 'revaluation of all values' written before his final collapse. He had certainly planned such a work, but in all probability had abandoned it. He had not prepared it for publication, and thus probably did not want it published; he would have been appalled with it in its final form. The simple fact is that Nietzsche did not write a book called *Will to Power*; Elisabeth did.

The book that Elisabeth, with the help of Peter Gast, published in 1901 under the title *The Will to Power: Studies and Fragments* was in fact nothing less than a cobbling together of philosophical flotsam Nietzsche himself had rejected or used elsewhere. It grew in later years, as further fragments were added, and the title changed to the more emphatic *The Will to Power: Attempt at a Transvaluation of All Values*, firmly establishing Nietzsche as a prophet or 'value-legislator'. Elisabeth claimed, however, that this was Nietzsche's major work, thus giving it a quite spurious importance, and, by grouping otherwise unconnected jottings, notes and aphorisms, imposed an order on it where none existed. For example the fourth section of *Will to Power* is misleadingly called '*Zücht und Züchtung*', Breed and Breeding. True, Nietzsche had in one of his many drafts used this title, but he had abandoned it. In fact, what little he says here about breeding is ambiguous to say the least, and there is almost nothing about biological breeding (as Förster, Elisabeth and later the Nazis conceived it); yet this title was used to cover almost a quarter of what was trumpeted as Nietzsche's 'chief work'. Elisabeth tended to conceive editorial licence as mere censorship: while Gast was compiling the notes for *Will to Power*, for example, she wrote telling him to remove an unflattering reference to the House of Hohenzollern, which *she* admired greatly.

Will to Power does contain ugly elements. Perhaps the most famous concerns Napoleon: 'The Revolution made Napoleon possible; that is its justification. For the sake of a similar prize one would have to desire the anarchical collapse of our entire civilisation. . . .' Given that this is precisely what almost happened under Hitler, that remark has a most disquieting ring to it. It is true that Nietzsche wrote this and other apparent incitements to totalitarianism; but it is equally true that he rejected them. In the second volume of the condensed version of her biography (published in 1914) she was to write: 'it looks as though my brother's fervent advocacy of the Will to Power as a law of nature had come in the nick of time. . . . we cannot become leaders and discoverers; we shall be glad that we may perhaps be allowed "to submerge ourselves" in a great type' – which makes it clear enough how Elisabeth wanted the *Will to Power* to be received. Elisabeth was waiting for a 'great type' on to whom she could unload Nietzsche's thinking.

Her sixtieth birthday was the occasion for major celebrations at Villa Silberblick; bundles of birthday cards arrived, flowers and visitors. That year her portrait was painted by the Norwegian artist, Edvard Munch; Hans Olde was commissioned to paint another. The Italian nationalist and poet, Gabriele D'Annunzio, wrote a poem in Nietzsche's honour which he dedicated to Elisabeth, the 'Antigone of the North'. She thanked him by letter, and he replied fulsomely:

> I have read, Madame, your unexpected letter with overwhelming emotion. The 'sad shadow of Antigone the Greek' comes towards me and speaks to me! As for my Ode: no praise for it equals this gift of yours.
>
> Please accept, Madame, this expression of my gratitude. My poem is dedicated to you, entirely and for ever.
>
> I write to you from the coast of Tyrrhenia. I would like to send you, for the Hero's sepulchre, a large pine branch.
>
> You can have faith, Madame, in my admiration and unlimited devotion.
>
> G D'A.

It was exactly the sort of letter Elisabeth loved, even if she didn't particularly want lumps of wood cluttering up her shrine, and precisely the sort of letter writer she approved of. D'Annunzio was a fervent nationalist whose ideas helped to lay the groundwork for Italian fascism. Her biographies had been enthusiastically received, her name was linked with the foremost intellectuals of the age and the collected Nietzsche was selling fast.

EVEN in Paraguay, things seemed to be improving. In 1906, a volume of Paraguayan reminiscences was published in Germany by one Baron Heinrich von Fischer Truenfeld, an adventurer of the old school who had been employed by the dictator Francisco Solano Lopez to build the Paraguayan railway system and had later taken over the country's communications system, such as it was. His memoirs make interesting reading: it was he who, at the height of the terrible War of the Triple Alliance, had developed a way of making newspapers out of *caraguatá* pulp and thus kept the Paraguayans informed about the course of the war; in return for this useful discovery, Lopez had had him imprisoned. But Elisabeth was most intrigued by the Baron's survey of the colony New Germany, which included many flattering references to Bernhard Förster – 'an idealistic genius pursuing dreams and ideals for the happiness of man and who sought to achieve this with self-sacrificing loyalty and indefatigable work'.

According to Truenfeld, one German colonist in Nueva Germania called Fritz Neumann, originally of Breslau, 'after six or eight years of tireless experimentation', had discovered a way to make *yerba* seeds germinate artificially. The truth was rather more prosaic than that. Neumann had one day, quite by accident, noticed that the areas where the jungle birds roosted tended to produce large quantities of *yerba*. He deduced that the birds' digestive system was acting on the seeds they had eaten and accelerating germination. He concocted a mixture of acid and charcoal and, by steeping the *yerba* seeds in it, achieved the same result; thus Fritz Neumann of New Germany had the brief honour of being the world's first (if you discounted the Jesuits) and only *yerba maté* plantation owner. In 1903, the community produced eight thousand kilos of *yerba*, or *ora verde*, green gold, as they now called it; in 1904, thirty thousand kilos were shipped downriver to Asunción, where the new 'artificial' *yerba* commanded a far higher price than the wild variety. Neumann had become a rich man and leader of the colony. He built himself a house at Tacarutý, a few miles outside town, with glass in the windows and a real piano. The population of the colony doubled, mostly from migrant Paraguayan peons looking to harvest the crop, but some new German settlers came too, drawn by the new prosperity. The slanders of a few disenchanted people in the past had, said Baron Truenfeld, delayed the development of the colony but they could not prevent it now after Neumann's scientific breakthrough: 'For New Germany and *yerba* have become synonymous. And as the future production of *yerba* is increased, so the further development of New Germany is assured.' Elisabeth was delighted. At last, in her sixtieth year, the two great projects of her life seemed to be coming to fruition.

The royalties from Nietzsche's works, as well as her own, were pouring into the Archive, but the money was pouring out again just as fast. Thanks to the small army of lawyers and the rather larger army of servants in permanent attendance, Elisabeth was perennially short of cash – a problem that was compounded by her taste for expensive entertaining. In 1905 she had received a letter from a forty-five-year-old Swedish banker called Ernest Thiel, complimenting her on her biographies. Thiel was to become the economic mainstay of the Nietzsche cult. But, in addition to being exceedingly wealthy, a dedicated Nietzschean and skilled translator of Nietzsche's works, Thiel was an orthodox Jew. This perhaps explains why Elisabeth's first reaction was to hire a private detective in Stockholm to look into his background before she accepted money from him. But accept she did – the first instalment being RM 300,000 in September 1907. Her anti-semitism was of an opportunistic sort; when it became clear that Thiel was prepared to donate large amounts to the Archive, Elisabeth conveniently put her racist scruples aside; indeed she became genuinely fond of Thiel and his family. Whenever Elisabeth ran short of money she would turn to him, and he, uncomplainingly, would dig ever deeper into his copious pockets. Over the next thirty years he gave hundreds of thousands of Marks, most of which Elisabeth quite happily spent.

It was a sign of how far Elisabeth's star was in the ascendant that in 1908 a group of German university professors nominated her for the Nobel prize for literature; it was the first of three occasions that Elisabeth would be proposed (the others were 1915 and 1923) and each time she was turned down, much to her annoyance. But she could take heart from the fact that the Archive in Weimar was fast becoming a place of pilgrimage for every German intellectual worth his salt; foreign dignitaries and even Persian grandees (noting that Zoroaster, or Zarathustra, was Persian) came to pay homage to Nietzsche, whose 'death room' was preserved intact, and to the sister who had saved him for posterity and immortalised him in her biographies.

Years before, Nietzsche's old friend Overbeck, himself a victim of Elisabeth's will to power, had written of her biographical efforts: 'Rarely has the reading public been so duped as in [Elisabeth] Förster[-Nietzsche]'s book. It reads sometimes as though Frau Förster wants to prove that she is far wiser than her brother. She is often praised now as a saint among sisters. But this will change. The time may come when she will be considered a prime example of the type: dangerous sisters.' And not all of those who came to Weimar to pay homage to Nietzsche were taken in by his sister's posturing. Oscar Levy, the foremost British Nietzsche scholar of the period and the man who would later and quite unfairly be linked with the translation of the forged *My Sister and I*, visited her in August 1908. He gave this account to a friend following a four-and-a-half-hour encounter with her:

> I came here with some trepidation, because I have recently read her brochure 'The Nietzsche Archive and Its Enemies', in which she stresses at several points her willingness for sacrifice – and whenever someone mentions 'willingness for sacrifice', I invariably feel sick. . . . It was even worse than I anticipated, and I scanned the streets of Weimar for a whole day wondering how it could be possible that such a man could have such a sister! By and large, however, I feel sorry for this woman who pays rather heavily for her 'celebrity'. She is nervous, talks incessantly, interrupting the flow only in order

to fetch some book or other in order to verify something hastily, only to change the subject and to talk about something which has no relation to the previous topic. This is punctuated by a lot of unconscious sighs which would reveal an inner restlessness if the outer one were not already a sufficient indication of it. She also complained to me a good deal about being the subject of attacks, though, as she thinks, 'her enemies would soon be the worse for it.' 'But it is all too much for a single woman,' she added dolefully – this is my opinion too: 'mais Diable! c'est ce qu'elle fait dans cette galère!' There were also a lot of other utterances – gushingly insincere à la Meysenbug – women's views of the first calibre – high-sounding phrases peppered with the constant words: 'acted in the interests of my brother'. She is also vain, not only in relation to her appearance for which, as a woman and a good-looking old lady, she would have every justification. She still has pink cheeks, rather pronouncedly defined, so that I thought at first she had put rouge on her face – besides, although she is small rather than tall and somewhat plump, she is 'very mobile' and 'I am already 62 years old.' But she is not only vain about her exterior, but also – quelle horreur! – even more so about her literary achievements. About her Introductions [to Nietzsche's works], for instance, all of which she wants to have translated into English. In short, she is one of those women against whom her brother always thundered!! I can well believe that she often made life miserable for him – and if the great man wrote some tender letters to her, this only proves *his* generosity of the soul and conciliatory nature in spite of all the vexation . . . and worse: would you believe it possible that this woman, thanks to her prestige as the sister of Nietzsche, has entered into relationships with all the so-called poets of Germany and beyond, with a Dehmel, with a Hoffmannsthal, with Bernard Shaw, with D'Annunzio, with Gerhard Hauptmann – people her brother would have expelled from the Temple and from the Archive! She also exchanges enthusiastic messages with Graf Zeppelin, the inventor of aviation. Quite up to date – and all this should not make a woman irascible, nervous and contentious!

In the noise of adulation surrounding Elisabeth in these years, such voices of dissent, let alone of criticism, were seldom heard. Elisabeth might talk and write about her enemies, but her friends grew ever more numerous and influential as the Nietzsche cult grew. She herself suggested the foundation of an International Nietzsche Memorial Committee. Van de Velde was entrusted with the design, and Count Kessler did most of the organising: his plans included a Nietzsche shrine overlooking Weimar, a temple and a vast classical stadium where young Europeans could compete in the spirit of Nietzsche. Using his energy and contacts he gathered extraordinary international support from men such as André Gide, H. G. Wells, D'Annunzio and many others. The plan was scuppered by the war.

Eight years earlier Elisabeth had signed a letter to *The Times* in London along with other 'distinguished representatives of Science, Literature and Art' – including Kessler, Richard Strauss, Siegfried Wagner and someone called Engelbert Humperdinck – emphasising their respect for Britain and playing down the possibility of war: 'none of us, though living in widely distant parts of Germany and moving in different spheres of German society and party life, has ever heard an attack on England seriously discussed or approved of by any man or section of the German public worth noticing. . . . no feelings the German people are ever likely to harbour, can ever rightly endanger the friendship between both nations.' If that really represented Elisabeth's view in 1906 (which is doubtful), it certainly didn't by 1914. When war came, Elisabeth was elated. The news that the German armies were advancing stirred her jingoism, never far below the surface. Her brother had written of war as a vital factor in human affairs, of the productive nature of conflict and of the heroic qualities produced by battle. He had spoken of his own 'warlike soul', but he had also written of himself as 'the good European' who wanted to subsume nationalist rivalries. He used militaristic language, to be sure, but he was very far from supporting war as an end in itself, and certainly not a war of conquest between European countries. But Nietzsche was a peacemaker too:

> Perhaps there will come in the future a great day on which a nation distinguished for wars and victories and for the highest

> development of military discipline and thinking will declare of its own free will: *'we shall shatter the sword!'* – and demolish its entire military machine, down to its last foundations. *To disarm while being best armed,* out of an *elevation* of sensibility – that is the means to real peace. . . . the tree of the glory of war can be destroyed only at a single stroke, by a lightning bolt: Lightning, however, as you well know, comes out of a cloud and from on high.

Elisabeth's approach was unambiguous. She trumpeted Nietzsche as a militarist and an imperialist. She wrote long articles in the press describing *Zarathustra* as 'the great challenge to Germans to rise up and fight. . . . there is a fighter in every German, no matter what party he belongs to and this soldier in him comes to the fore whenever the Fatherland is threatened. . . . Our German mission has not been fulfilled.' She joined the Party of the German Fatherland (Deutsche Vaterlandspartei) to push for victory and hosted receptions for wounded soldiers at Villa Silberblick. *Zarathustra* became a best-seller: between 1914 and 1919 more than 165,000 copies were sold and the book was even distributed to soldiers at the Front. She developed a remarkable line in militaristic rhetoric, as when she talked of 'one of the greatest and most solemn moments in world history when four powers have brought enemies and opponents to us everywhere, to annihilate a young and ambitious people; but divine justice and the shining power of the German people allow us to overcome this huge, malevolent storm so we can be certain with God that Germany will come through this terribly difficult time, despite countless, heartbreaking sacrifices, as a legendary hero and victor'. Elisabeth's propagandising had its effect abroad as well as in Germany; when the first translation of Nietzsche appeared in England, newspaper placards told book-buyers to 'read the devil in order to fight him better'.

Elisabeth had never contemplated defeat and when it came, in a welter of revolutionary upheaval, she was furious and blamed the Social Democrats for stabbing her brave German soldiers in the back. She even wrote to the Chancellor, Prince Max von Baden, urging him to continue the fighting. Versailles was a humiliation from which she believed Germany would never recover.

It was Elisabeth's war rhetoric that began to sow doubts in Count Harry Kessler's mind about the old lady he had supported for years. In 1919 he noted in his diary, 'Even in her seventh decade, she remains a flapper at heart and enthuses over this or that person like a 17-year-old. . . . In spite of her name she is . . . the embodiment of precisely what her brother fought against.' The Weimar Republic was anathema to Elisabeth's every political instinct and her own interpretation of her brother's philosophy. Her conservatism refused to contemplate that a Superman could emerge from the morass of democracy. 'She insists that she is a "nationalist",' noted Kessler gloomily, 'whereas her brother did not even want to be a German, but a Pole. She has had her head turned by all these countesses and excellencies.' Later he noted, 'the good old lady simply refers to the right-wing radicals as "we"!' She poured scorn on the republic, which turned to dismay when a socialist government was elected in Weimar and to fury when it became clear that Germany was slipping into economic chaos. Being nominated (and rejected) for the Nobel literature prize for the third time in 1923 did little to improve her mood.

That same year, though Nietzsche's books still sold well and Thiel hovered in the background ever ready with more cash, Elisabeth (now *Frau Doktor*, after the University of Jena presented her with an honorary doctorate on her seventy-fifth birthday) was suddenly reduced to near penury. Her entire capital was wiped out at a blow by the government's decision to replace the old currency with the Rentenmark. Inflation raged, but Elisabeth took it on her redoubtable chin and, as ever, decided it was time to look elsewhere for patronage. Even Kessler, increasingly disillusioned, was impressed by her fortitude: 'Admirable, the resignation and courage with which this old woman of eighty mentioned the complete loss through inflation of the accumulated funds (800,000 gold Marks in round figures) of the Nietzsche endowment. . . . This courage of hers, which in situations of this sort comes out so strongly, borders on the heroic and compels admiration for Nietzsche's sister.'

But, though he could still find praise for the old woman, he found her political views, and their effect on Nietzsche's interpretation, deplorable. One of the most influential figures to be found in Weimar was Oswald Spengler, author of *The Decline of the West* and a man whose notions of German cultural decay and Prussian imperialism directly coincided with Elisabeth's. In 1919 he had been awarded the Nietzsche Prize, a considerable sum donated by a wealthy Hamburg shipping agent, Christian Lassen. (Thomas Mann had won it the previous year for his *Reflections of a Non-Political Man* – his attack on Western democracy. Ernst Bertram was another prize-winner.) Spengler's views, emphasising the decline of cultural values and prophesying a new age of high technology and 'caesarism', laid the cultural groundwork for the rise of Nazism. Spengler was later to oppose the fascist regime, but in the 1920s he was the movement's intellectual wet-nurse, and was present as an observer at Hitler's trial after the failed Munich *Putsch* in 1923. Though Spengler had reservations about the young Nazis' coup attempt, Elisabeth had few; the *Putsch*, she thought, was quite simply 'patriotic', and the trial was 'deplorable'.

With both Spengler and Kessler on the board of the Nietzsche Archive, the two antithetical approaches to Nietzsche were represented: Spengler the authoritarian, militaristic, radical conservative; Kessler, the social democrat, the consummate 'good European' and a pacifist as a result of his war experiences. They did not like each other. When in 1927 Spengler was due to give a lecture at the Archive, Kessler initially refused to come because of Spengler's 'political methods and intellectual arrogance'. When he relented and attended, he wished he had not. Spengler was 'a fat parson with a fleshy chin and brutal mouth' who 'spouted the most trite and trivial rubbish. Everything uniformly shallow, dull, insipid and tedious. In short Spengler succeeded in making Nietzsche a bore.' Kessler however was no longer the force he had once been in Elisabeth's life; increasingly men like Spengler were entrusted with the work of disseminating and interpreting her brother's work. It was Spengler, not Kessler, who gave the lecture 'Nietzsche and Our Time' on 15 October 1924, the philosopher's eightieth birthday. It was a sign of her continued determination to 'reconcile opposites' that she tried to encourage Kessler and Spengler to work together, and a sign of her superficial approach to politics that she was surprised when they could not.

In 1927 she achieved the reconciliation of two opposites that were dearest to her heart. The story of the Nazification of Wagner is almost as unedifying as the story of the intellectual perversion of Nietzsche. With the help of Houston Stewart Chamberlain, Cosima Wagner systematically sought to interpret and disseminate her dead husband's work in the light of her own racist, nationalist ideology. Chamberlain's theories of the supremacy of the Aryan race influenced the young Adolf Hitler and are at least partially reflected in *Mein Kampf*; Cosima went to the grave in 1930 believing that 'the race most capable of culture is the Germanic, which on that account is destined to dominance'. She even traced Nietzsche's apostasy to his putative Slav origins. With Elisabeth fast pushing Nietzsche's philosophy down the nationalist path, a rapprochement between the two clans was perhaps inevitable. Her mendacious biographies made it clear that she never really accepted the breach between Nietzsche and Wagner, in spite of her brother's repeated public denunciations of his former mentor; now, her control over Nietzsche absolute, she sought to 'mend' the relationship. Her chance came when Weimar hosted a festival of folk operas written by Siegfried Wagner, Wagner's son, who had paid several visits to the Archive in 1926; it was also the opportunity for her to return, with interest, a little of the Wagner patronage.

> Elisabeth went on to tell me about the reconciliation of the Wagner clan [recalled Kessler]. Last year, during the festival held for Siegfried Wagner, and after preliminary reconnaissance by Countess Gravina, the whole Wagner family called on her. Subsequently she gave a luncheon party for them. On this occasion the reconciliation was formally sealed when they all held hands around the table, and she read them her brother's 'Star Friendship'. Siegfried Wagner issued an official invitation to her to share the family box at Bayreuth. She cannot be cross with him, she added, for she still sees him as

the little boy who announced that he 'loved her more than anything else in the world'. The Wagner–Nietzsche feud has petered out in an atmosphere of social cosiness, and in a manner of the courtly style so typical of the Bayreuth crowd. The Princess of Albania was present and duly took cognisance of the reconciliation. The whole business is infinitely commonplace, and removed in sentiment by several thousands of miles from the closing chord of *Götterdämmerung*, let alone the ending of *Zarathustra*.

CHAPTER VIII

Mother of the Fatherland

AS A young Italian schoolteacher, Benito Mussolini believed he had found in Nietzsche's *Will to Power* a central political truth. In an essay of 1908, 'Philosophy of Strength', he had written that Nietzsche had 'the most congenial mind of the last quarter of the nineteenth century'. He was later to claim that Nietzsche had 'cured' him of his socialism, and in 1924 he was quoted as saying, 'You are right in assuming that I have been influenced by Nietzsche ... I have read them without exception ... I was deeply impressed by Nietzsche's wonderful precept "Live Dangerously". I have lived up to that I think.' This was more than the mere political magpie at work, picking up stray, brightly coloured political phrases. Mussolini certainly read Nietzsche – to say that I think he misunderstood him perhaps falsely implies that I do. My point is simply that Nietzsche would have despised Mussolini, although he might initially have applauded his bravado. He would have found Mussolini's appeal to base, mass instincts, and in particular the new religion of fascism, quite repugnant. Mussolini was clearly attracted by Nietzsche's potent language and his cult of the great individual who can and should override mere institutions to achieve his ends. It is, of course, impossible to say to what extent Mussolini was 'inspired' by Nietzsche (however he misread him) and how far Nietzsche was merely a useful propaganda tool.

Elisabeth had no such qualms about Mussolini. Perhaps through D'Annunzio, she knew he was a reader of her brother's works, and when Mussolini marched on Rome she wrote to congratulate him and he replied stressing his admiration for Nietzsche. Elisabeth and Mussolini were never to meet, but throughout the 1920s they corresponded with increasing warmth, to their mutual advantage. If Nietzsche was not merely propaganda when Mussolini discovered him, he most certainly was by the time Elisabeth had discovered Mussolini.

Max Oehler, Elisabeth's fascist cousin, wrote an article on 'Nietzsche and Mussolini' which was widely published; as chairman of the Nietzsche Archive, Elisabeth herself gave a 'speech of admiration' for the Duce in Villa Silberblick on 5 June 1928; on the same occasion, Consul Wilhelm Mann lectured on 'Fascism as a Spiritual Movement'. When Mussolini concluded the Latean Treaty with the Pope and the Italian monarchy, Elisabeth wrote to the Italian Ambassador in Berlin:

> 'I can no longer restrain myself from expressing to your Excellency my whole-hearted admiration for the President Minister Mussolini. ... His Excellency is not only the pre-eminent statesman of Europe, but of the whole world and I am truly proud that I was able to detect how some of Nietzsche's philosophy is revealed in the strength in action of this highly esteemed president. With what pride would my brother gaze at this wonderful man, upon someone happy, powerful and triumphant, who offers mankind the happy chance of salvation, so that it is possible to hold firm to faith in mankind itself.

For Elisabeth, Mussolini represented the triumph of her interpretation of Nietzsche's thought. She called him 'the genius who rediscovered the values of Nietzsche's spirit', and wrote long letters stating how 'my brother loved Italy more than any other country. How happy he would be now that this country has been so closely connected with his thoughts and ideas by your Excellency's wonderful influence.' If Mussolini came to think of himself as some sort of Superman, it was partly at Elisabeth's urging. 'Without exaggeration I can say that Nietzsche would have regarded him as his most splendid disciple,' she wrote, 'and the only one who has implanted to a great degree Nietzsche's philosophy –

humility, discipline and control – into the youth of Italy.' It was not true, of course, as Kessler was quick to recognise. In 1926 he noted that Elisabeth had written to him 'bursting with news of her Mussolini friendship and demanded to know whether I had heard of it. Yes, indeed, I said, I had both heard and regretted it, for Mussolini compromises her brother's reputation. He is a danger to Europe, that Europe which her brother longed for, the Europe of all good Europeans. She will be 80 soon, and it is beginning to show.'

To mark that birthday President Hindenburg awarded her an honorary pension on 16 July 1926, slightly alleviating her financial problems, which were threatening to become serious after 1930 when the copyright on Nietzsche's books would expire. The long-suffering Ernest Thiel, though he continued to send money to the Archive, was facing cash difficulties of his own. Elizabeth was determined that the Archive should be made financially secure. She needed a permanent patron, someone who could ensure her future and her lifestyle, and the future of her Archive. She chose the Nazis.

Of the brood of second-rate bullies and braggarts that made up the National Socialists, Dr Wilhelm Frick was perhaps the least colourful. A civil servant by training, an antisemite by conviction and a bureaucrat by taste, he was a devoted follower of Hitler from the earliest days. They had been tried and sentenced together after the Munich Beer Hall *Putsch* in 1923. Grey-haired and slight, he drifts around in the background of those early puff-chested Nazi photographs, like a lost bank clerk. Yet he played a vital role in the Nazi rise to power, sharing every part of Hitler's twisted philosophy and helping him to consolidate his hold on power. As early as 1924 he was in the Reichstag, where he proposed a bill to dismiss Jews from the civil service. 'We deem it below our dignity to be ruled by people of that race,' he averred. And it was Frick who later, as Reich Minister of the Interior, created the pseudo-legal apparatus for the oppression of communists, social democrats and Jews which culminated in the Nuremberg Laws. In 1930, as Minister of the Interior in Thuringia, he became the first National Socialist minister in a provincial government. Elisabeth had

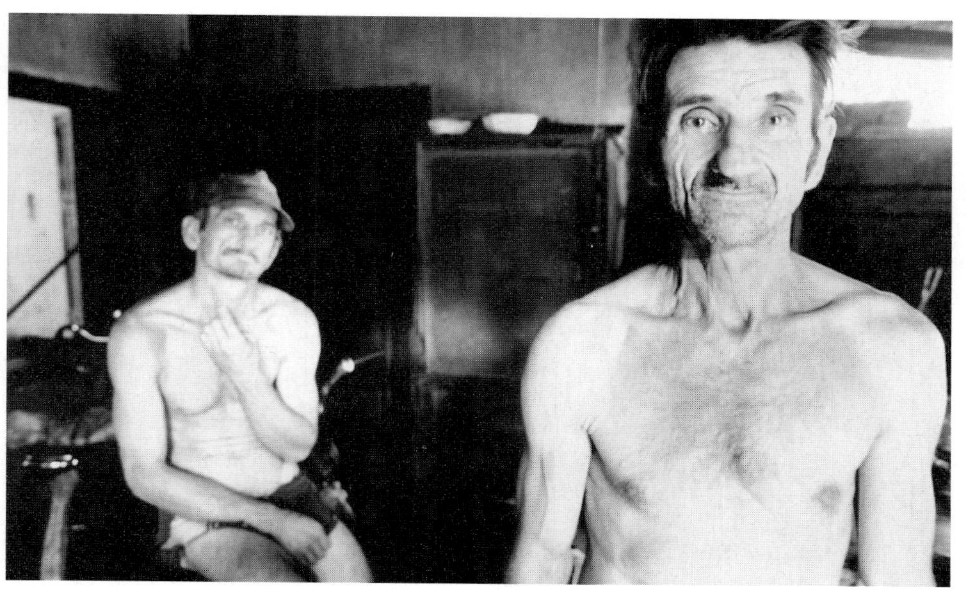

The Schweikhart brothers, Nueva Germania, 1991. Their Paraguayan neighbours refer to them as 'gente perdita', the lost people.

Rolf Richter, Colonia Independencia, 1991. Under President Stroessner, Paraguay became a haven for fugitive Nazis and ex-combatants, including Josef Mengele, the doctor of Auschwitz.

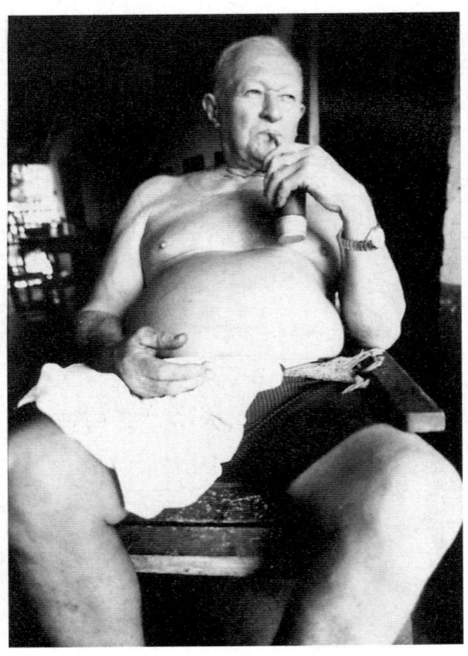

The Germans of Nueva Germania have become as addicted to *yerba maté*, or Paraguayan tea, as the Paraguayans themselves.

Heinrich and Martha Schütte with their grandchildren, Nueva Germania, 1991. His grandfather travelled on the steamer *Uruguay* with the first group of settlers.

Pablo Flascam plays 'The Mennonite Waltz' on a squeeze-box brought by his grandfather from Chemnitz in 1886.

Magdalena and Bernhard Fischer, Nueva Germania, 1991.
'We are dying out, the pure Germans,' she says.

The grave of Bernhard Förster in the overgrown cemetery at San Bernardino near where he poisoned himself in 1889. In 1934 Hitler sent a package of German soil to be strewn on the grave, in honour of a fallen martyr to the anti-semitic cause.

The insane Nietzsche on the balcony at Villa Silberblick in Weimar, shortly before his death in 1900. From time to time Elisabeth would dress him up to be exhibited to special guests.

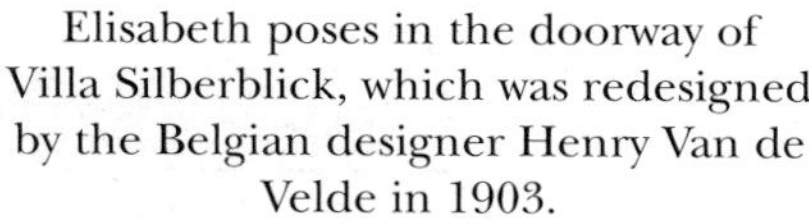

Elisabeth poses in the doorway of Villa Silberblick, which was redesigned by the Belgian designer Henry Van de Velde in 1903.

The cosmopolitan diarist Count Harry Kessler, whose early support of Elisabeth's activities in the Nietzsche archive gradually turned to bitter disillusionment.

Elisabeth *c.* 1925. 'She is still a flapper at heart,' said Count Kessler.

Adolf Hitler gazes thoughtfully at the bust of Friedrich Nietzsche. There is no evidence, however, to suggest that he ever read a single word of Neitzsche's philosophy.

Elisabeth, aged 87, greets Adolf Hitler outside the Nietzsche Archive after the Nazis come to power. 'What I like most about Hitler is his simplicity and naturalness,' she wrote, 'he wants nothing for himself but thinks only of Germany. I admire him utterly.'

Elisabeth on her deathbed, November 1935. Wreaths were sent by all the most prominent Nazis.

'You could see from the Führer's face how deeply moved he was.' In the main reception room at Villa Silberblick Adolf Hitler and the Nazis pay homage at Elisabeth's coffin to 'the fearless, determined and motivated guardian of a great German genius'.

The Nietzsche memorial 'built in the sixth year of the Third Reich under the direction of Adolf Hitler' is officially opened in August 1938. It is now Weimar radio station.

already noted his ascent with approval, and when Frick won office she was among the first to congratulate him on the election 'victory' of the NSDAP. His reply was immediate and fulsome, ending with a transparent recognition of the propaganda use that could be made of Nietzsche's sister: 'I am not giving up hope that you too, my dear lady, will one day devote yourself to the liberty movement of the German people, as a fighter like your highly esteemed brother Nietzsche.'

A month later, as an added incentive to Elisabeth to put her considerable cultural clout behind the Nazis, Frick offered to introduce a bill in the Reichstag which would extend the thirty-year copyright on Nietzsche's works, and thus provide Elisabeth with a continuation of the royalties she so badly wanted. She accepted with alacrity and, though the bill failed, Frick promised official subsidies for the Nietzsche Archive. Elisabeth had taken the bait; not that she needed much encouragement, the hearts (if they had them) of men like Frick beat in time with hers. By 1931 she was ready to write a letter to thank Frick for a donation of 5000 Marks which comes close to admitting its own perjury:

> It is certain that my brother wrote against nationalism forty years ago, but then forty years ago the situation was completely different. In those days, Germany was neither as big nor as powerful as it is today. Everything has changed so much. I understand what Herr Hitler has found in Nietzsche – and that is the heroic cast of mind which we need so desperately. There is one quotation by my brother which I always connect with the feelings of the best National Socialists, 'Don't throw away the golden guinea in your soul and always preserve your greatest hope.' I'm quite sure this 'hope' of Nietzsche's lies especially in your heart, surrounded as you are by difficulties. Whenever Germany's enemies make their stupid remarks that Nietzsche has nothing to do with National Socialism, you should reply in general that the link between National Socialism and Nietzsche is the heroism in both their souls.

In contrast to Mussolini, Hitler almost certainly never read a word that Nietzsche wrote, either now or at any other time. Though he might occasionally style himself a poet–politician, he never mentioned Nietzsche in his writing, and only once, in passing, during his table-talk. Nietzsche's works, and the mythical reputation built up around him by Elisabeth and her Weimar acolytes, were little more than useful propaganda tools. They provided Hitler with an armoury of (admittedly emotive) words and phrases, 'will to power', 'the Superman', 'live dangerously', which, quoted partially and out of context, could be used to provide the Nazi ideology with a spurious philosophical basis.

Elisabeth's finances improved when, at the end of 1931, a court ruled that she should be considered co-author of the works she had compiled out of her brother's *Nachlass*, most notably *Will to Power*. It was further proof that these were really her creations, not her brother's. The royalties from these works would still go to her account, as did the royalties on her own works to which she was adding with a book entitled *Nietzsche and the Women of His Time*, a final swingeing attack on the now ageing Lou Andreas-Salomé. Otherwise, the Archive and its large staff survived on handouts, from Thiel, Frick and a wealthy cigarette manufacturer Philipp Reetsma, who between 1929 and 1945 donated an annual sum of 20,000 Reichsmarks; he was later tried at Nuremberg for attempting to bribe Hermann Gœring. Mussolini sent 20,000 lire to the Archive, with sincere congratulations on Elisabeth's eighty-fifth birthday. She told the Italian Ambassador that it would be 'the happiest day' of her life if 'the deeply venerated Duce were to visit the Archive'. Six months later she saw her opportunity to persuade him by an appeal to his vanity.

Mussolini had co-written a play about Napoleon, *Campo di Maggio* (*The Hundred Days* in English) in which Bonaparte is portrayed as a hero brought down by the intrigues of his enemies. Elisabeth liked the play, perhaps because it echoed her own fictional accounts of the heroic deaths of her husband and brother; it certainly mirrored Mussolini's view of his own greatness, particularly since he portrayed Napoleon as a man whose one fatal mistake was to give in to democracy.

It is not clear what part Elisabeth played in arranging to have the play performed, for the first time in German, at the Weimar National Theatre in February 1932, but she wrote to Mussolini:

> Can I dare to dream that your Excellency might attend this magnificent work with us? How happy I would be if, before my death, I could tell your Excellency how grateful I am that you have implanted the thoughts and doctrines of my brother Friedrich Nietzsche – respect, bravery, discipline – into numerous young hearts. It would be the most beautiful and joyous day of my life if I could receive your Excellency at the Archive, which would give me the opportunity to thank your Excellency for all the great help you have given the Archive in recent times. . . .

Mussolini declined, but on the opening night the theatre was packed with the most important people in Weimar, including one who was about to become very important indeed. When Hitler strode down the aisle, flanked by storm troopers, the audience, including Elisabeth in her box of honour, was thunderstruck. During the interval, Hitler paid a courtesy visit to the sister of the great writer and presented her with a large bunch of red roses. Elisabeth was deeply impressed. 'His eyes', she told Kessler, 'are fascinating and stare right through you.'

Elisabeth was by inclination and upbringing a conservative monarchist; her instincts lay more with the right-wing politicians who helped to bring Hitler to power than with the Nazis. She corresponded regularly with the Empress Hermine, the Kaiser's wife, now in exile in Holland – a relationship Kessler considered 'grotesque' – and talked of a restoration of the monarchy. She was above all a snob; a Hindenburg, the grand old man of German politics, was always more to her taste than an Austrian ex-corporal. Like other conservatives she was prepared to expand her political views to embrace the Nazi cause. Yet her espousal of Nazism was not simply opportunistic. Before Hitler came to power she told Frick of her admiration for the National Socialists. In July 1932, following that first breathless encounter with

Hitler, she wrote of the explosive political situation: 'there is great agitation here at the Nietzsche Archive, because all the men of the Archive have associated themselves so much with the Hitler movement, as I have too.' Kessler had already noted that 'inside the Archive everyone, from the door-keeper to the director, is a Nazi . . .'. Elisabeth's enthusiasm for Hitler was little short of hysterical, eclipsing even the lavish praise she had heaped on Mussolini. But it was not just hyperbole. Elisabeth found in Hitler an idol, another object of veneration, a new Superman.

On 30th January 1933, Max Oehler, Elisabeth's cousin and head of the Archive and now a committed Nazi, made an entry in his diary which is ringed in red and blue crayon and surrounded by exclamation marks: 'Hitler in power!!' Three days later Elisabeth wrote to Frick:

> A wave of joyous enthusiasm is coursing through Germany, because the beloved Führer, Adolf Hitler, is now at the head of the German Reich; German Nationalists and Stahlhelm [two right-wing parties] are included in this joyful flood. This is a situation which hearts of national sensitivity have dreamed of and there are not sufficient words to describe the deep impression made by the Führer's superb action in taking German Nationalists and Stahlhelm into the Reich cabinet. But I have a particular reason to be filled with happiness, for I think of you as a good friend, and am proud that you have become Reich Minister of the Interior and also delighted that my concern, the Nietzsche Archive, is under your special care. My constant anxiety is that I may die and leave the Nietzsche Archive in strange hands. But I can now look happily into the future, for not only have all Germany's economic needs been smoothed away, but now also cultural concerns are being taken over by a Reich government that has a heart for it.

To Thiel she talked of the 'wonderful, indeed phenomenal personality of our magnificent Chancellor Adolf Hitler'. She even used the new Führer's rhetoric: 'We have suddenly achieved the *one* Germany . . . which we have all been waiting for: *Ein Volk, ein Reich, ein Führer*.' These are not the extravagant ravings of senility, they are the effusions of a believer.

Less than a fortnight after the Nazis came to power, Elisabeth met the Führer again, at a performance of Wagner's *Tristan und Isolde*. Hitler's enthusiasm for Wagner's music had already turned Bayreuth into a centre for Nazi propaganda with the willing connivance of Wagner's heirs; now he and his 'cultural advisers' turned to Elisabeth Nietzsche and Weimar, and she welcomed them with open arms. On the same day as the performance, Hitler came to Villa Silberblick. It was to be the first well-publicised visit of many, as the Nazis contrived, with Elisabeth's help, to entwine the tendrils of Nazism around Nietzsche's name.

Harry Kessler, who said he felt like weeping to see what had become of Nietzsche and was shortly to leave Germany for exile in Paris, was not the only person whose gorge rose as Elisabeth paid court to the Nazis. Dr Fritz Rütishauser, a Swiss democrat and member of the board of the Nietzsche Archive, wrote to Elisabeth from Switzerland soon after Hitler's first visit, appalled at events in Germany and their effect on Nietzsche's name: 'It is becoming ever clearer that the land of poets and thinkers, this great people, is becoming a phalanx to fight everything that is not *völkisch* – a place where people are set upon in the streets. . . . that Nietzsche's name is associated with these events is evidence of the deep turmoil in the German spirit.' Elisabeth justified herself to him with customary vigour:

> We are very happy at Nietzsche's adoption by Mussolini and Hitler. . . . you can't understand it because you do not live in our country. If you were here you would understand. . . . The Nietzsche archive has become a centre not only of the German Reich, but of the whole intellectual world. I could tell you so many good things: our splendid Führer has visited me three times in eleven months, and he is the most honourable man you can imagine. If my brother had ever met Hitler his greatest wish would have been fulfilled. It amazes me that in these unintellectual times such a hero can still emerge. He will change Germany completely, but we must be patient. . . . what I like most about Hitler is his simplicity and naturalness, and he wants nothing for himself but thinks only of Germany. I admire him utterly.

Rütishauser replied, regretfully severing links with Elisabeth for ever. 'A trip to Weimar is, for me, like a trip to the Holy Land. But the new political orientation has become an ideology. You and the Archive are taking part in this event, and adhering to that ideology. The development is dreadful, and I oppose it.'

Even her old Jewish protector, Ernest Thiel, was belatedly beginning to have doubts. 'Yes, Elisabeth, you are living in a great time,' he replied to one of her more effusive protestations of Hitler-worship, but added, 'you make no culture through a police force. . . . both Nietzsche and I belong to a different culture'. Elisabeth was no stranger to criticism and was adept at ignoring it. If Dr Rütishauser, Kessler and Thiel disagreed with her, then they were wrong. She wrote long, adoring letters to the Führer, repeatedly urging him to visit her in Weimar. And, since the propaganda value of Nietzsche as a Nazi prophet was immense, he accepted no less than seven times. He was photographed staring avidly into the eyes of Nietzsche's bust, apparently deep in reverential thought, or poring over copies of Nietzsche's works in the Archive; on every visit, children would line the road to the Archive and present the Führer with flowers before he paid homage to the philosopher's sister. Elisabeth happily connived at the propagandising: on 2 November 1933 she presented Hitler with Nietzsche's walking stick and, even more symbolically, with a copy of the anti-semitic petition that Bernhard Förster had presented to Bismarck in 1880. If Hitler had taken the trouble to read it, he would have found sentiments which prefigured his own.

Max Oehler described in lavish detail each of Hitler's visits: the result was pure grist to the Nazi propaganda mill, such as this account of July 1934:

> The Statesman comes to the house of the leading philosopher of the state; he comes not as a politician visiting a philosopher, but as a well-intentioned visitor making a personal and friendly call on the 'sister' who has now reached such advanced years and whose unparalleled loyalty we have to thank for the consciousness of our new aims.

So, in the olden days, might a great mother have greeted her great son, so might a prophet have received a hero, and a great man the holy flame of a watchful priestess. . . . Hitler spake – and we can still hear the quiet and admirable tone of his voice – of Mussolini: He is a completely great and powerful man. He has not followed his genius for his own sake, but he must make his people completely powerful. He is a Roman from days long past. Hitler moved on to the subject of our own boys and girls, as simple and serious as a father with his own children. . . . Frau Förster-Nietzsche took the opportunity to speak. She thanked Hitler for honouring with his affection the two geniuses of Weimar and Bayreuth, who were of equal birth and whose friendship made in the stars had lasted beyond a later falling out which had been preordained. How above all else, he was putting everything to right and joining together what was opposed only in appearance. She compared her own hard task with that of Cosima: to protect the inheritance of a genius and to fulfil it despite difficulties that only the bravest could overcome.

The Führer then spoke meaningfully. In misfortune, misunderstanding and even in evil, fate finds its way for the best, and he considered that it was fortunate for himself and us that Wagner and Nietzsche had been kept apart to preserve their purity. The leader of the Archive now explained, in her lively, inimitable style, about Tribschen and Bayreuth and of those great days which are certainly in store for us, amid much serious but also light-hearted talk. . . . the circle around them became lively in his great presence and he told how he had found in her a worthy follower. It was, as Cosima had once explained, the most important moment in German history after Goethe, when Wagner, with Nietzsche in the carriage, had driven to lay the foundation stone at Bayreuth, so that in that half-hour young Germany had found the most profound expression of German unity, which has been achieved so recently.

No one who saw it will ever forget how the man to whom the whole world looks with the liveliest interest took his immortal leave of the elegant old lady as they both stood in the bright sunlight.

In Hitler's wake, the tribe of moral cripples and pseudo-academics that made up the thinking part of the Nazi Party trooped to Weimar to pay homage.

Hans Frank, the Nazi Party's leading jurist, Hitler's personal lawyer and later the sadistic Governor General of Poland, flattered Elisabeth after their first meeting: 'both personally and objectively', he wrote, as Reich Commissar for Justice, 'it is of importance to me that Nietzsche of all people has become the mentor of German jurisprudence'. Frank of course was rather more interested in eliminating the Jews than in Nietzsche's notions of justice. In 1940 he told his troops: '. . . in one year I can do away with neither all the lice nor all the Jews . . . but in the course of time that will be made attainable.' If that could be achieved more effectively by twisting Nietzsche and then hiding behind him, so much the better. In May 1934, Frank had visited the archive in the company of Alfred Rosenberg, a German Balt of vicious anti-semitic inclinations with a large appetite but little aptitude for intellectual activity. As editor of the Nazi newspaper, the *Völkischer Beobachter*, he, along with Frick and Frank, had played a vital role in the early days of Nazism. Hitler was impressed by his 'great intellect' and made him the theoretician of Nazi racism and head of cultural propaganda, although he later fell from favour. His book *The Myth of the Twentieth Century* helped to form the Nazi view of culture and history. It was his opinion that 'German post-war art is that of mestizos laying claim to the licence of depicting bastard excrescences, the products of syphilitic minds and painterly infantilism.' As part of Nietzsche's ninetieth-birthday celebrations, he had a wreath bearing the words 'To the Great Fighter' laid on Nietzsche's grave. (Never mind that Nietzsche's great mind was itself, in all probability, syphilitic.) The *Völkischer Beobachter* carried an official tribute: 'We honour Friedrich Nietzsche . . . who called us, and still calls us, to arms, to the arms of the German spirit and to service in the spirit of German arms, to the tragic-heroic soldierdom of the whole nation.' In the grip of a man like Rosenberg, Nietzsche's philosophy was doomed. In 1933 a copy of *Thus Spoke Zarathustra*, perhaps the most poetic work of anti-dogmatism ever penned, was laid in the vault of the

Tannenburg memorial to the German victory over Russia in the First World War; alongside it were placed Hitler's *Mein Kampf* and Rosenberg's *Myth of the Twentieth Century*.

As Elisabeth observed to Margarethe Frick, wife of Wilhelm, 'Hitler and the party prove that it is not just academics who show an interest in Nietzsche.' It was an unintentional admission that the National Socialist approach was anything but scholarly. Any careful (or even careless) reading of Nietzsche would have revealed his loathing of anti-semitism and of nationalism and his scorn for the German Reich, facts which Nietzsche's newest disciples conveniently ignored, or perverted by quoting out of context. It was Nietzsche's language, his myth-spinning martial exhortations and his celebration of strength that appealed to the Nazis; the rest they ignored. The fascists, in fact, fulfilled Nietzsche's dictum about 'the worst readers. . . . who behave like plundering troops: they take away the few things they can use . . .'. As Elisabeth did herself. In a paper entitled 'Was Nietzsche a National Socialist?' she spoke of his 'passionate patriotism' and stressed that Nietzsche had been a soldier himself in the Franco-Prussian war. By quoting him out of context, and partially, she implied anti-semitism in his writing where there is none. She concluded that 'Nietzsche had always seen very clearly how alien Jewish behaviour has been in Germany.'

The effect of all this on Nietzsche's reception both inside Germany and elsewhere can be gauged by the fact that for two decades after the war Nietzsche's name was philosophical mud. Bertrand Russell suggested he was 'merely megalomaniac', a hill-top Lear, impotent and dangerous, a prophet of the police state. The war against fascism safely won, Russell could state that 'his followers have had their innings, but we may hope that it is rapidly coming to an end'. That was in 1946. Nietzsche was accused of inciting genocide in the preceding years. George Lichtheim wrote: 'It is not too much to say that but for Nietzsche the SS – Hitler's shock troops and the core of the whole movement – would have lacked the inspiration to carry out their programmes of mass murder in eastern Europe' – though Nietzsche always claimed to be Polish. Even P. G. Wodehouse's excellent

Jeeves cannot find a good word for him. Nietzsche, he tells Bertie Wooster, is 'fundamentally unsound'. This must be one of the few occasions on which Jeeves is demonstrably wrong. Nietzsche was an elitist conservative; he opposed equally democracy and socialism, though both democrats and socialists have claimed him as their own. He demolished the traditional values of humanism and championed the right to greatness in individuals, couched in Platonic terms, in the face of mass mediocrity. His works do not support Nazism, or anything like it, and Nietzsche himself, I feel certain, would have looked with horror on what was done in his name. He opposed German nationalism and every mass movement; he distrusted ideologues; and he loathed anti-semitism. He criticised Judaism, certainly, but with the same criteria that he used to attack Christianity; the Jews, he said, were responsible for bringing Christianity, 'the lie of millennia', into being in the first place. That was not racism; on the contrary, he looked forward to the 'great task and question [which] is approaching: how shall the earth as a whole be governed? And to what end shall man as a whole – and no longer as a people or race – be raised and trained?' The Jews, he said, were 'beyond doubt the strongest, toughest and purest race at present living in Europe. The Jews could, if they wanted – or if they were compelled as the anti-semites seem to want – even now predominate, indeed quite literally rule over Europe [this is where the Nazi citation tended to stop, but he continues]. . . . that they are *not* planning and working towards that is equally certain. . . . it would perhaps be a good idea to eject the anti-semitic ranters from the country.' If he had heard Bertrand Russell's understandably facile remarks, he would have surely reiterated what he wrote in *Ecce Homo*: 'I have a duty against which my habits, even more the pride of my instincts, revolt at bottom – namely to say: *Hear me! for I am such and such a person. Above all, do not mistake me for someone else.*'

ELISABETH's support of the Nazi cause brought material as well as personal satisfaction to the old woman. Early in 1934, she received a letter from Hans

Heinrich Lammers, the Führer's secretary. 'The Chancellor of the Reich', it said, 'has felt moved to recognise your great service in maintaining and spreading the life-work of your brother, who will be for ever famous, who is so perpetually significant for our Fatherland and the world, and therefore grants you for your lifetime an honorary stipend of 300 Reichsmarks a month.' Given that she was almost ninety, this was hardly a long-term financial commitment, but it was followed, just over a year later, by another act of Nazi munificence. The Führer gave orders that RMs 2,000 should be transferred immediately to the Archive, and moreover that his own 'special fund' was 'always gladly at the disposal of Frau Förster-Nietzsche'.

Suddenly, she was bombarded with letters from the victims of her new patrons, urging her to intercede with the National Socialists on their behalf. Most of these were Jewish: schoolteachers, journalists, composers, civil servants, artists, all of whom had lost their jobs and livelihoods under the Nazi's discriminatory legislation. Some are pathetic in their wheedling flattery; many are heart-rending. 'I am not an Aryan,' wrote a journalist, Rudolf K. Goldschmit, 'I was a volunteer in 1914 but now non-Aryans have to give up all activities in the press. This would be the destruction of my life. Can you send some word to Frick and Goebbels on my behalf, then I could get on to the list of accepted journalists . . .?'

In some instances Elisabeth did try to intercede, if the supplicant was sufficiently important or culturally recognised, like the sculptor Richard Engelmann. Elisabeth's snobbery had always been even stronger than her anti-semitism. She even wrote to Lammers on behalf of Ernst Praetorius, a celebrated Wagnerite composer now reduced to driving a taxi in Berlin. But she was far more concerned with the fate of Schulpforta, Nietzsche's old school, which was threatened with closure after a sex scandal. She was relieved when Lammers told her it was to become a National Socialist school: 'I'm so glad this is happening. . . . I'm looking forward to this new future for the school, because I perceive that the pupils will be educated in the image of our splendid Reich. It will remain a school for the elite, nothing could be better than that.' Among the begging letters she received at this time is one from a schoolteacher called Schmid, a Jew, who had been sacked from Schulpforta under the new laws to 'cleanse' the civil service – laws for which Elisabeth's friend Wilhelm Frick was largely responsible. 'I will be sacked now because of the law,' he told her; 'even former pupils have said they are appalled at my sacking.' There is no evidence that Elisabeth tried to help him. She gloried in her new-found political influence. 'I am now the good old lady of Weimar,' she told Frick proudly, 'receiving all the problems of everyone around because I know, indeed I am a friend of Frick. Everyone knows that.'

EVERYONE included the inhabitants of New Germany, Paraguay. Elisabeth's interest in the colony had been rekindled by the news that the situation had improved there; she started to take a renewed interest in its future, particularly when the principles on which it had been founded were apparently coming to fruition in Germany itself. She often used to regale her friends and associates with stories of colonial life in Paraguay and, recalled Kessler, 'of the atrocities performed under the Lopez dictatorship, tales that sounded as if recounted by Hudson or Cunningham Grahame [*sic*].' To Kessler's annoyance, she claimed that her nationalism was the result of being an 'expatriate German', though she had left Paraguay more than three decades earlier: 'Painful to hear such nonsense from Nietzsche's sister in the environment of the Nietzsche Archive.' Through the German Consulate in Asunción, and correspondence with chosen protégés, the Ercks, the schoolteachers, and even Fritz Neumann, the son of her former enemy, Elisabeth kept a watchful eye on the colony, her rediscovered 'adopted child'.

The boom brought about by Fritz Neumann's discovery of *yerba* cultivation had been short-lived. He had been too generous with the secret method of germination, and *yerba* plantations began to spring up everywhere, not just in Paraguay but also in Argentina and Bolivia. Still hampered by inadequate communications and isolation, New German *yerba* soon lost its corner of the market and the settlement swiftly lapsed back into economic torpor. In 1929 Elisabeth had received a discouraging report from the German Consulate. Exports of *yerba* had dwindled, and the demand from Argentina was negligible.

Three years earlier, a young, nationalistic German schoolteacher called Cornelie Nürnberg had arrived in the colony, filled with determination to revive the settlement's flagging *geist*, though the school in the colony had been closed for two years. She found the colony in a 'miserable state'. A tiny house of just two rooms served as the school, one of which she slept in. There were, in addition, four benches, one slate, one table, two chairs, some mouldy pictures and a map. To remind themselves of Germany and German culture the original settlers, now considerably outnumbered by their descendants, sang old German folk songs. The children spoke only German and had been brought up strictly under a primitive patriarchal system at home; they were disciplined severely and taught to work for their parents. But they had a clear idea of their German Fatherland, Frauline Nürnburg recounted, 'with which they associated everything that was good, happy and great on earth'. Their greatest joy was to hear their schoolteacher tell stories about Germany, about German life, German schoolchildren, German winter and Christmas. On the rare occasions that the Paraguayan authorities visited the school, she would make the children sing the Paraguayan national anthem. Normally, of course, they sang the German one and flew the Prussian flag on every special occasion.

On her return to Germany in 1928, Cornelie Nürnberg had found Elisabeth keen to use her influence to help the struggling colonists. She persuaded the Foreign Office to pay for another teacher, Alfred Meyer, a fascist in the making, and a man after Elisabeth's heart. In 1930, Fritz Neumann the younger had sent a letter which described the colony as a knot of beleaguered Germans, their German values surviving against all the odds. It was the sort of heroic image so beloved of Elisabeth. 'The colony', he wrote, 'can be very proud that, although it is still so small, it has not disappeared over the last fifty years. While it is a desperate place, the colony can still claim some fame as a centre of true Germanness, even though it is so small.'

The German Consulate reported that under Meyer the school was making good progress; when the schoolteacher wrote to ask for copies of Nietzsche's works ('though I believe the works of your husband might find a larger audience'), Elisabeth promptly complied. If she couldn't build New Germany in person, she would do it by proxy. It was a blow when Meyer wrote again from Argentina to tell Elisabeth that he had decided to leave New Germany. In the harsh, unhealthy conditions at the settlement, his young son had simultaneously contracted malaria, paratyphoid and colic, and Meyer had decided to take up a teaching post in more hospitable climes. He was happy, he said, to 'remain true to the service of foreign Germanness' by teaching in South America, but he yearned 'for Germany, where finally my like-minded compatriots and comrades are in government'. 'I feel most disloyal,' he grovelled to his sharp-tongued patroness, 'but I have the consolation that I have made a foundation on which others can build. . . . I implore you not to be angry. Please understand and write me a few friendly lines to assure me of your understanding and forgiveness.'

In July 1933 Elisabeth wrote again to the German Consulate inquiring about the 'cultural health' of her colony. The reply was not immediately encouraging: some of the settlers were doing reasonably well and 'old Fritz Neumann is living in reasonable circumstances. The younger generation had managed a few profitable *yerba* harvests, but they are all suffering because of falling prices. Obviously no one has saved any money, so they have to struggle to survive and thus their spiritual interests are rather neglected.' Spiritual and cultural interests meant only one thing: the Nazification of Germans living abroad. It was a central tenet of Nazi thinking that the huge numbers of expatriate Germans should be incorporated into the National Socialist fold. The first Nazi Party outside Germany was established in Paraguay and the Hotel del Lago in San Bernadino, where Förster had killed himself half a century earlier, became a centre for Nazi meetings. The Nazis canvassed for support in South America with almost the same energy as in Germany, and with the undisguised backing of the embassies. The German pastor of Asunción, Carlos Richert, under orders from the Evangelical Church in Berlin, travelled the country spreading Nazi propaganda. When he appeared in New Germany, with a portable film projector on which he showed his propaganda films, the settlers were first amazed and then enthusiastic. Elisabeth was delighted when Fritz Neumann reported that the Nazi doctrine had been well received by the colonists. 'It is a great pleasure to hear that the National Socialist Party is strong in the colony,' she wrote. 'One day they will all become National Socialists. Our wonderful Chancellor Adolf Hitler is such a splendid gift from heaven that Germany cannot be grateful enough.'

The historical link between events in Germany and a tiny colony in the middle of the Paraguayan jungle did not go unnoticed by the German authorities: the *Volksbund für das Deutschtum in Ausland* (a sort of Nazi British Council) wrote to Elisabeth with the news that it intended to commemorate the main passion in her husband's life by publishing an article detailing 'the enmity of the Jews that Herr Bernhard Förster exposed'; the grave where he lay buried in San Bernadino was tidied up and fresh flowers planted around it. There was even talk of setting up a memorial to the fallen martyr in the anti-semitic struggle. Elisabeth began to receive letters from people she had never met describing her husband as a national hero. One such arrived just before Christmas 1934, from a Frau Böckel, containing a poem which she said her husband had written back in 1889 about Bernhard Förster. The poem ended, 'May God give the German people many such men.' The Nazi Party plainly agreed. One afternoon in 1934 the German schoolchildren of San Bernadino were rounded up by their teachers and amid much excitement were taken to the cemetery overlooking the lake. A large package had arrived from Germany on Hitler's orders, containing real German soil, something very few of the inhabitants of San Bernadino ever expected to see. Ceremonially it was strewn over Bernhard Förster's grave, while the children sang.

Elisabeth wrote to the Consulate offering to intercede with the new government to alleviate the poverty of New

Germany: 'I want to help the colony. I know Frick, so if there is a problem just let me know.' When it came to it, the colonists were too proud and too patriotic to accept the Reich's handouts. One of the colonists, Martin Schmidt, had become an energetic Nazi and later tried to enlist younger settlers to go and fight for a country they had never seen. He spread the rumour that the Führer would send a submarine to Buenos Aires to fetch them if there was a war. Despite the fact that plunging prices had left the colony almost destitute, Schmidt later wrote on the colony's behalf: 'Because of the Reich's foreign debts,' he said, 'we don't want to add more of a burden by asking for money . . . but from private people we would accept gifts and perhaps books because we want to make our children understand the Germany of today, the Reich of Adolf Hitler and his aims.' Cornelie Nürnberg thought this reflected the pride of the settlers, who were determined to stay whatever the cost; but their refusal to accept money also showed the 'dull inflexibility of their minds, which the idealistic founders must also have had to overcome'.

Elisabeth quickly convinced herself that she enjoyed not only Hitler's admiration and his economic protection, but his friendship as well. She sent him a birthday card and a copy of her new book, *Nietzsche and the Women of His Times*, with a handwritten dedication; when she injured her arm by falling downstairs one day, late in 1933, she sent him a long letter describing the circumstances of the accident and asking him to visit. Hitler obliged, and Elisabeth was embarrassed that with her arm in a sling she was unable to give him the correct Nazi salute. She then sent him a series of letters detailing the progress of her recovery.

While she treated the Führer to the minutiae of her medical condition, she continued to shower praise on Mussolini; when he narrowly escaped assassination she wrote 'in admiration, veneration and with deepest joy at his deliverance'. When her two political idols met on 14 June 1934 in Venice, Elisabeth sent a telegram suggesting that 'the spirit of Nietzsche hovers over this meeting of the two greatest statesmen of Europe'. Mussolini and Hitler were far more concerned with the immediate problem of defusing the political situation in Austria than with the finer (or less fine) points of Nietzschean thought; yet both took the trouble to reply, confirming that, yes indeed, they had sensed the spirit of the great philosopher above them. Hitler later told Elisabeth that as the two leaders sailed down the Lido together they had discussed her and her sterling work in her brother's name. It probably wasn't true, but Elisabeth was deeply flattered. The little bourgeois girl from Naumburg, with the provincial Saxon accent that would not go away (after she gave a radio talk in Weimar, she was complimented on her speaking voice; in fact, an actress had been brought in to cover the embarrassing country tones), was still a praiseworthy subject for the most powerful men in the world. By 1935, her ego was in better shape than it had ever been in all the eighty-nine years it had gradually expanded. Her body, however, was less robust, though she still hurtled around the Archive bullying her staff with scarcely diminished energy.

In June she had to go into an eye clinic in Jena for a cataract operation. As usual, she assumed that the Führer of all Germany, busy as he might be, would nonetheless want to know the details of his friend's health. She wrote:

> In my long time of suffering, waiting impatiently for the return of my sight, I had to keep myself in inactivity which is not part of my nature (and took all my strength) and this strength I found for myself in your wonderful book *Mein Kampf*, which I had, of course, already read years ago, but which now I could study thoroughly as if for the first time. [It was, presumably, read to her.] Those wonderfully and deeply strong perceptions and insights into the new creation of the German character took hold of me, so that I would advise anyone who is an invalid to sink themselves into the individual chapters of this wonderful book and to find there strength and courage to oppose the trials of fate.
>
> With these words of heartfelt thanks, my deeply revered Führer, I sign myself, yours, in deepest respect and admiration, Elisabeth Förster-Nietzsche.

Hitler responded by visiting her again, this time in the company of Albert Speer, the Nazi architect. To mark the official adoption of Nietzsche by the Nazi Party, Hitler had decided, he told Elisabeth, to order the construction of a Nietzsche memorial and auditorium adjoining Villa Silberblick. It was to contain a vast conference hall, with busts of the philosopher and a library for the writings of both brother and sister – an ugly parody of the Nietzsche memorial Kessler, now in exile, had once planned. Hitler diverted RMs 50,000 from his personal fund for the project. Elisabeth, though frail after her operation, was overjoyed; 'one cannot but love this great magnificent man', she wrote of Hitler, 'if one knows him as well as I do'.

Her own Machiavellian talents never alerted her to the same skills in others. Elisabeth believed that she and the Führer thought as one, and she saw genuine respect in the attention lavished on her by the Nazis. That was not the impression gained by others. Speer later recalled: 'We went to Nietzsche's house where his sister Frau Förster-Nietzsche was expecting Hitler. This solitary eccentric woman obviously could not get anywhere with Hitler; an oddly shallow conversation at cross-purposes ensued. The principal purpose of the meeting, however, was settled to the satisfaction of all parties; Hitler undertook to finance an annexe to the old Nietzsche house and Frau Förster-Nietzsche was willing to have Schultze-Naumberg [one of the prime architectural exponents of so-called National Socialist Realism] design it.' She was sad, she told Hitler, that her brother could not share her deep joy at his 'enormous interest in Nietzsche's works'.

At the beginning of November 1935 a bout of flu confined her to her bed, but she continued to dictate letters at her old rate. On the 8th Max Oehler noted that she seemed to have thrown off the infection and had got up. But in the afternoon, she felt a little weak and decided to take a nap. She felt much better, she said, and would take her dinner in bed. The housekeeper, Frau Blankenhahn, brought the meal to her room at 7.00. Elisabeth had tried to get up, but had fallen back on the bed, where she now lay dead, fully clothed.

The Führer, Rosenberg, Frick and Fritz Sauckel, the Gauleiter of Thuringia, were informed immediately. Hitler was in Munich, celebrating the anniversary of the 1923

Putsch; a state memorial service, he said, should be arranged for the 11th, which he would attend. Six hundred death notices were sent from Villa Silberblick, and letters of commiseration poured in: from leading members of the Nazi Party, from Mussolini and, several weeks later, from the colonists of New Germany. As Elisabeth lay in state in the downstairs room of the Archive, surrounded by flowers, the staff frantically arranged the funeral.

By 1.00 on the day itself, a Nazi guard of honour – the SA, the SS, the Hitler Youth – lined the street leading up the hill to Villa Silberblick; behind them crowded the people of Weimar. In the garden of the Villa, SS officers bore wreaths, while the photographers milled around. Every prominent Nazi had been invited to attend, and many did, including Baldur von Schirach, leader of the Hitler Youth, and Winifred Wagner – the Welsh-born wife of Cosima's son Siegfried and a keen Nazi sympathiser. Goebbels had flu, but sent his regrets and a wreath, as did Frick, whom work confined to Berlin. At 3.00 Hitler's car drew up and he inspected the guard of honour before entering the building and taking a seat at the foot of the coffin, flanked by Fritz Sauckel on one side and the President of Thuringia on the other. A Palestrina Mass was played. When the music stopped, the packed room fell silent.

'You could see from the Führer's face', noted Oehler, 'how deeply moved he was. He hardly uttered a word.' It says something for Hitler's acting talents that he could produce crocodile tears for a woman he had needed rather than liked and whose brother's works he had almost certainly never read.

Fritz Sauckel had been chosen to read the funeral oration. He was, perhaps, an appropriate choice. An ex-sailor and factory worker of minimal intellect, Sauckel was distinguished only by his slavish adherence to Nazi doctrine and by his devotion to Hitler. It is probably safe to assume that he could not spell Nietzsche, let alone understand him. (Later he would become Plenipotentiary General for Labour Mobilisation, and an honorary general of the SS. It was Sauckel who was responsible, under Albert Speer, for organising slave labour in the Third Reich, for the transportation of foreigners to Germany and the extermination of Jewish workers in Poland.) On behalf of the government, the party, the whole of National Socialist Germany and the Third Reich, he gave thanks to the deceased, 'the fearless, determined and motivated guardian of a great German genius'. He compared her to the woman she had modelled herself on for fifty years. 'Who has not been struck', he asked, 'by the wonderful character of this woman (and here we think of Bayreuth), who has used her energy in the fight to create a true German master, and who had cemented a friendship with the single-minded Frau Cosima Wagner? Our German people should be eternally happy to praise this noble and magnificent woman in the same breath as the greatest statesmen, heroes, generals and the most powerful creators of culture.' He promised that the Nazis would protect and for ever be grateful to her for the important intellectual legacy she had preserved.

Finally he turned to Hitler. 'You have, *mein Führer*, spoken to us with great respect and admiration of this great German woman, whom eternal providence has gathered to join her incomparable brother the searcher for truth, the prophet of the struggle, the exalted and heroic Friedrich Nietzsche.' Hitler rose and placed his own laurel wreath on the coffin. A special truck had to be used to carry the wreaths and flowers to the graveyard at Röcken, and storm troopers lined the roadside. Above the Nietzsche family graves, the little church was draped with swastikas. A nephew of Bernhard Förster spoke a few words over the coffin.

Nietzsche had been buried next to his father and brother. An exactly matching gravestone had been prepared for Elisabeth, and she had taken the precaution of leaving a space between Nietzsche and her father for herself, a position where the eye was immediately drawn to it. At least one person, who knew her personally and whose mother attended the funeral, believes Elisabeth had to move Nietzsche's gravestone about four feet to the left to make room for herself. If this is so, the stone which supposedly marks Elisabeth's grave actually stands over that of Friedrich Nietzsche.

Elisabeth had not lived to see the Nazis declare war on Europe, finally smashing Nietzsche's ideal of European solidarity, or their glorification of a Reich that Nietzsche wanted to 'sew up in a metal jacket'. She did not see the Nazi programme of mass Jewish extermination, those people whom Nietzsche had lauded as the most robust and useful race on earth. But perhaps she would not have objected. She would certainly have delighted in the monster of Nazi architecture which arose beside the Nietzsche Archive, bearing the inscription 'In memory of Friedrich Nietzsche, built in the 6th year of the Third Reich under the direction of Adolf Hitler.' Officially opened on 3 August 1938, the final memorial consisted of a ninety-metre high central hall (which was never completed) to house the busts of sixteen thinkers and mystics who had influenced Nietzsche's development, a reception room, formal terrace and research institute, as well as a library with glass cases containing a variety of Nietzscheana. One newspaper stated: 'One cannot but feel melancholy and bitterness at the memory of the attempts to stifle the passionate writings of the great upholder of values, Friedrich Nietzsche. The compensation for a terrible wrong is represented by those pictures in the Nietzsche Archive, which show the repeated visits to this house of Adolf Hitler, Führer and best of Germans, as well as a picture of the Duce, Mussolini, which he personally gave to Elisabeth Förster-Nietzsche.' The building is now a radio station.

The Nazis had found it hard to choose the appropriate statue to commemorate the great philosopher; Mussolini finally sent a replica statue of Dionysus, the classical god whom Nietzsche had used as a symbol of his philosophy. Max Oehler, Elisabeth's faithful Nazi henchman, drove to collect it from Weimar station, as British bombers battered the city with explosive in 1943. Two years later, when the Red Army marched into the city, both Max Oehler and the statue disappeared. Dionysus eventually reappeared in a Berlin museum. Max Oehler never did.

Elisabeth had written about Nietzsche's love of Weimar in his last years, even though he was already insane when she first brought him there. 'How he rejoiced every day', she wrote, 'in the beautiful view over Weimar and towards the lights on the Ettersberg hills, always repeating, "This now is Weimar."' It was in those Ettersberg hills, facing the house where Nietzsche died and where Elisabeth resurrected him as a myth, that the Nazis built the concentration camp of Buchenwald.

ON 16 October 1946, four men whom Elisabeth had considered her friends were executed in the gymnasium of Nuremberg jail. They died within half an hour of each other. Alfred Rosenberg, the Nazi intellectual, was the first to hang, which he did defiantly and without a word. When Hans Frank, the butcher of Poland, was led to the gallows he pleaded with his newly discovered Catholic God for mercy. Wilhelm Frick, Elisabeth's protector, the dour, dowdy Nazi bureaucrat, died next, aged sixty-nine. 'Long live eternal Germany,' he said, before he dropped through the trap. Fritz Sauckel, the Gauleiter of Thuringia and organiser of Nazi slave labour, the man who had been chosen by Hitler to read the funeral oration over Elisabeth's coffin, was the last of the four to die. The prosecutor at Nuremberg had called him 'the greatest and cruellest slaver since the Pharaohs of Egypt'. It was rather a grand description for such a pitiful and profoundly dense man. (In IQ tests carried out on the Nuremberg defendants, only two of the leading Nazis were found to be less intelligent than him.) Sauckel was defiant. 'I am dying innocent!', he bellowed from the platform. 'The sentence is wrong. God protect Germany and make Germany great again. Long live Germany!'

The long shadow of Elisabeth Förster-Nietzsche had touched the judicial proceedings at Nuremberg. In the course of the trial, the French prosecutor had stated: 'If it is certain that the higher races should exterminate the people considered subordinate and decadent, the people who are incapable of living as they are supposed to, then which method of extermination will be shied away from?' This was, he said, 'the morality of immorality, the result of Nietzsche's purest teaching, which regards the destruction of any conventional moral as the highest duty of man'.

There were some notable gaps in the ranks of the Nuremberg war criminals. Martin Bormann, the man usually to be found at Hitler's right hand, was tried and sentenced to death *in absentia*. But he was never caught and the sentence was never carried out; it was often rumoured that he had disguised himself as a priest and, like Adolf Eichmann, instrument of the Final Solution, and Josef Mengele, the Auschwitz doctor, had headed for the anonymity of South America.

CHAPTER IX

Nueva Germania, March 1991

I STOOD in the middle of Försterhof, Elisabeth's great mansion, and watched a couple of piglets wrestling across the tiles of what was once her dining room. Nothing was left but some posts of *quebracho* wood which had supported the verandah roof, riddled with termite holes. You could make out the avenue of orange trees she had planted leading to the house, now twisted and overgrown. The mandioca was growing wild where the vegetable patch had been, and the jungle had rioted over her garden, quickly taking over the land painfully cleared by her 'childlike' peons. 'Only the palm trees silhouetted against the red glow of the night sky remind us that we are not in our old dear German home,' she had boasted. The palm trees were still there. 'I never imagined it to be half so magnificent,' she had told her mother. 'Everything is marvellous. Everything looks so professional and grandiose. . . . before falling asleep I lie in bed wondering how we got the money for such a grand enterprise. God must have blessed it. . . . we own a magnificent property, a large house, five small ranchos and three medium-sized ones. We have hundreds of head of cattle, eight horses; we own a store with six thousand Marks' worth of stores; we pay an official administrator, an agricultural administrator, a store-keeper, a land surveyor and an agent who escorts colonists from San Pedro. Besides we employ twenty peons, servants, cooks etc. . . . It is God's blessing on honest work.' Look on my works, ye mighty.

Someone with a long memory has carefully stencilled on to a tin board 'Luisa N. de Forster', and hung it from a post where the muddy track runs down to the river. I doubt if the painter knew what the 'N' stood for.

When Elisabeth had left Paraguay for the last time in 1892, she sold Försterhof to a Baron von Frankenberg-Lüttwitz, and from him it passed to Alfredo Neumann. Alfredo was a bad farmer, and he in turn was forced to sell the house to an Italian–Paraguayan family which came to the colony after the war. It was still the grandest building in the colony, appropriately, since the new owner, Dr Risso, was not only a medical doctor but an important local *caudillo* in the Colorado Party. The family was proud of the heavy old furniture they had bought with the house, Elisabeth's piano and the daunting engraving of an angular German knight which hung on the wall.

Risso had an annoying habit of lecturing the colonists about the benefits of the Colorado Party, and he made few friends. The Germans paid scant attention to the complexities of Paraguayan politics, but when they did they considered themselves Liberales; their Paraguayan workers tended to be Colorados. Not that anyone, except Risso, was too sure of the difference, but politics was something you inherited and were proud of, like the colour of your skin and eyes. Indio Risso, his son, was just eight years old in the Revolution of 1947. The Liberales had already taken San Pedro and were advancing on Nueva Germania, working their way along the river towards the town and shooting anyone who tried to stop them. When they were a few miles away, and you could hear the gunfire down by the Aguarya-guazu, Dr Risso packed his young family into a cart and fled into the forest. The rebels arrived a few hours later and set up their headquarters in Elisabeth's house. It was two weeks before they were driven off by Colorado troops, in a pitched battle through the settlement. When they headed back to San Pedro, they took everything of value – pictures, furniture, crockery; the rest they smashed or burned on a bonfire next to the well. They fired their rifles through the roof, and tried to set fire to the house but the walls were too thick. Somewhere in Paraguay there must be a house with a Dürer engraving on the wall and a gilt-edged Goethean motto, 'Over all obstacles, stand your ground'. Or perhaps the rebels, like Eliza Lynch, just pitched their loot into the river.

Old Risso came back from the forest and patched up the roof. He replaced the glass windows with wooden shutters and climbed down the well to take out the dead animals. The only piece of furniture left intact was Elisabeth's dressing table, which the invading Liberales had moved to an outhouse and then forgotten to take with them. The glass had been smashed, and the sight depressed him, so Dr Risso had left it there, and the chickens laid eggs in the drawers. It is still there.

Rain and heat had seeped into the old house as Indio Risso grew up, and the thatch began to give off a strange smell. Then, a few years ago, the walls began to bulge and one of the beams holding up the roof turned to termite dust. Risso decided to move out and build a new house behind the old one, and the pigs moved in. There was a high wind the very next year, and the verandah collapsed, killing a chicken. Risso took out the sound timbers and used them to build a shed.

THE next day I ate water melon in Tacarutý with toothless, hearty old Magdalena Fischer, under a *yuyra pyta* tree. It had great yellow flowers, like candles, which smelled strong and sweet. She was seventy-four now, but remembered Försterhof well: 'He would say that about the Liberales, Risso would, he's a Colorado. It's the Colorados that did all the killing and raping. People we had known for years, our neighbours, all Paraguayans, just came and took everything.' Magdalena and her young family had also hidden in the forest until the fighting was over. 'All the Germans are Liberales,' she said and rocked back on her chair to look out over the little Tacarutý valley. It seemed rather beautiful suddenly, in the hazy afternoon sun. You could just see the river from here, and the forest behind it. Her nephew was herding the cow home; you could hear him talking to it in German. Elisabeth had told her colonists: 'You will tear yourselves with bleeding hearts from your native soil, from the land which you have loved and which has nourished you. You are certainly not leaving through any thoughtless desire for change, but for a higher faith. Loyalty to the beliefs and customs of your fathers. Come to us, you are warmly welcome; plant your ideals, your steadfastness in this distant beautiful land, which you can rule as your own land, with nothing but God and justice above you.'

Magdalena said she wouldn't go back to Germany now, even if she had the money. The saddest thing, she said, and her pink face fell, was finding the right people for her children to marry. She had wanted them to marry Germans but there weren't enough around. She had to send them to the Mennonite colony downriver to find suitable white partners. The old Alsatian yawned and licked her bare feet. 'The Paraguayans are lazy, they have no idea of how to work or save money. That is the main difference between us. They are a faithless people. Until the Revolution, none of the Germans married Paraguayans but now some are leaving the old ways.' She pointed through the trees to where her brother and sister-in-law and two children had built houses, identical two-roomed huts. 'We are dying out, the pure Germans, but they still call this area *costa* Fischer. At Christmas and weddings, we play German songs and dance the old way.' There was defiance in her voice.

She talked of the war in Europe and how they had closed the German school in Nueva Germania because Hitler had lost. 'Sure, everything was "Heil Hitler",' she giggled suddenly; it was something you did, like supporting the Liberales. It didn't mean much. After the war, some of the men who had gone to fight in Europe came back. Some, like Martin Schmidt and the Neumann lads, never did. And others came too. In the 1950s, a man calling himself Brandt came to the colony selling agricultural equipment. Magda remembered him well. He stayed with her brother-in-law, Robert Fischer. He was a doctor too, and used to travel around the *montes* tending the poor German families; he was very good with the children. But he kept to himself and you didn't inquire too closely. In those years a lot of people came and went. Then, after about 1960, he didn't come any more. They hadn't even heard of Josef Mengele then, so how could they know who he really was? It wasn't until much later that they realised Herr Brandt's real identity. Magdalena Fischer is adamant about that.

Mengele was forty-eight when he applied for and was granted Paraguayan citizenship. He found a welcoming home in Paraguay, where the fascist sympathies which already ran high in parts of the German community were kept alive by an influx of escaping Nazis. Paraguay could boast the first Nazi Party to be formed in South America, in 1932, and the last to be dissolved, in 1946. It was only with reluctance that the Paraguayan government had declared war on Hitler, three months before the Allied victory. 'The Axis powers will know full well what Paraguay's real sentiments are and will take them into account when they finally triumph,' the Paraguayan foreign minister optimistically assured the German community.

Mengele's anti-semitism never dimmed in all his years of exile, nor his belief that through genetic engineering the characteristics of the Aryan race could be maintained. The unspeakable cruelties he had visited on thousands of inmates of Auschwitz had been carried out in the name of racial purity. Perhaps that was what brought him to Nueva Germania, where those ideas of breeding and genetic manipulation had been in action, haphazardly, for a half a century. The war over, *die Spinne*, as the Germans called it, the spider's web of Nazi sympathisers in South America, protected Mengele in Argentina, Paraguay and Brazil, for thirty-three years. Journalists, bounty-hunters and professional Nazi trackers were convinced that Mengele was still in hiding somewhere in Paraguay. The Mengele-hunting industry provided much-needed foreign capital for the country, for the Mengele myth was almost the only thing Europeans could tell you about Paraguay. His powers of escape became legendary; for some he was a symbol of resistance, and the stories multiplied: he was Stroessner's personal physician; he lived surrounded by bodyguards in the Chaco; he used to drive into Asunción in his limousine and bang his revolver on the bar of his favourite club. In fact he was living in a Brazilian backwater, a fractious old neurotic, having left Paraguay some time in the early 1960s. He died in a swimming accident in 1979 and in 1985 his body was exhumed and positively identified by an international team of experts. That ended the myth, briefly; most of the Nazi-hunters went home, or elsewhere, but a few stayed on because they didn't know how to do anything else. Then, in 1991, one of those experts said that the body dug up from Embu graveyard in São Paulo might not have been Mengele's. The evidence was, he said, inconclusive. And the myth began again.

In Nueva Germania, Hermann Stern owns a shop which sells *yerba* and machine parts. This is his story: 'In 1979 a man called Friedrich Ilg came to the colony. He was about seventy years old with grey hair and one of his front teeth was missing. He said he had been a Luftwaffe pilot. He was very Nazi and was always saying that Hitler had been misunderstood. He talked about Josef Mengele and he said that Mengele was just doing his job. We became friends. I would travel to Asunción now and then for supplies, and I would pick up money for Ilg sent from Germany to a bank in Asunción. He had bought himself a little plot and he worked hard on it. But he was depressed here, a very nervous man. I was the only one he talked to. He never seemed to sleep – even at three or four in the morning you could see a candle burning in his hut. He had hundreds of medical books which he read all the time. In return for collecting the money he gave me a Polaroid camera, but he would never let me take a photograph of him. But I took one anyway.'

Hermann handed over a faded snapshot, blurred and indistinct, of an old white-haired man, twisting his head away, trying to get out of the shot. 'Things started to go wrong when I sold Ilg some machinery. He accused me of charging too much for it and refused to pay. He got angrier and angrier, then one day he appeared at my house with a pistol and called me a Jew and threatened to kill me. He said Stern was a Jewish surname.' Hermann was surprised. No one had called him a Jew before and, frankly, he wasn't exactly sure what a Jew was because he had never met one. Hermann's grandfather had been just seventeen when he joined Bernhard Förster on the steamer in Hamburg. He was a carpenter from Frankfurt, that was all Hermann knew for sure. Grandfather Stern had trapped parrots in the forest which he trained to speak and then sent back downriver to be sold in Germany. He kept hundreds of them in cages behind his house. When Hermann's father was about fifteen, old Stern had decided to go gold-prospecting in the forest. Some said he had found the lost treasure of President Lopez. He returned about three months later, looking worn and frightened; a week after that he left again and never came back. The other Germans thought he must have caught yellow fever or fallen in a river or died of snakebite. But the older ones said he had found the lost gold, and his Paraguayan peons had killed him for it. He hadn't said anything about being Jewish. 'There is a saying here in Paraguay, "*un negocio buen judeo*", a right Jewish shopkeeper, so maybe I am Jewish,' Hermann laughed. 'The pastor thinks that my grandfather slipped on to the boat without telling Förster he was Jewish.' Hermann keeps a picture of Bernhard Förster on his wall.

Friedrich Ilg was convinced that Stern, the Jewish shopkeeper, was persecuting him. He became angrier and more depressed. 'After that he was completely *loco.* He would run up the road without any clothes on waving his pistol and shouting "Heil Hitler!" and "Who is Friedrich Ilg?" Some Germans took him to the lunatic asylum in Asunción, and soon after that one of them came back saying he was a friend of Ilg's. He took away all his books and other bits and pieces, and nailed planks across the door.' In July 1985, Ilg killed himself. 'He threw himself under a bus, the number 30, outside the Victoria cinema in Asunción. There was an article on the front page of the newspaper the day after it happened, and then nothing else, not a word. I thought that was strange at the time.'

It wasn't until a year later that Hermann saw an early photograph of Josef Mengele in a newspaper article about the exhumation of a body thought to be that of the Auschwitz doctor. Stern recognised his erstwhile neighbour and began to do his own investigations. The German Embassy had no record of a Friedrich Ilg entering the country, but that wasn't so surprising, since thousands of Germans had slipped into the country under false names. 'This Ilg used to hold his knife in a particular way when he ate, like a pencil. They say Mengele used to eat that way too.' The corpse dug up in Brazil had been buried in 1979, the year Friedrich Ilg arrived in Nueva Germania. If that body was not Mengele's, might he not have taken refuge back in Paraguay having carefully faked his own death? After years of fruitless searching, he might reasonably have thought that Paraguay was the last place the bounty-hunters or Mossad would now look. Hermann showed me the tumbledown hut, two rooms and a hearth, where he said Mengele had lived for six years. It smelled of decay; I hoped Mengele *had* gone mad in such a place. 'That man was Mengele, I know it,' said Hermann Stern.

'Ilg was a Nazi all right,' said Magdalena Fischer, 'but he wasn't Mengele. Mengele was shorter than that, and he had a gap between his teeth. He came here in 1959 or 1960. He was rather strange. Whenever you gave him a meal he would put some in his pocket *for later*.'

'That old Doctor Risso, he was Mengele,' said someone else.

'Oh yes, he was here,' said Gonzalez at the municipality, 'he looked after the Germans in the *montes*.'

Everyone had their own Mengele story. They wanted him to have been here. No one ever talked about what he had done. Perhaps no one knew.

One evening a little German boy ran into Gregoria's bar, sent by his mother, Frau Küke, to tell me that my country was at war. By climbing on top of the chicken coop, I found I could pick up the BBC World Service on my short-wave radio. Above the sound of the cicadas and the whistling interference, I could just hear the translation of Saddam Hussein's latest speech: the anti-semitic rhetoric sounded familiar, and the Scud missiles had, it seems, been landing in Tel Aviv for over a month.

I had been in Nueva Germania too long. A month of Gregoria's weighty cooking, of mandioca with every meal, of night raids by mosquitos and heat that made the blood thunder in your head. It had rained only twice; violent electrical storms had exploded overhead, bringing down sheets of water so heavy that the chickens had come running for cover in my bedroom. Avalo said there was usually much more rain, and he worried for his crops. Gregoria said it was the ozone layer. In the heat of the day, ever concerned, she would periodically stagger with another bucket of water, in which the larvae wriggled, over to where I lay panting under her orange tree. I would trickle it deliciously over my head and down my back. It was tepid, but felt momentarily freezing. My gums had begun to turn a delicate ochre, and every morning involved a minute search for evidence of *polverino* bugs, whose eggs, a faint rash of yellow under the skin, I would daub with disinfectant. The mosquito net seemed to make no difference; putting on the insect repellent at night meant peeling the coarse pillow from my face in the morning. Gregoria produced some forest herbs to go with my *yerba maté*, which I had taken to again. She said it would ease the stomach cramps.

Most days I would wake at first light and trek off in the cool dawn to a different part of the colony, a different family of Germans, as I tried to piece together their history. In accordance with Förster's original directions, the houses were widely dispersed, at least a mile between each tiny settlement, and I spent much of the day on horseback. Seven or eight of the original fourteen families which had accompanied Elisabeth and Bernhard Förster were still here, I calculated, mostly in Tacarutý. I carried with me a photocopy of Elisabeth's list of colonists, in her angular handwriting: Fischer, Schubert, Stern, Schütte, Halke, Küke, Hähner, Schweikhart. There was no trace of the aristocratic Maltzans, who must have left soon after Elisabeth, nor of the Ercks.

They were a strange people, these remnants of Elisabeth's racial experiment, hospitable but distant. Initial uncertainty usually turned to wary acceptance, although some became tight-lipped and strained when I asked too many questions. One hot afternoon I went to the Schweikhart hut, deep in the forest. The Schweikhart brothers were gaunt-looking men who had not looked up when I had greeted them on the track a few days before. 'Their accent is so strong, even I don't understand a word they say,' Dr Schubert had warned me. I had called out at the door, but there was no answer; a fire was burning with some meat stew over it and a battered Lutheran Bible lay open on the table, but the room when I entered was empty. The brothers must have seen me coming and had vanished. I could hear someone moving in a back room behind a tattered curtain: old Frau Schweikhart, another Fischer before her marriage. 'She is very old, very ill, very sad.' Dr Schubert had said. 'I doubt she will talk to you.' I didn't want to draw the curtain, and slipped away again.

Usually it was the older people who wanted to talk, who stared most avidly at my garish postcards of Berlin and wrestled with their memories to recall what their parents and grandparents had told them. I played them my tapes of Wagner and they smiled, but it meant nothing. I listened in their musty adobe huts while they told me about a Germany I couldn't recognise and they had never seen; a few proudly showed me tattered passports. They talked of the economic crisis which had driven their ancestors from Europe as if it had happened last year. They had been promised a paradise, they said, where you didn't have to pay for your hunting and the food grew on trees and the river teemed with edible fish. Förster they remembered as an arrogant man; their grandfathers had been ready to beat him up for swindling them, they said, but he had killed himself first. But of Elisabeth the memories were always kinder: 'A brave woman,' they said, 'and beautiful.' Her charm was horribly enduring.

You could easily miss their little houses, the walls as red as the earth, thatched with greying rushes, tucked away on the forest's edge along narrow tracks. They remained what their ancestors had been, nineteenth-century German peasants, even poorer now than they had been then. In a hundred years they had made little impact on the countryside. Their fields were neat, but pitifully small; you could almost sense the forest biding its time. These were the 'spiritual heirs of Richard Wagner', clinging to their language and religion like a raft which was sinking under them. The young were drifting away, they said. Some of the youngsters didn't even care about the German language any more, preferring to speak Guaraní. The pastor, a young energetic German with piercing eyes, sent by the Evangelical Church, said it was their religion that had kept the community together for so long. 'God gave them the strength.'

But it was something else too. Often, after some beer from Gregoria's bar, they spoke loftily of the Paraguayans; a stupid people, they said, lazy and feckless. A few migrant Paraguayans came to Tacarutý at harvest time, but they didn't live there. None of the Germans could afford to employ Paraguayan workers all the time; 'and anyway', said Heini Schütte, 'you can't trust them.' The old ones of Tacarutý, as the pastor called them, held tight to a belief that they were, in some way they couldn't describe, not just different, but chosen, holier. A querulous little vein of anger sometimes ran through their voices when they talked of their dark-skinned neighbours. It was racism of a sort, not the political racism that had motivated the founders, but something more visceral. In the absence of any Jews, anti-semitism had quickly withered, as had the other motivating principles of Elisabeth's colony; but their residue could be felt in a few fossilised and now quite meaningless ideals. 'We eat vegetables,' Magda told me proudly, 'but the Paraguayans only eat meat.' She couldn't remember why.

Much later I found the headstone over Bernhard Förster's grave in San Bernadino, partly overgrown and beginning to crumble, in a cemetery overhung with Spanish moss. Weeds were growing in the soil Hitler had sent from Germany, and a cracked vase held some dead flowers. The cemetery keeper, old Max Hermann, said people still came to visit it sometimes, to lay flowers. Förster had never doubted that his ideas were right or that his suicide was honourable. 'Here lies with God', reads the headstone, 'Bernhard Förster, founder of the colony Nueva Germania'. Förster died full of anger, but without shame. 'He clings firmly out of defiance to a cause which he has seen through – but he calls it "loyalty",' said Förster's brother-in-law, of man in general. But he also said, 'An anti-semite is not made more decent because he lies on principle.' Like Förster, Elisabeth never questioned herself or her opinions, nor acknowledged the forgeries she had carried out or the lies she had told. Even Mengele, in the last solitary years of his life, denied that he had ever hurt anybody. He told his son that, when he had stood at the Auschwitz railhead, deciding which Jews should live, which should die and which should be used for his obscene experiments, he had actually been saving lives. He may even have convinced himself of his innocence. Nietzsche described a familiar process. '"I have done that," says my memory. "I cannot have done that" – says my pride, and remains adamant. At last – memory yields,' since 'the hypocrite who always plays one and the same role finally ceases to be a hypocrite. . . . if one obstinately and for a long time wants to *appear* something it is in the end hard for him to *be* anything else.' And I remembered another grave, one I had seen in Asunción: the mausoleum where the remains of Madame Eliza Lynch, transported back from Paris in 1964 by President Stroessner, had been laid amid pomp and false praise. A statue on top of her tomb depicts Eliza, spade in hand, having just buried her lover, the dictator, on a riverbank; a plaque pays tribute to a woman who 'with self-sacrifice supported the greatest hero of Paraguay, Francisco Solano Lopez, until Cerro Corá'. From the ferocious look in her marble face, you can tell that she too was untroubled by conscience.

IN Independencia, a more recent German colony not far from Asunción, I met Rolf Richter. On his wall hung pictures of Hitler, Adenauer and a tiny print of Goethe in a field of daisies. A pigeon-chested seventy-year-old, Richter had fought first on the Russian Front, and had been injured and finally captured by American forces at Nancy. He had joined the Foreign Legion after his release. Full of anger at his wartime treatment and humiliated by life in post-war Germany he came to Paraguay in 1953 on a boat from Amsterdam, the *Cordoba*. Richter hated that ship – it was just like the one that had taken him away as a prisoner from France. An amateur photographer, his curling snaps show the war of a 'loyal' believer.

'You see this one,' he said. 'It was in Warsaw. This sign says "No Jews on the sidewalk". These are Polish Jewish girls, walking on the sidewalk just before they pushed me off. They were trying to provoke me.' He feels vindicated by that photograph. These days he farms a little, but mostly he collects pornography and foreign magazines, out of which he cuts evidence of the Jewish conspiracy. He has assembled his clippings in scrap books, neatly filed on wooden bookshelves, now so numerous they covered the wall of his hut. 'I can show you all sorts of things, but you probably don't want to see. People can't bear the truth.' Nietzsche had thought the same, I said, had he read any of his books? 'Nietzsche was a great philosopher,' he replied, 'except about religion, he didn't understand that. Otherwise he was very good.' Richter showed me a poem he had written and framed, a poem to tell me how uninterested he was in changing his beliefs:

> YOU should feel comfortable here
> I am not wretched in my house, 'the house of all things',
> only the master.
> YOU are political –
> I too.
> YOU have another opinion.
> I respect it.
> YOU may express it – but not on my toes.
> I thank you

I had thought I would find men like Richter in Nueva Germania, but I did not. He hated on account of his race, where they merely feared for it.

In my last few days in the settlement, I often found myself at the house of Pablo Flascam, grandson of one of the first settlers, Emil Schubert, a musician. The Flascams always received me kindly, squeezing out some fresh grapefruit juice and talking for hours; sometimes Walter played the Mennonite Waltz on his squeeze box. But each visit was painful. Frau Flascam's eyes were always red with crying, and her husband carried a revolver in a holster even when he was drinking. A few weeks before, four masked men had come to the house at dusk and killed their twenty-three-year-old son. They had shot him repeatedly in the head. 'Paraguayans, I'm sure of it,' said Pablo, 'banditos, drug smugglers or something like that.' He looked very tired. 'I have told the police, but they will do nothing, they are Paraguayans too. It was better under Stroessner. He was German, and he looked after the Germans.' Gonzalez at the municipality shrugged. 'Maybe the boy saw them planting marijuana in the forest. What can we do?' I thought of Ector's death. The bandits and the river and the hookworm don't discriminate between races. But it wasn't the bandits who threatened their ideals and their community, it was the unanticipated biological legacy of those ideals.

Dr Schubert took me around his garden, where he grew every kind of vegetable. 'If you treat the plants right, you can grow anything here,' he said, pointing to some out-of-place aubergines. 'It's a mystery to me why the first settlers had such problems. But you have to tend them constantly. If you leave them the jungle quickly overruns everything. It's the same with people. The Germans are caught in a trap. They know they cannot go back to a country they would never understand, but they are determined to maintain their cultural independence. They are inbred, and it is getting worse. You can already see the effects. I try to tell them. I say, "Look at the way you breed animals," and they nod and carry on as before. They can't help it.' Child mortality was increasing, he said, a number of the younger people had severe mental as well as physical problems, and there were clear patterns of hereditary disability. The pastor was now refusing to marry couples who were related, but the German families were now so biologically enmeshed you couldn't tell who was related to whom. It was most noticeable in the youngest children. A slack, bespittled jaw here, there a drooping eye. A few were obviously retarded, but most were just slow, the gears of heredity grinding, as cousin married cousin, as the handful of old, 'pure' German families lived off their dwindling genetic capital.

The text books are firm: 'Fairly recent isolation of a small section of a population with consequent inbreeding, such as can occur when a group emigrates to a country with different social and religious customs, will result in a higher incidence of recessive genetic disease than in the original parent population.' The fourteen peasant families who travelled on the steamer *Uruguay* held in their genetic makeup, as do all of us, a number of deleterious genes. 'Such genes are usually recessive. Under a system of random mating such as exists in most civilised countries, the accident of marriage sometimes brings such recessive genes together, which will then express themselves to some degree in the offspring issuing from such a union.' In the case of marriage between cousins, the likelihood of both partners being heterozygotes, carrying one copy of the recessive gene inherited from mutual grandparents, and thus of an accident occurring, is obviously far higher; first cousins carry one-eighth of their genes in common. With every generation that intermarries, the likelihood of a manifestation of deleterious genes grows.

Take albinism, the congenital lack of pigmentation which results in abnormally white skin and red eyes. Roughly speaking, one person in fifty is heterozygous for this condition (that is they carry, but do not manifest, the recessive gene associated with albinism); so the chances of marrying someone with a similar gene at random is 1/50 × 1/50 = 1/2500. The expectation among offspring is one in four, so the frequency of albinos in the population is 1/10,000. (Actually it is rather less frequent than that.) The mathematics for cousins is very different. If an individual marries a cousin, his chance of being heterozygous for albinism is 1/50, but the chance of her *also* being heterozygous is 1/8, thus 1/50 × 1/8 = 1/400, more than six times more likely. If an albino marries a cousin, there is a 1/4 chance that she carries the recessive gene for albinism, and that they will have equal numbers of albinos and children carrying the recessive gene. If two albinos have children and are related, they will have albino children. Among the San Blaz Indians of Peru, albinos are not permitted to marry.

Dr Schubert said there were no albinos in Nueva Germania, yet.

The idea of breeding human beings is an old one; Plato suggested the breeding of a race, by controlling human variability. Elisabeth and Bernhard Förster's attempt to create a pure-blooded German colony was unscientific in the extreme, but it carried at its centre the fiction of all racism – that racial traits can be characterised as 'better' and 'worse', and that the 'valuable' traits can be preserved by breeding. They could not know it, but preserving 'valued' traits could work only if they could have plotted the genetic inheritance of each individual, for otherwise how could they know which harmful traits were being bred along with the ones they valued?

In 1839 Charles Darwin, the 'father of evolution', married

his first cousin, Emma Wedgwood – both were of impeccable intellectual and social pedigree. They had ten children: some of Darwin's children were people of marked scientific ability, and three were members of the Royal Society; but most were also sickly and delicate, three died as infants, and the last child, Charles Waring Darwin, was mentally deficient and died aged two without ever learning to walk or talk.

Was this the end of Elisabeth Nietzsche's pure Aryan colony, a tribe becoming more blonde and blue-eyed with every generation, but simultaneously degenerating? In the four or five generations since the first colonists had arrived, the families had so interbred that they had even begun to look the same; perhaps that was because so many of the founders had come from the same part of Germany, or was the effect of the environment and nutrition; one physical type, tall, with high cheekbones, blue eyes and fair hair, seemed gradually to be predominating, just as the Saxon accent brought by the majority of the original settlers had subsumed other local German dialects.

If you take two mice and breed them, and then inbreed their offspring, and then their offspring, within twenty generations you create clones, mice that are genetically identical, the same mouse. 'You can't explain it to the people here,' said Dr Schubert. 'It's partly that they don't understand, but also they don't want to understand. They need to preserve their separateness to maintain their pride; without that what would they have? But if they do not change their ways, who knows what will happen to them?' The identical mice at the twentieth generation are sterile mutants.

For the older inhabitants, it was only by defending a dividing line between thee and me, brown and white, chalk and cheese, that they could preserve their sense of moral worth. For, after all, what else is morality than a codification of what is good for oneself, or so Nietzsche thought:

> Zarathustra has seen many lands and many peoples: thus he has discovered the good and evil of many peoples. Zarathustra has found no greater power on earth than good and evil.

> No people could live without evaluating: but if it wishes to maintain itself it must not evaluate as its neighbour evaluates.
>
> Much that seemed good to one people seemed shame and disgrace to another: thus I found. I found much that was called evil in one place was in another decked with purple honours.
>
> One neighbour never understood another: his soul was always amazed at his neighbour's madness and wickedness.

It was the older Germans in Nueva Germania who still felt they could not live without evaluating their Paraguayan neighbours. The younger ones found it easier to overcome racial *Ressentiment* (Nietzsche sometimes called it passion) and mixed easily with the Paraguayans. Nietzsche believed that 'The man who has overcome his passions has entered into possession of the most fertile ground; like the colonist who has mastered the forest and swamps . . . the overcoming itself is only a means and not a goal.'

'The older generation don't like it,' said Dr Schubert, 'but thank God there is nothing they can do. Look at Jorge Halke – he is the future.' Jorge was a tall, fit youth of about twenty-five, partly descended from one of Förster's henchmen, partly of Paraguayan origin, with blue eyes and brown skin. He lived in the only house still standing from Elisabeth's time, an incongruous, square structure with stone pillars and a wide verandah, on the edge of the Stadtplatz, the patch of field in mid-village. Jorge had a taste for catching anacondas, which he kept in a wooden crate behind the house. He said he had a good idea where we could find Eliza's treasure. Before setting off we sat down on his verandah to eat, and I asked him which race he felt most like: German, Spanish or Indian. 'I have forgotten,' he said, laughing and peeling another *guabirá* fruit.

Notes

QUOTATIONS from Nietzsche are from the works translated by R. J. Hollingdale and published by Viking Penguin (marked by *), or from his *A Nietzsche Reader*, London 1977. Any translation not otherwise credited is my own.

Human All Too Human, first published 1878. Second edition 1886.

Assorted Opinions and Maxims, first published as first supplement to *Human All Too Human*, 1879.

The Wanderer and his Shadow, first published as second supplement to *Human All Too Human*, 1880.

Daybreak, first published 1881. Second edition 1886.

The Gay Science, first published 1882. Expanded edition 1887.

**Thus Spoke Zarathustra*, London, 1961: first published 1883–92.

**Beyond Good and Evil*, London, 1973: first published 1886.

Towards a Genealogy of Morals, first published 1887.

The Case of Wagner: a musician's problem, first published 1888.

**Ecce Homo*, London, 1979: written in 1888, first published 1908.

**Twilight of the Idols* and *The Anti-Christ*, London, 1990 edn: first published 1889 and 1895.

The Will to Power, first published 1901.

The main sources for the history of Neuva Germania are Bernhard Förster and Elisabeth Förster-Nietzsche:

ELISABETH FÖRSTER-NIETZSCHE
Dr Bernhard Förster's Kolonie Neu-Germania in Paraguay, Berlin, 1891.

Das Leben Friedrich Nietzsche, volume 1, 1895; volume 2 part one 1897; volume 2 part two, 1904 (all Leipzig). Shortened and updated versions *Der Junge Nietzsche*, Leipzig, 1912, translated as *The Young Nietzsche*, A. M. Ludovici, London, 1912, and *Der Einsame Nietzsche*, Leipzig, 1914, translated as *The Lonely Nietzsche*, Paul V. Cohn, London, 1915. Reference is to the translated version.

BERNHARD FÖRSTER
Deutsche Colonien in dem oberen Laplata Gebiete mit besonderer Berücksichtigung von Paraguay, Naumberg, 1886. [*German Colonisation in the Upper La Plata District with Particular Reference to Paraguay: The Results of Detailed Practical Experience, Work and Travel 1883–1885*]

Das Verhältniss des modernen Judenthums zur deutschen Kunst, Berlin, 1881. [*The relationship between modern Jewry and German art*]

The principal secondary sources are:

Ronald Hayman, *Nietzsche: A Critical Life*, London, 1980.

R. J. Hollingdale, *Nietzsche: The Man and His Philosophy*, Baton Rouge and London, 1965.

S. L. Gilman and D. J. Parent, *Conversations with Nietzsche*, New York and Oxford, 1987.

Walter Kaufmann, *Nietzsche: Philosopher, Psychologist, Antichrist*, Princeton, 1950, fourth edition 1974.

H. F. Peters, *Zarathustra's Sister*, New York, 1974.

E. F. Podach, *Gestalten um Nietzsche*, Weimar, 1932.

J. P. Stern, Nietzsche, London, 1978.

Reference in the Notes to these texts is in the form of the author's surname and the year of first publication; thus 'Nietzsche, 1886, 26'.

FOREWORD

'one has . . .' Nietzsche, 1886, p. 42–3

'Footfalls echo . . .' T. S. Eliot, *Four Quartets,* 'Burnt Norton', 1

CHAPTER I: ASUNCIÓN DOCKS , PARAGUAY

'Others will follow,' Podach, 1932, p. 145

'wasting away in . . .' ibid., p. 152

'despite the many difficulties . . .' Förster, 1886, p. 221

CHAPTER II: TERRA INCOGNITA

Morgenstern (or Morgenstein) de Wisner (variously Colonel Enrique, Francois Enri, and Francisco), was born in 1800; the date of his death is unknown. This sketch of his life and my account of nineteenth-century Paraguay derives from the following sources: H. G. Warren, *Paraguay. An Informal History* (Oklahoma, 1949) and *Paraguay and the War of the Triple Alliance* (Texas, 1978); Alyn Brodsky, *Madame Lynch and Friend: The true account of an Irish Adventuress and the dictator of Paraguay who destroyed that South American Nation* (New York, 1975); C. J. Kolinski, *Independence or Death! The Story of the Paraguayan War* (Florida, 1965) and *Historical Dictionary of Paraguay. Latin American Historical dictionaries No. 8* (New Jersey, 1973); *The Times*, 25 August 1871; Alfredo Sieferheld, *Los Judeos en el Paraguay* (Asunción, 1981); H. Morgenstern de Wisner, *Collected documents of José Gaspar*

Rodriguez de Francia (Argentina, 1923); T. J. Page, *La Plata, The Argentine Federation and Paraguay. Being the narrative of the exploration of the tributaries of the River La Plata and adjacent countries during the years 1853, '54, '55 and '56* (London, 1859). R. Andrew Nickson, *Paraguay*, vol. 84 in the world bibliographical series (Oxford, 1987), is a detailed bibliographical guide to the country.

The account of Elisabeth's arrival in Asunción is derived from the oral histories of inhabitants of Nueva Germania, Elisabeth's own descriptions and contemporary records of the city (see below).

R. B. Cunninghame Graham's life is described in H. F. West's biography, *A Modern Conquistador. Robert Bontine Cunninghame Graham: his life and works* (London, 1932). The best of his own books are *The Ipané* (London, 1899), *Mogreb al Acksa; Journey in Morrocco* (London, 1898), *A Vanished Arcadia* (London, 1901), *The Conquest of the River Plate* (London, 1924) and *Portrait of a Dictator* (London, 1933).

'my way of thinking . . .' Nietzsche, 1882/7, 32

'Whatever the type . . .' *Jungle Survival*, PAM (AIR) 214, Crown Copyright 1984, p. 7

'Report on the State of Paraguay . . .' Col. H. von Morgenstern de Wisner, *The Times*, 25 August 1871

'Several small boats . . .' *Sudamericanische Coloniale Nachrichten*, October 1888

'the odd luxury . . .' Förster, 1886, p. 220

'The next worst bug . . .' ibid., p. 62

'Excellent diagrams . . .' *Dictionary of Scientific Biography*, ed. Charles Coulton Gillispie (New York, 1970), vol. II, p. 127

'My first worry . . .' Förster, 1886, p. 139–145

'While every noble morality . . .' Nietzsche, 1887, 'Good and Bad' 5

'Whoever believed . . .' Nietzsche, 1908, 'Why I Write Such Excellent Books', I 'to *want* to remain a riddle . . .' Nietzsche, 1886, 6

'a shrunken . . .' ibid., 61–2

'the contemptible sort . . .' Nietzsche, 1889, 'Expeditions of an Untimely Man', 38

'a great service . . .' Nietzsche, 1879, 58

'Overcome, you higher men . . .' Nietzsche, 1883–92, IV 'Of the Higher Man', 3

'We would not let . . .' Nietzsche, 1880, 333

'he never fell into the error . . .' Oscar Wilde, *The Picture of Dorian Gray* (London, 1891), chapter 11

'Remain true . . .' Nietzsche, 1883, quoted in H. F. West, op. cit., p. vi

'A drive and impulse . . .' Nietzsche, 1878 (1886 edn.), Preface 3–6

'His getting into prison . . .' George Bernard Shaw, *Three Plays for Puritans*, quoted in H. F. West, op. cit., p. 77

'I care not . . .' Cunninghame Graham, 1901, p. 211

'when I think . . .' ibid., p. xviii

'I have no theory . . .' quoted in H. F. West, op. cit., p. 126

'The main things . . .' Förster, 1886, p. 220

'To make plans . . .' Nietzsche, 1879, No. 85.

CHAPTER III: UP THE CREEK

My main source on the life of Eliza Alicia Lynch is Alyn Brodsky's admirable *Madame Lynch and Friend* (New York, 1975). In addition to sources cited above, material is derived from William E. Barrett, *Woman on Horseback. The biography of Fransisco Lopez and Eliza Lynch* (London and New York, 1938), and Gordon Meyer, *The River and its People* (London, 1965). Information on the nature and origins of Guaraní myths is primarily taken from H. G. Warren, *Paraguay. An Informal History* (Oklahoma, 1949).

'Would as soon . . .' quoted in Alyn Brodsky, op. cit., p. 182

'It is somewhat . . .' G. F. Masterman, *Seven Eventful Years in Paraguay. A narrative of personal experience among the Paraguayans,* (London, 1869), p. 51

'The Paraguayan women . . .' Cunninghame Graham, 1933, p. 89

'everything great, fruitful and noble . . .' Arthur, Comte de Gobineau, 'Essay on the Inequality of Human Races', quoted in the 1991 Reith Lectures by Dr Steven Jones

'the whole history of nations . . .' Ernst Haeckel, quoted in Richard Milner, *The Encyclopedia of Evolution* (Oxford and New York, 1988), p. 312

'I sat on the ground . . .' From the sworn deposition of Alonso Taylor, quoted in C. A. Washburn, *The History of Paraguay. With notes of personal observations, and reminiscences of diplomacy under difficulties* (Boston, Mass., 1871), vol. II, p. 510

'It was a sad sight . . .' ibid., vol. II, ch. VII, p. 94

'he who wants to live on . . .' Nietzsche, 1879, 307

'Her eyes were of a blue . . .' quoted in William Barrett, op. cit., p. 333

'Sadism . . .' Cunninghame Graham, 1933, p. 241

'gross animal look . . .' C. A. Washburn, op. cit., vol. II, p. 48

'Even the meanest . . .' Nietzsche, 1879, 95

'quite too busy . . .' Alyn Brodsky, op. cit., p. 60

'J'espere . . .' ibid., p. 59

'The colour . . .' Captain Richard Burton, *Letters from the Battlefields of Paraguay* (London, 1870), p. 138

'As a steamer slips . . .' Cunninghame Graham, 1901, p. 39

'A large round fish . . .' Förster, 1886, p. 61

'A long tail . . .' ibid., p. 61

'. . . they flee . . .' ibid., p. 60

'with marvellous . . .' H. G. Warren, op. cit., p. 9

'a hoggish appearing . . .' ibid., p. 9

'in order to find Indians . . .' Father Ruiz de Montoya, *Conquista Espiritual del Paraguay*, introductory chapter

'carelessly washing . . .' ibid., quoted in H. G. Warren, op. cit., p. 10

'a white, long-haired animal . . .' A. K. Macdonald, *Paraguay: Its People, Customs and Commerce* (London, 1911), p. 479

'an amphibious animal . . .' Father Ruiz de Montoya, in H. G. Warren, op. cit.

'Sipping the infusion . . .' G. F. Masterman, op. cit., p. 51–2

'if the ceremony . . .' W. H. Koebel, *Paraguay* (London, 1917), p. 286

'the effects of *yerba maté* . . .' Förster, 1886, p. 50

'the one god . . .' Nietzsche, 1882/7, 143

'The population is Christian . . .' Förster, 1886, p. 80

'that the sounds . . .' Father Martin Dobrizhoffer, *History of the Abipones, an Equestrian people of Paraguay* (Vienna, 1784; English translation London, 1822). Quoted in Cunninghame Graham, 1901, p. 25

'Sleep was out of the question . . .' Sir Christopher Gibson, *Enchanted Trails* (London, 1948), p. 61

'the organ of fear . . .' Nietzsche, 1881, 250

CHAPTER IV: THE WHITE LADY AND NEW GERMANY

'in the blood . . .' Cunninghame Graham, 1933, p. 118

'That Lopez . . .' ibid., p. 239

'She could drink more . . .' Masterman, op. cit., p. 42

'he would indulge . . .' C. A. Washburn, op. cit., quoted in Cunninghame Graham, 1933, p. 243

'I know not . . .' Förster, 1886, p. 70

'I'm also convinced the trail . . .' Jim Woodman, *The Ancient Inscriptions of Paraguay*, Epigraphic Society of South America, (Asunción, 1989) Section IV.

'A tame tiger cat . . .' Wilfred Barbrooke Grubb, *An Unknown People in an Unknown Land. An account of the life and customs of the Lengua Indians of the Paraguayan Chaco, with adventures and experiences met with during twenty years pioneering and exploration amongst them* (London, 1911), p. 267

'That attitude was briefly . . .' ibid., p. 27

'They had . . .' R. P. François-Xavier de Charlevoix, *Histoire de Paraguay* (Paris, 1756; London, 1769), liv. IV. p. 183, quoted in Cunninghame Graham, 1933, p. 6

'The men and women . . .' Hulderilke Schnirdel (variously Schmidel and Schmidt), *Historia y Descubrimiento de el Rio de la Plata y Paraguay*, contained in the collection made by Andres Barcia, *Historiadores Primitivos de las Indias Occidentales*, Madrid, 1749. This translation from *The Faber book of Reportage*, ed. John Carey (London, 1987)

'they eat the flesh . . .' *Commentariós de Alvar Nuñez Cabeza de Vaca*, contained in Barcia, op. cit., quoted in H. G. Warren, p. 27

'a community . . .' Father Martin Dobrizhoffer, op. cit., quoted in Cunninghame Graham, 1901, p. 229–30

'for youthful, vigorous barbarians . . .' Nietzsche, 1879, 95

'They died like plants . . .' Padre del Techo, *History of Paraguay*, quoted in Cunninghame Graham, 1901, p. 234

'which was in former times . . .' Nietzsche, 1881, 204

'The principal characteristics . . .' Förster, 1886, p. 73–4

'a harmless race . . .' Elisabeth Förster-Nietzsche, 'A Sunday in Nueva Germania', *Bayreuther Blätter*, vol. IX, 1889, p. 285, Peters, 1974, p. 103

'Throughout Paraguay . . .' Förster, 1886, p. 169

'for it heats the blood . . .' Förster-Nietzsche, 1891, p. 41

'No one who . . .' Förster, 1886, p. 61

'The snakes are dangerous . . .' ibid., p. 60

'In a lagoon . . .' Förster-Nietzsche, 1891, p. 51

'We travelled . . .' Förster, 1886, p. 145

'It is grand . . .' Elisabeth Förster-Nietzsche to Franziska Nietzsche, 18 March 1888, Peters, 1974, p. 99

'Clearly the carpenter . . .' Förster-Nietzsche, 1891, p. 118

'the radiant German children . . .' ibid., p. 45

CHAPTER V: KNIGHTS AND DEVILS

The principal unpublished sources for this and subsequent chapters are contained in the Goethe–Schiller Archive in Weimar (henceforth GSA) and in the private collection of Mr Albie Rosenthal. H. F. Peters' *Zarathustra's Sister*, as the only published work on Elisabeth Nietzsche, has proved a useful starting point. For biographical information on the life of Nietzsche I have relied on the following works: R. J. Hollingdale, *Nietzsche: The Man and His Philosophy*; Ronald Hayman, *Nietzsche: A Critical Life*; and E. F. Podach, *Gestalten um Nietzsche*. S. L. Gilman and D. J. Parent, *Conversations with Nietzsche*, has also been helpful. The most lucid critical work on Nietzsche is still Walter Kaufmann, *Nietzsche: Philosopher, Psychologist, Antichrist,* which contains a detailed examination of the Nazis' textual misuse of Nietzsche. J. P. Stern, *Nietzsche*, is a good short introduction. Nietzsche's letters are contained in *Nietzsche Briefweschel Kritische Gesantasgabe*, edited by G. Colli and M. Montinari (Berlin and New York, 1975), henceforth C & M; some references are to the earlier *Friedrich Nietzsche Briefe*, eds W. Hoppe and K. Schlechta (Munich 1938–42).

'in the life . . .' Förster-Nietzsche, 1912, p. 135

'Do you desire ...' Friedrich Nietzsche to Elisabeth Nietzsche, 11 June 1865, ibid., p. 137

'It is much easier ...' *Friedrich Nietzsche Briefe*, vol. I, p. 419, Peters, 1974, p. 21

'the wonderful way ...' Förster-Nietzsche, 1911, p. 8

'feminism is ...' Förster-Nietzsche, 1915, p. 302

'My brother's ideal ...' ibid., p. 304

'In everything God has ...' Friedrich Nietzsche, 'Aus meinem Leben', Hayman, 1980, p. 26

'the inspector ...' Förster-Nietzsche, 1912, p.63

'I have a pleasant ...' Friedrich Nietzsche to Franziska Nietzsche, 19 November 1862, Hayman, 1980, p. 49

'A letter is ...' Nietzsche, 1880, 261.

'Dresden will be ...' Friedrich Nietzsche to Franziska Nietzsche, end of February 1862, Hayman, 1980, p. 46

'Marie Deussen is ...' Friedrich Nietzsche to Franziska and Elisabeth Nietzsche, 8 October 1864, Hayman, 1980, p. 59

'the story of ...' Anonymous, *My Sister and I* (Amok Books, 1990), reproduced p. lxvi

'It first happened ...' ibid., p. 6

'for a flat fee' Walter Kaufmann, *Nietzsche: Philosopher, Psychologist, Antichrist,* Princeton, 1950, p. 503n

'What I fear ...' *Friedrich Nietzsche*, ed. Karl Schlecta (Aus den Jahren 1868–9), vol. III, p. 148, Peters, 1974, p. 22

'I am quivering ...' Friedrich Nietzsche to Erwin Rohde, 28 October 1868

'wonderfully lively ...' Friedrich Nietzsche to Erwin Rohde, 9 November 1868, Hollingdale, 1965, p. 49

'Together we could march ...' Friedrich Nietzsche to Erwin Rohde, 9 December 1868, Hayman, 1980, p. 100

'I know that they are all talking . . .' Elisabeth Nietzsche to Friedrich Nietzsche, 13 February 1869, Peters, 1974, p. 23

'I offer all . . .' Nietzsche, 1908, 'Why I am so Clever', 5

'Richard came in . . .' Cosima Wagner, *Diaries*, Hayman, 1980, p. 133

'Ariadne, I love you . . .' Friedrich Nietzsche to Cosima Wagner, beginning of January 1889, Hayman, 1980, p. 335

. . .'My wife, Cosima Wagner . . .' Records of the clinic at Jena, 27 March 1889

'The whole of Tribschen . . .' Förster-Nietzsche, 1912, p. 222

'I can still . . .' ibid., p. 223–4

'nothing more beautiful . . .' Richard Wagner to Friedrich Nietzsche, beginning of January 1872, Hayman, 1980, p. 146

'I am in no mood . . .' *Friedrich Nietzsche Briefe*, vol. III, p. 112, Peters, 1974, p. 30

'because of my sister's . . .' *Friedrich Nietzsche Briefe*, vol. IV, p. 233, ibid., p. 31

'as an old maid . . .' Elisabeth Nietzsche to Franziska Nietzsche, 13 July 1868, ibid., p. 19

'great, brave and indomitable . . .' *Friedrich Nietzsche*, ed. Karl Schlechta, Munich, 1960, Vol III, p. 303, Peters, 1974, p. 34

'We shall love . . .' Friedrich Nietzsche to Erwin Rohde, 15 December 1870, Hayman, 1980, p. 132

'Truly a hair-raising crowd!' Nietzsche, 1908, 2

'philistines and housewives', Förster-Nietzsche, 1912, p. 378

'peeped into the room . . .' ibid., p. 383

'It was really . . .' *Friedrich Nietzsche Briefe*, vol. IV, p. 467, Peters, 1974, p. 42

'pint pot capacity . . .' Ernest Newman, *The Life of Richard Wagner* (London and New York, 1972), vol. IV, p. 520

'Finally Israel intervened . . .' Cosima Wagner to Maria von Schenitz, May 1878, Hayman, 1980, p. 204

'criticise everything . . .' Richard Wagner, *Bayreuther Blätter*, August 1878

'When we hear . . .' Cosima Wagner, 2 April 1881, *Diaries*, Martin Gregor Dellin and Dietrich Mack, eds (Munich, 1976–7), trans. Geoffrey Skelton (London and New York, 1978)

'Either we rid ourselves . . .' Förster, 1881, p. 53

'The true German . . .' ibid., p. 20

'let that most . . .' ibid., p. 54

'ridiculously servile . . .' Cosima Wagner, *Diaries* trans. Skelton, op. cit., entry for 6 July 1880

'how embarrassing . . .' ibid., 12 June 1881

'I almost think *Carmen* . . .' Friedrich Nietzsche to Peter Gast, 8 December 1881, Hayman, 1980, p. 236

'The true man . . .' Nietzsche, 1883–92, 'Of Old and Young Women'

'man should be trained . . .' ibid.

'What stars . . .' Lou Andreas Salomé, *Lebensrückblick*, ed. Ernst Pfeiffer (Zurich, 1951), Hayman, 1980, p. 245

'Don't get the idea . . .' *Friedrich Nietzsche, Paul Rée, Lou von Salomé: Die Dokumente ihrer Begegnung*, ed. Ernst Pfeiffer, (Frankfurt, 1970), p. 254, Peters, 1974, p. 65

'that rabid egotism . . .' Elisabeth Nietzsche to Clara Geltzer, 24 September 1882, Hayman, 1980, p. 251

'a disgrace . . .' Friedrich Nietzsche to Franz Overbeck, mid-September 1882, ibid., p. 251

'I have the Naumburg . . .' Friedrich Nietzsche to Franz Overbeck, 18 September 1882, Hollingdale, 1965, p. 183

'I warn Miss Salomé . . .' and 'low, sensuous, cruel . . .' Ernst

Pfeiffer, *Nietzsche, Rée, Salomé*, op. cit., p. 291, Peters, 1974, p. 70

'I am a headache-plagued half-lunatic ...' Friedrich Nietzsche to Lou Salomé and Paul Rée, mid-December 1882, Stern, 1978, p. 34

'I have suffered ...' Friedrich Nietzsche to Franz Overbeck, Christmas Day 1882, Hollingdale, 1965, p. 184

'dried up, dirty ...' Friedrich Nietzsche to George Rée, Hollingdale, 1965, p. 187

'How charmingly ...' Nietzsche 1883–92, 'Of Chastity' p. 92

'You are visiting women? ...' ibid., 'Of Old and Young Women'. Nietzsche's views on women are contradictory. What appears at times to be wholesale condemnation of the female sex is often tempered by profound and sympathetic insight into female psychology, and relations between the sexes. The following are exerpted from the section on 'Woman and Child' in *Human all too Human*: 'The perfect woman is a higher type of being than the perfect man: also something much rarer' (section 377). '... a good marriage is founded on the talent for friendship' (section 378); 'Everyone bears within him a picture of woman derived from his mother: it is this which determines whether, in his dealings with women, he respects them or despises them, or is in general indifferent to them' (section 380). There are many other examples. Nietzsche opposed nineteenth-century feminism on much the same basis that 'post-feminists' now attack their predecessors. An excellent examination of Nietzsche's ideas on women is contained in the article 'Who is the "Ubermensche"? Time, Truth and Woman in Nietzsche' by Keith Ansell-Pearson in *The Journal of the History of Ideas*, 1992.

I am grateful to Dr Ansell-Pearson for pointing out that the much-quoted 'whip' passage needs to be read in context. 'Woman' in this passage (spoken by an old woman, it should be noted) is arguably a metaphor for life and that Nietzsche is once again exhorting the reader to master life and its secrets by using all necessary means, including coercion – which does not preclude the possibility that he had Lou Salomé in mind when he wrote the passage. A fuller discussion of this question is contained in the appendix of R. Hinton Thomas, *Nietzsche in German Politics and Society 1890–1918* (Manchester, 1984).

'a sneaking, slanderous . . .' Friedrich Nietzsche to George Rée, summer 1883, Hollingdale, 1965, p. 187

'I am being broken . . .' Friedrich Nietzsche to Franz Overbeck, 25 December 1883, Hayman, 1980, p. 254

'morally bloated' Friedrich Nietzsche to Elisabeth Nietzsche, end of November 1882, Hayman, 1980, p. 254

'It is painful . . .' Friedrich Nietzsche to Franz Overbeck, March 1883, ibid.

'For a year now . . .' Ernst Pfeiffer, *Nietzsche, Rée, Salomé*, op. cit., p. 344, Peters, 1974, p. 74

'There can be no question . . .' Friedrich Nietzsche to Malwida von Meysenbug, early May 1884, Hayman, 1980, p. 273

'A cry for help . . .' Quoted in Podach, 1932, p. 125

'the ferocity with which . . .' *The Times*, 1 February 1883

'He is filled . . .' Elisabeth Nietzsche to Peter Gast, 7 January 1883, Peters, 1974, p. 71

'a real rebirth' Richard Wagner, 'Religion and Art', *Bayreuther Blätter* 1880, in E. Newman, *The Life of Richard Wagner* (London and New York, 1972), vol. IV, p. 617–8

'The National anti-semitic movement . . .' Quoted in Podach, 1932, p. 125

'already being systematically . . .' Förster, 1886, p. 7

'the most representative Jew-baiter . . .' *The Times*, 1 February 1883

'let them make fun . . .' Bernhard Förster to Julius Cyriax, 30 March 1883, from the Rosenthal collection

'I find Fritz's views . . .' Elisabeth Nietzsche to Franziska Nietzsche, 4 April 1883, Peters, 1974, p. 72

'someday Förster . . .' Elisabeth Nietzsche to Franziska Nietzsche, ibid.

'Greetings from Wagner . . .' Richard Wagner to Bernhard Förster, 1 February 1883, GSA

'We hear . . .' Cosima Wagner, *Diaries*, trans Skelton, op. cit., entry for 9 February 1883

'What a thunderbolt . . .' Bernhard Förster to Julius Cyriax, 30 March 1883, Rosenthal collection

'the man one most . . .' Friedrich Nietzsche to Peter Gast, 19 February 1883, Hayman, 1980, p. 261

'I regard you today . . .' see Hayman, 1980, p. 261

'My son Zarathustra . . .' Friedrich Nietzsche to Heinrich von Stein, 22 May 1884, Hollingdale, 1965, p. 216. Nietzsche's 'übermensch' is traditionally translated as Superman, and I have used this translation for the sake of consistency. 'Overman', though more cumbersome, is a more accurate translation of the German and also accurately conveys the notion of 'self-overcoming' while Superman misleadingly implies mere superiority. See Keith Ansell-Pearson in the *Times Higher Educational Supplement*, 16 March 1991.

'My brother's goal . . .' Elisabeth Nietzsche to Bernhard Förster, 15 September 1883, Peters, 1974, p. 74

'Here is a man . . .' Nietzsche, 1882, 359

'This accursed anti-semitism . . .' Friedrich Nietzsche to Franz Overbeck, 2 April 1884, Hollingdale, 1965, p. 214

'To enthusiasm . . .' Friedrich Nietzsche to Franziska and Elisabeth Nietzsche, 14 March 1885, C & M no. 581.

'Is it right to leave my brother? . . .' Elisabeth Nietzsche to Bernhard Förster, 12 October 1884, Peters, 1974, p. 83

'shall bind . . .' Bernhard Förster to Julius Cyriax, 19 April 1885, Rosenthal collection

'From my own point of view . . .' Friedrich Nietzsche to Franziska Nietzsche, end of May 1885, C & M no. 604

'two horses . . .' Friedrich Nietzsche to Franz Overbeck, 6 October 1885, ibid., no. 632

'My husband . . .' Förster-Nietzsche, 1915, p. 218

'I am in the company . . .' Podach, 1932, p. 145

'How lonely your Fritz feels . . .' Friedrich Nietzsche to Franziska and Elisabeth Nietzsche, 6 September 1885, Hayman, 1980, p. 287

'I have lost . . .' Friedrich Nietzsche to Emily Fynn, February 1886, C & M, no. 671

'I would give everything . . .' Friedrich Nietzsche to Elisabeth Förster-Nietzsche, 7 February 1886, C & M no. 669

CHAPTER VI: ELISABETH IN LLAMALAND

'partly to complete . . .' Podach, 1932, p. 145

'I shall have . . .' Bernhard Förster to Julius Cyriax, 15 February 1886, Rosenthal collection

'jolly suggestion . . .' Friedrich Nietzsche to Elizabeth Nietzsche, February 1886, Podach, 1932, p. 147

'You say that New Germany . . .' Friedrich Nietzsche to Elisabeth Nietzsche, June 1886, C & M vol. V, p. 726

'I hear that . . .' Elisabeth Nietzsche to Franziska Nietzsche, 28 Feb 1890, Peters, 1974, p. 102

'Just think how grand . . .' Elisabeth Nietzsche to Bernhard Förster, 28 November 1883, Peters, 1974, p. 78

'I am getting old . . .' Bernhard Förster to Julis Cyriax, Rosenthal collection

'the few years . . .' Elisabeth Nietzsche to Franziska Nietzsche, 21 December 1887, C & M no. 507

'I hope that . . .' Franziska Nietzsche to Friedrich Nietzsche, 1 March 1887, ibid., no. 439

'In front of every farm house . . .' Elisabeth Nietzsche to

Franziska Nietzsche, 18 March 1888, Peters, 1974, p. 98

'I have no . . .' Friedrich Nietzsche to Reinhart von Seydlitz, 24 February 1887, Stern, 1978, p. 36–7

'nothing whatever to . . .' Friedrich Nietzsche to Heinrich Köselitz (Peter Gast), 20 May 1887, C & M no. 851

'indeed, I'm . . .' Friedrich Nietzsche to Elisabeth Nietzsche, 3 November 1886, C & M no. 773

'My position is . . .' draft letter Friedrich Nietzsche to Elisabeth Nietzsche, before 5 June 1887, C & M no. 854

'the shrewdest comment . . .' Friedrich Nietzsche to George Brandes, 2 December 1887, Hayman, 1980, p. 314

'Between ourselves . . .' Friedrich Nietzsche to Reinhart von Seydlitz, 12 February 1888, ibid., p. 315

'Your brother . . .' Friedrich Nietzsche to Elisabeth Nietzsche, end of October 1888, ibid., p. 328

'Personally I would have wished . . .' Elisabeth Nietzsche to Friedrich Nietzsche, 6 September 1888, Peters, 1974, p. 107

'It is time we . . .' draft letter Friedrich Nietzsche to Elisabeth Nietzsche, mid-November 1888, see Hayman, 1980, p. 334

'We are dreaming . . .' *Bayreuther Blätter*, end 1888, Peters, 1974, p. 102

'After supper we sit . . .' 'A Sunday In Nueva Germania', *Bayreuther Blätter*, January 1889, reproduced in Elisabeth Förster-Nietzsche, 1891, p. 43

'a healthy climate . . .' Elisabeth Nietzsche to Bernhard Förster, 20 August 1884, Peters, 1974, p. 82

'rather have spent time . . .' Förster-Nietzsche, 1891, p. 42

'the little queen . . .' Friedrich Nietzsche to Heinrich Köselitz (Peter Gast), 20 May 1887, C & M no. 851

'you can imagine . . .' Friedrich Nietzsche to Franz Overbeck, 3 February 1888, C & M no. 984

'There have been settlers . . .' *Sudamericanische Coloniale Nachrichten*, October 1888

'If we make a start . . .' ibid.

'the colony's management is . . .' Bernhard Förster to General Bernadino Caballero, 24 September 1888, GSA

'literary propaganda . . .' ibid.

'for all this . . .' ibid.

'filthy little egotist . . .' see Förster-Nietzsche 1891, chapter VII, p. 145–173

'remarkable industry . . .' ibid., p. 81

'There have been . . .' Julius Klingbeil, *Enthüllungen über die Dr Bernhard Förstersche Ansiedlung Neu-Germanien in Paraguay*, (Leipzig, 1889), p. 106

'There have been . . .' ibid., p. vi

'My experiences . . .' ibid., p. v

'in Paraguay . . .' *Friedrich Nietzsche*, ed. Karl Schlecta, (Munich, 1960), vol. III., p. 1345, Peters, 1974, p. 107

'Oh, you anti-semites . . .' reproduced in Förster-Nietzsche, 1891, p. 45

'bringing the German flag . . .' letter from Bernhard Förster to *Sudamericanische Coloniale Nachrichten*, 1889, ibid., p. 54

'My dear heart-Bern . . .' Elisabeth Nietzsche to Bernhard Förster, 1 May 1889, GSA

'With me a catastrophe . . .' Friedrich Nietzsche to Franz Overbeck, 14 April 1887, Hayman, 1980, p. 305

'one of my diseases . . .' Nietzsche, 1908, preface

'chewing the cud . . .' ibid., part III

'The Germans . . .' Nietzsche, 1889, 'What the Germans lack', I

'When truth . . .' Nietzsche, 1908, 'Why I am Destiny'

'In two months' . . .' Friedrich Nietzsche to Carl Fuchs, 11 December 1888, Hayman, 1980, p. 132

'I have ordered . . .' Friedrich Nietzsche to August Strindberg, undated, ibid., p. 132

'I want, I want to be mad . . .' August Strindberg to Friedrich Nietzsche, January 1889, ibid., p. 334

'I have just seized . . .' Friedrich Nietzsche to Meta von Salis, 4 January 1889, ibid., p. 335

'Ariadne . . .' Friedrich Nietzsche to Cosima Wagner, beginning of January 1889

'I have just had all anti-semites . . .' Friedrich Nietzsche to Franz Overbeck, *c.* 4 January 1889, C & M no. 1249

'He never said . . .' Elisabeth Nietzsche to Franziska Nietzsche, end of March 1889, GSA

'Bernhard does not show . . .' Elisabeth Nietzsche to Franziska Nietzsche, end of March 1889, Peters, 1974, p. 108

'Don't worry . . .' Elisabeth Nietzsche to Bernhard Förster, 1 May 1889, GSA

'I am in a bad way . . .' Bernhard Förster to Elisabeth Nietzsche, 2 June 1889, GSA

'suddenly rose from his couch . . .' Förster-Nietzsche, 1891, p. 64

'the false friends . . .' ibid., p. 64, see Podach, 1932, p. 159

'This one discovery . . .' Förster-Nietzsche, 1891, p. 65

'My body and mind . . .' Bernhard Förster to Elisabeth Nietzsche, 2 June 1889, GSA

'he and his wife . . .' Podach 1932, p. 160

'the artist leaves . . .' Förster, 1881, p. 2

'not only led us . . .' reprinted in Förster-Nietzsche, 1891, p. 63

'Do not call him . . .' reproduced in Podach, 1932, p. 161, and Förster-Nietzsche, 1891, p. 60

'passionately reproaching my husband . . .' Förster-Nietzsche, 1915, p. 391

'in excellent order...' Elisabeth Förster-Nietzsche, *Bayreuther Blätter*, September 1889, reproduced in Förster-Nietzsche, 1891, p. 67

'bitterly reproached...' Förster-Nietzsche, 1915, p. 391.

'The whole letter...' ibid.

'paralytic psychic disturbance...' diagnosis of the Jena Clinic: see Hayman, 1980, p. 339

'I am dead...' Franziska Nietzsche to Franz Overbeck, 26 September 1892, Hayman, 1980, p. 344

'like a Prussian soldier...' Förster-Nietzsche, 1915, p. 403

'As mother of the colony...' GSA, see Hayman, 1980, p. 345

'a battling hero...' Förster-Nietzsche, 1891, p. 68

'the climate of Paraguay...' ibid., p. 116

'colony tiger...' ibid., p. 120

'we don't pay...' ibid., p. 120–135

'Society...' Friedrich Nietzsche 1889, 36

'I do not think Germany...' George Streckfuss to Max Schubert, December 1892, Podach, 1932, p. 165

'if there is not an improvement...' ibid., p. 166–7

'the favourable letters...' Walter Glitza to Max Schubert, 8 July 1892, ibid., p. 168

'truth and not delicacy...' ibid., p. 169 and 171

'but how insignificant...' Elisabeth Förster-Nietzsche in *Bayreuther Blätter*, January 1895, Podach, 1932, p. 175–6

'My dear Llama...' Friedrich Nietzsche to Elisabeth Nietzsche, 5 July 1885, C & M no. 611

CHAPTER VII: WILL TO POWER

'I do not...' Förster-Nietzsche, 1915, p. 407

'a popular error . . .' Nietzsche, *Gesammelte Werke*, Musarion ed. (23 vols, 1920–9), vol. XVI, 318, Kaufmann, 1950, p. 19

'His life I am . . .' Elisabeth Förster-Nietzsche to Peter Gast, 17 September 1893, Peters, 1974, p. 131

'Frau Förster-Nietzsche is . . .' Rudolf Steiner, *Das Magazin für Litteratur*, 10 February 1900, Kaufmann, 1950, p. 5

'Whoever saw Nietzsche . . .' quoted in C. A. Bernoulli, *Franz Overbeck und Friedrich Nietzsche. Eine Freundschaft* (Jena, 1908), vol. II, p. 370, Hollingdale, 1965, p. 304

'wonderfully beautiful . . .' Förster-Nietzsche, 1912, p. 13

'The only female relative . . .' ibid., p. 39

'He used not to speak . . .' ibid., p. 323

'I more than anyone . . .' Förster-Nietzsche, 1915, p. v

'My sister is not . . .' ibid., p. 45

'helpful trusting soul . . .' ibid., p. 211

'listens not only . . .' Förster-Nietzsche, 1912, p. 307

'Never in our lives . . .' Förster-Nietzsche, 1915, p. 222

'a forerunner of . . .' ibid., p. 131

'essentially distasteful . . .' ibid., p. 121

'malicious brood of . . .' ibid., p. 390

'marked out . . .' ibid., p. 240

'if Förster had not . . .' ibid., p. 251

'it was principally . . .' ibid., p. 240

'he was far too good . . .' ibid., p. 222

'an intriguing young lady . . .' ibid., p. 187

'he dreaded . . .' ibid., p. 241

'various adverse . . .' ibid., p. 251

'had not the slightest . . .' Förster-Nietzsche, 1912, p. vii

'story of a friendship . . .' ibid., p. 372

'whatever people may say . . .' ibid., p. 296–7

'often indulged in . . .' Förster-Nietzsche, 1915, p. 368

'he cherished a . . .' ibid., p. 376

'a real liking . . .' ibid., p. 373

'he never forgot . . .' ibid., p. 373

'the most difficult task . . .' Förster-Nietzsche, 1912, p. 137

'this extraordinarily rich . . .' ibid., p. 41

'apparently she does . . .' Count Harry Kessler, entry for 24 April 1929, *Diaries of a Cosmopolitan* (London, 1971)

'he was asleep . . .' ibid., 8 August 1897, Hayman, 1980, p. 348–9

'How I felt . . .' Isabella von Ungern-Sternberg, 31 March – 1 April 1900, trans. David J. Parent in Sander L. Gilman, ed., in *Conversations with Nietzsche* (New York and Oxford 1987), p. 259

'prefer to be understood . . .' Nietzsche, 1879, p. 138

'he wrote me a . . .' Förster-Nietzsche, 1915, p. 404

'one day . . .' ibid., p. 404–5

'At two o'clock . . .' ibid., p. 410

'"Lisbeth," said my brother . . .' ibid., p. 65

'I have a terrible fear . . .' Nietzsche, 1908, 'Why I am Destiny' I

'Hallowed be thy name . . .' Förster-Nietzsche, 1915, p. x

'pink satin . . .' Förster-Nietzsche, 1912, p. 223

'Did you know . . .' Cosima Wagner to Daniela, 28 February 1900, Cosima Wagner, *Briefe an ihre tochter Daniela Bulow* (Stuttgart and Berlin, 1933), p. 514

'She seems to have . . .' Cosima Wagner to Houston Stewart Chamberlain, 14 August 1900, ibid., p. 541

'The Revolution made . . .' Nietzsche, 1901, p. 271. For a more detailed examination of the pleasures and pitfalls of

Nietzsche's *nachluss*, see Hollingdale, 1965, and Kaufmann, 1950

'it looks as though . . .' Förster-Nietzsche, 1915, p. 334

'I have read, madame . . .' Gabriele d'Annunzio to Elisabeth Förster-Nietzsche, 7 July 1906, GSA

'an idealistic genius . . .' Baron von Fischer-Truenfeld, *Paraguay in Wort und Bild* (Berlin, 1906), p. 248

'after six or eight . . .' ibid., p. 250

'For New Germany . . .' ibid., p. 253

'Rarely has . . .' C. A. Bernoulli, *Franz Overbeck und Friedrich Nietzsche*, op. cit., vol., II p. 431, in Peters, 1974, p. 184

'I came here . . .' Oscar Levy to Mrs Crosland, Weimar, 7 August 1908, Rosenthal collection

'none of us . . .' *The Times*, 12 January 1906

'Perhaps there will come . . .' Friedrich Nietzsche, quoted by Keith Ansell-Pearson in the *Times Higher Educational Supplement*, 16 March 1990, p. 13

'the great challenge . . .' Elisabeth Förster-Nietzsche, 'Nietzsche and the War', GSA

'one of the greatest . . .' fragment of document, undated, GSA

'read the devil . . .' quoted by Keith Ansell-Pearson, *The Jewish Quarterly*, Autumn 1990, p. 28

'Even in her seventh decade . . .' Count Harry Kessler, *Diaries of a Cosmopolitan*, op. cit., 23 February 1919

'She insists that . . .' ibid., 9 May 1920

'the good old lady . . .' ibid., 20 July 1922

'Admirable, the resignation . . .' ibid., 20 April 1925

'political methods . . .' ibid., 12 October 1927

'a fat parson . . .' ibid., 13 October 1927

'the race most . . .' *Briefwechsel zwischen Cosima Wagner und Fürst Ernst zu Hohenlohe Langenburg* (Stuttgart, 1937), p. 45, trans. E. Newman, *Life of Richard Wagner* (London and New York, 1972), vol. III, p. 285

'Elisabeth went on . . .' Count Harry Kessler, op. cit., 22 October 1927

CHAPTER VIII: MOTHER OF THE FATHERLAND

'the most congenial. . .' Benito Mussolini, 'Philosophy of Strength', *Pagine Libere*, Lugarno, 1908

'You are right . . .' Interview by Dr Oscar Levy, *New York Times Magazine*, 9 November 1924

'I can no longer . . .' Elizabeth Förster-Nietzsche to Mussolini, quoted in *New Weimar Journal*, 30 May 1929

'my brother loved . . .' Elisabeth Förster-Nietzsche to Mussolini, 23 July 1931, GSA

'Without exaggeration . . .' Elisabeth Förster-Nietzsche to Count Baroni, Italian Ambassador to Berlin, 13 October 1931, GSA

'bursting with news . . .' Count Harry Kessler, op. cit., 11 February 1926

'We deem it . . .' Pfundter, ed., *Dr Wilhelm Frick und sei Ministerium* (Berlin, 1937), p. 180–1

'I am not giving . . .' Wilhelm Frick to Elisabeth-Förster Nietzsche, 20 September 1930, GSA

'It is certain . . .' Elisabeth Förster-Nietzsche to Wilhelm Frick, 7 February 1931, GSA

'the happiest day . . .' Elisabeth Förster-Nietzsche to Count Baroni, 13 October 1931, GSA

'Can I dare . . .' Elisabeth Förster-Nietzsche to Mussolini, 14 January 1932, GSA

'his eyes . . .' Count Harry Kessler, op. cit., 7 August 1932 'inside the archive . . .' ibid., 7 August 1932

'A wave of joyous enthusiasm. . .' Elisabeth Förster-Nietzsche to Wilhelm Frick, 2 February 1933, GSA

'wonderful, indeed phenomenal. . .' Elisabeth Förster-Nietzsche to Ernst Thiel, 12 May 1933, Peters, 1974, p. 220

'It is becoming ever clearer . . .' Fritz Rütishauser to Elisabeth Förster-Nietzsche, 24 July 1933, GSA

'We are very happy . . .' Elisabeth Förster-Nietzsche to Fritz Rütishauser, undated, GSA

'A trip to Weimar . . .' Fritz Rütishauser to Elisabeth Förster-Nietzsche, 14 October 1934, GSA

'Yes, Elisabeth, you are . . .' Ernst Thiel to Elisabeth Förster-Nietzsche, 14 May 1934, GSA

'the Statesman comes . . .' Max Oehler, 'Hitler's visit to the Archive', 20 July 1944, GSA

'both personally and objectively . . .' Hans Frank to Elisabeth Förster-Nietzsche, 4 May 1943, GSA

'in one year . . .' *Trial of the Major War Criminals* (Munich and Zurich, 1984), vol. XXIX, p. 415

'German post-war art. . .' quoted in Paul Otwin Rave, *Kunstdiktatur im Dritten Reich* (Hamburg, 1947), p. 13, trans. Richard Grunberger, *A Social History of the Third Reich* (London, 1971), p. 532

'We honour Freidrich Nietzsche . . .' Quoted in *The Times*, 18 October 1944

'Hitler and the party . . .' Elisabeth Förster-Nietzsche to Margaritha Frick, 5 July 1934, GSA

'the worst readers . . .' Nietzsche, 1879, 137

'Nietzsche had always . . .' Elisabeth Förster-Nietzsche, 'Was Nietzsche a National Socialist?', date unclear, probably 19 and 20 July 1934, GSA

'merely megalomaniac . . .' Bertrand Russell, *A History of*

Western Philosophy (London, 1946), p. 734

'his followers . . .' ibid., p. 739

'It is not too much to say . . .' George Lichtheim, *Europe in the Twentieth Century* (New York, 1972), p. 152

'fundamentally unsound . . .' P. G. Wodehouse, *Carry On Jeeves* (London, 1960), p. 26

'great task and question . . .' Nietzsche, 1908

'beyond doubt the strongest . . .' Nietzsche, 1878, 475

'I have a duty . . .' Nietzsche 1908, foreword, I

'The Chancellor of the Reich . . .' Hans Heinrich Lammers to Elisabeth Förster-Nietzsche, 19 April 1934, GSA

'special fund . . .' Lammers to Elisabeth Förster-Nietzsche, 27 June 1935, GSA

'I am not an Aryan . . .' Rudolf K. Goldschmit to Elisabeth Förster-Nietzsche, 16 March 1935, GSA

'I'm so glad . . .' Elisabeth Förster-Nietzsche to Hans Heinrich Lammers, undated, GSA

'I will be sacked . . .' Schmidt to Elisabeth Förster-Nietzsche, 14 April 1935, GSA

'I am now . . .' Elisabeth Förster-Nietzsche to Wilhelm Frick, 14 August 1934, GSA

'of the atrocities . . .' Count Harry Kessler, op. cit., 22 October 1927

'Painful to hear . . .' ibid., 13 October 1927

'miserable state . . .' Cornelie Nürnburg, undated article, 'My Experiences as a teacher in New Germany', Nietzsche Archive, 1936, GSA

'with which they associated everything . . .' ibid.

'The colony can be very proud . . .' Fritz Neumann to Cornelie Nürnburg, 23 April 1930, GSA

'though I believe . . .' Alfred Meyer to Elisabeth Förster-Nietzsche, 25 May 1932, GSA 'remain true to ...' Alfred Meyer to Elisabeth Förster-Nietzsche, 10 April 1933, GSA

'old Fritz Neumann ...' German Consulate in Paraguay to Elisabeth Förster-Nietzsche, 17 July 1933, GSA

'It is a great pleasure ...' Elisabeth Förster-Nietzsche to Fritz Neumann, 21 August 1933, GSA

'the enmity of the Jews ...' *Volksbund für das Deutschtum in Ausland* to Elisabeth Förster-Nietzsche, 16 May 1935, GSA

'May God give ...' Frau Böckel to Elisabeth Förster-Nietzsche, November 1934, GSA

'I want to help ...' Elisabeth Förster-Nietzsche to German Consulate in Paraguay, 19 October 1933, GSA

'Because of the Reich's foreign debts ...' Martin Schmidt to Cornelie Nürnburg, New Year 1937, GSA

'dull inflexibility ...' Cornelie Nürnburg to Max Oehler, 11 February 1937, GSA

'the spirit of Nietzsche ...' Elisabeth Förster-Nietzsche to Adolf Hitler and Benito Mussolini, 5 June 1934, GSA

'In my long time ...' Elisabeth Förster-Nietzsche to Adolf Hitler, 19 June 1935, GSA

'one cannot but love ...' Elisabeth Förster-Nietzsche to Ernst Thiel, 31 October 1935, Peters, 1974, p. 222

'We went to Nietzsche's house ...' Albert Speer, *Inside the Third Reich* (London, 1970), p. 64

'enormous interest ...' Elisabeth Förster-Nietzsche to Adolf Hitler, 26 August 1935, GSA

'You could see ...' entry for 11 November 1935, Max Oehler's diary, GSA

'the fearless, determined ...' funeral address read by Fritz Sauckel, 11 November 1935, GSA

'One cannot but ...' *Thuringer Gauzeitung*, 4 August 1938, GSA

'How he rejoiced ...' Elisabeth Förster-Nietzsche, undated radio broadcast, *Plauderei zu dem Weimar*, GSA

'Long live eternal Germany . . .' report of Kingsbury Smith of Illustrated News Service, 16 October 1946

'I am dying innocent . . .' Smith, ibid.

'If it is certain . . .' Speech by French prosecutor François de Menthos during sitting of 17 January 1946; see *The Trial of the Major War Criminals*, op. cit., Vols. V–VI, p. 474

CHAPTER IX: NUEVA GERMANIA, MARCH 1991

'Only the palm trees . . .' Förster-Nietzsche, 1891, p. 43

'I never imagined it . . .' Elisabeth Förster-Nietzsche to Franziska Nietzsche, 18 March 1888, Peters, 1974, p. 98

'You will tear yourselves . . .' Förster-Nietzsche, 1891, p. 134

'The Axis powers . . .' quoted in G. Posner and J. Ware, *Mengele: The Complete Story* (London, 1986), p. 170

'He clings firmly . . .' Nietzsche, 1882, 229

'An anti-semite is not . . .' Nietzsche, 1895, 183

'"I have done that" . . .' Nietzsche, 1886, 68

'the hypocrite who . . .' Nietzsche, 1878, 51

'fairly recent isolation . . .' J. A. Fraser Roberts and Marcus E. Pembrey, *An introduction to medical genetics* (Oxford, 1985), p. 56. See p. 48–56 for statistics on albinism.

'Such genes are . . .' Ashley Montagu, *Human Heredity* (New American Library, 1960), p. 311

'Zarathustra has seen. . .' Nietzsche, 1883–92, I, 'Of the Thousand and One Goals'

'The man who . . .' Nietzsche, 1880, 53

Index

R.T.C. LIBRARY, LETTERKENNY

BOLIVIA

Bahia Negra

CHACO

PARAGUAY

PARAGUAY

ARGENTIN

Rio Parag